What Saith the Lord?

halt · apt · variance · emulations · seditions

meat · commend · miserable · convenient ·

careful · spoil · equall · incontinent · enlarge

honest · excess · overcharge · communicate

conversation · corn · fetched a compass · fai

experience · moderation · suffer · help meet

so that · bastard · bowels · ass · holy ghost ·

quit · coasts · counsel · host · sodden · by my

flowers · offend · rumor · condemn · entreat

affect · that · wealth · peculiar · road · follo

bruise · brethren · passenger · constantly

oppose · in · of purpose · rage · imagine · pe

will worship · replenish · discover · debate ·

difference · shew · closet · issues · apple of t

virtue · hell · charity · staggered · desired ·

convinced · conversation · great waster · dis

commune · turtle · delicacies · grud

observe · lust · world · reins ·

grief, grieve · minister · scho

freely · doubts · room · naked

amaze · comfortably · spirit · c

mourn · evil · comprehend · d

generation · rid · target · n

"Everyone who loves God's Word should read this book! As one who is devoted to helping other people understand, believe, and follow God's truth, I greatly appreciate and loudly applaud this work from Mark Ward. In these pages Mark brilliantly and insightfully weaves together his passion for truth, his love for Jesus, and his love for Bible readers. He has done a great service to all those who love God's Word and God's people. I most appreciate Mark's respectful spirit, gentle tone, well-timed humor, disarming wit, and irrefutable coherence of logic. Whatever your position on English Bible translation, your knowledge of God's Word and your ability to edify others through God's Word will be greatly enhanced through the pages of this work. Thank you, Mark!"

Cary Schmidt, pastor at Emmanuel Baptist Church of Newington, Connecticut

"If we are to teach and preach from the KJV, we must take the time to explain those words whose meanings have shifted since the translation was first written. This is a responsibility we cannot take lightly, as the clarity of our message depends on it. For those seeking to understand the nuances of the KJV and how to navigate its challenges, I recommend Mark Ward's work. While I may not fully agree with the conclusions of other writings or presentations, his scholarship shines a much-needed light on the issues we face in using this historic translation in contemporary times. I truly believe this book represents a successful attempt to find common ground in an ongoing debate that often generates more heat than light. By shedding light on the challenges of the KJV without dismissing its value, Mark Ward offers a path forward for those who cherish this translation while acknowledging the need for clarity in our communication of God's Word. In a discussion often marked by division, this work is a breath of fresh air."

Joe Shakour, pastor at Tabernacle Baptist Church of Wilson, North Carolina

"I highly recommend this insightful and well-researched book to anyone who values the accuracy and preservation of the King James Version of the Bible. The author's thorough research and deep understanding of the KJV language make this work both informative and enjoyable. While I may not agree with all of the author's conclusions, I appreciated the fresh perspective and the focus on discerning the true meaning of Scripture. Approach this book as you would a valuable commentary or Bible study aid, and you will surely gain new insights and deepen your understanding of God's Word."

Dan Haifley, pastor at Maranatha Baptist Church of Mattoon, Illinois

"So long as language lives, it is subject to change both in terms of vocabulary and syntax. The reasons for change are haphazard and unpredictable, yet undeniable. All it takes is time. The positive influence of the King James Version on the English language is indisputable, even if many are unaware of the source of that influence. Yet, the language and literary style of the KJV has not been exempt from change. A lot can happen to a language over a span of more than four hundred years. Ward identifies significant examples of words used in the KJV whose meanings have been subject to change and thus are liable to misunderstanding. He consistently demonstrates that these words were not mistranslations but rather words whose current definitions differ from Elizabethan English. Apart from his occasional 'witticisms,' it's what preachers using the KJV do regularly and what the Reformation Heritage KJV Study Bible (of which I was the OT editor) did consistently. To this end, Ward's work can benefit those who prefer to use the KJV either in public worship or private reading. My guess is that if some of the modern versions could possibly enjoy the kind of longevity the KJV has, in four hundred years someone would have to address their archaisms as well."

Dr. Michael Barrett, Puritan Reformed Theological Seminary

What Saith the Lord?

KJV Words We're Getting Wrong—and How to Get Them Right

Mark Ward

BakerBooks
a division of Baker Publishing Group
Grand Rapids, Michigan

Published by Baker Books
a division of Baker Publishing Group
Grand Rapids, Michigan
BakerBooks.com

Printed in the United States of America

Library of Congress Cataloging-in-Publication Data
Names: Ward, Mark (Mark L.) author
Title: What saith the Lord? : KJV words we're getting wrong—and how to get them right / Mark Ward.
Description: Grand Rapids, Michigan : Baker Books, a division of Baker Publishing Group, [2026]
Identifiers: LCCN 2026008112 | ISBN 9781540905949 paperback | ISBN 9781493465477 ebook
Subjects: LCSH: Bible. English. Authorized
Classification: LCC BS186 .W37 2026
LC record available at https://lccn.loc.gov/2026008112

Cover and interior design by William Overbeeke

Baker Publishing Group publications use paper produced from sustainable forestry practices and postconsumer waste whenever possible.

26 27 28 29 30 31 32 7 6 5 4 3 2 1

Contents

Preface

My Agenda

I LOVE THE KING JAMES BIBLE. I grew up fishing exclusively in its waters. Even today, when I sail through the sea of my memory, cast an hook, and take up the fish that cometh up, the coin in its mouth is a farthing and not a quarter. (If that allusion to Matthew 17 was not as clever as I hoped, I just mean that my Scripture memory is all from the King James Version.) My years of work on the KJV since this book's prequel, *Authorized: The Use and Misuse of the King James Bible*, have only made me appreciate the KJV more.

In that former book, I gave considerable time to discussing something I'm against, which I called "Bible translation tribalism." If you want to know more about it, see that book. There I wade into some controversies that have disrupted Christian unity, including my own fellowship with believers I love. But this book is only about what I'm for: *I'm for readers of the KJV understanding God's Word.* That's my agenda in these pages. This book wades into no controversies because it is built on common ground—the common ground that I know I share with every

Christian, including every Christian who loves the KJV: We all want to understand our Bibles.

Indeed, I want you to notice the endorsements that were graciously given to *What Saith the Lord?*. If you know the current ecclesiastical landscape, you might perceive these endorsers include those who preach and teach exclusively from the KJV and those who do not. That's because I want this book to be useful for—and trusted by—those who read only the KJV and those who do not. In this book, the only modern translations I cite are based on the same (Masoretic) Hebrew and (Textus Receptus) Greek texts the KJV is based on. Textual criticism has 1,611 times less than nothing to do with this book. It's all about English. If a review of this book brings up textual criticism, or "missing verses," or if it includes the words "Sinaiticus," "Vaticanus," or "Westcott and Hort," you'll know the reviewer has changed the subject.

I've done extensive fishing in some of the deepest parts of the KJV sea, and I have some tips to share. This book will not merely hand you a few fish; it is meant instead to be a manual. I'm convinced that KJV readers will do far better if they understand *why* "conversation" in the KJV actually means "conduct" and not "chatter," *why* "prevent" means "come before" and not "block," and *why* people today commonly turn "an help meet" into "a helpmeet." I believe that understanding how to fish for "false friends" in the KJV is essential to reading it well. In this book I offer a tackle box and a set of tried-and-true lures.

We forget how the common language of English, and the common people who spoke it, were despised by the elite during the early Reformation. In the early 1500s, educated European people spoke and wrote in Latin. It was a mark of William Tyndale's profound love and respect for the common man that he was willing to devote his life to putting God's Word into the language of the plow boy.[1] The brilliant Catholic Englishman Thomas More

1. David Daniell, *William Tyndale: A Biography* (Yale University Press, 1994), 80.

sneered at Tyndale's choice to use the word "love" instead of the traditional (and Latinate) "charity." To More, "love" was a common word that might be used by "any Jack."[2] No one could have made Tyndale's point better. That was precisely it.

I am endeavoring, like my far greater forebear, to show respect to the fisher—or the potential fisher—by writing this book. I am putting what I believe to be important and powerful tools for reading the King James Version into your hands.

Happy fishing.

2. As quoted in Marilynne Robinson, *The Givenness of Things: Essays* (Farrar, Straus & Giroux, 2015), 18–19.

Introduction

"False Friends" and the Ways Language Changes

Everybody knows the King James Bible contains "dead words," or words we know we don't know—like "amerce," "bestead," and "ceiled."[1] But most English readers today don't realize there are words in the KJV they *don't* know they don't know—simple words like "halt," "study," and "remove." These are what I call "false friends."

These false friends are not the fault of the KJV translators, not in any way. They are not translation errors. And they are not the fault of modern-day readers or of too much screen time among our young. False friends are just what happens when language changes over time. And most historians agree that time has elapsed since the KJV was first released in 1611.

In this introduction, I'm going to define false friends. Then I'm going to explain a concept essential to false friends, a

1. A good list of these words can be found at "Archaic Words in the King James Bible," The Five Solas, accessed February 2, 2026, www.fivesolas.church/archaic-words-in-the-kjv/.

concept I find is widely misunderstood: language change. Then I'll give some practical explanations about how to read this book.

What Is a False Friend?

"False friend" is a label commonly given to words in two or more different languages that look or sound similar but mean different things. *Gift* in German might look like something you get on your birthday, but it means "poison." (No, Germans do not give poison as birthday gifts—I checked.[2]) Another classic example I learned in Spanish class is the word "embarrassed" in English and the word *embarazada* in Spanish. That Spanish word does not mean "embarrassed," even though it looks and sounds like it; it means "pregnant." Many beginning Spanish students have learned this the hard way, much to their pregnancy. "Embarrassed" and *embarazada* are false friends.

But I use "false friends" a little differently, and I need to acknowledge immediately that this is what I'm doing. I use the label to describe misleading mismatches *within the same language*, namely English. One of the most well-known of these, "conversation," quite obviously exists in both Elizabethan English and contemporary English. But "be ye holy in all manner of **conversation**" (1 Pet. 1:15) meant something different in 1611 than it means today. It meant "conduct," and not "a talk between two or more people." Because many contemporary English readers hear the new meaning in the KJV and not the old—*without realizing it*—it is a false friend.

Yes, the KJV is an English translation; and, yes, we still speak a language called "English." KJV English—or Elizabethan English, or, to be maximally precise, Jacobean English—and our English

2. My almost-lifelong, godly friend, David Lowry, son of missionaries to Germany, tells me that customs officials did treat his father very suspiciously one time when he wrote that he was bringing a "gift" into the country!

are even, broadly speaking, part of the same era of English called "modern English." KJV English and our English are not two entirely different languages.

But they are not entirely the same, either, as you almost certainly already know. And the reason is not that the KJV uses "biblical English" (there is no such thing[3]) or that modern English has been dumbed down, or that txting has like killed R motha tongue + stuff, or even that verbing weirds language.[4] The reason Elizabethan English and contemporary English are not the same is that four hundred years is a long time.

Some of the very same forces that, over time, turned Latin into what we call Spanish, Italian, and French have turned Elizabethan English into contemporary American, British, Australian, Kenyan, Indian, and Singaporean Englishes—Englishes with lots of overlap but also lots of distinctions. So, as with *embarazada,* we assume we know what a KJV false friend means, but in some contexts, we don't. At least I know I didn't: Literally all of the thirty-eight false friends in this book tripped *me* up as a KJV reader, totally unbeknownst to me, until I uncovered the principles and tools that revealed them.

I find it useful, then, to think of Elizabethan English as a different language—one that overlaps with ours substantially, of course, but is also its own complete system. Let me picture this with a classic Venn diagram:

---

3. All writing of sufficient size can be dated to a time and, usually, located in a place. The KJV clearly comes from early Jacobean England—though "Elizabethan" is the most common term for the English then used, and I will stick with that name in this book. As for "biblical English," the most that can be said for that concept is that the KJV does often follow Hebrew and Greek order in a way that isn't perhaps natural to English speakers but has come to be familiar nonetheless because of the ubiquity of the KJV. "By the skin of his teeth" and other phrases that are very literal translations of Hebrew and Greek idioms were not familiar to English speakers, but they became so because of the KJV (and other English Bibles).

4. Here I quote the other Calvin. See https://www.gocomics.com/calvinandhobbes/1993/01/25.

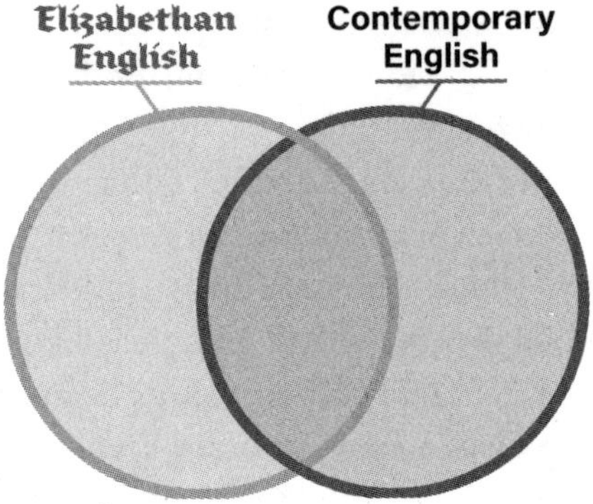

I have exaggerated the distance between the two Englishes here to make the diagram easier to decode, but here's the point: A false friend happens when our English and Elizabethan English look like they're overlapping but they're not. A false friend straddles the border between the two Englishes.

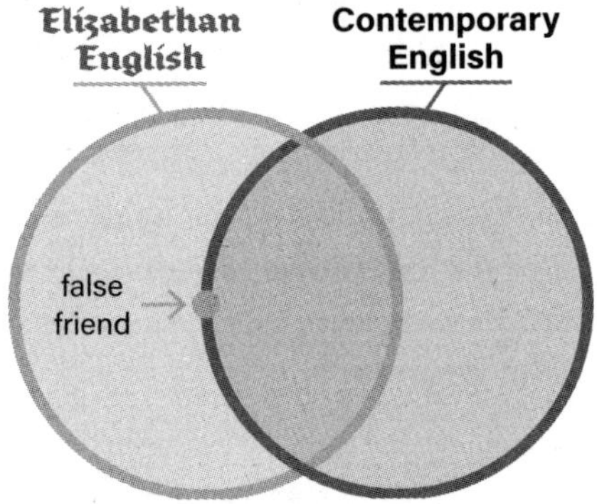

What is a KJV false friend, then, as I define it? It's three things:

1. It's a word in the KJV that we still use in contemporary English.
2. It's a word that today's English speakers use differently than the Elizabethans four-hundred-plus years ago did. That is, our English uses it with a different set of senses.

3. And it's a word used in such a way that this difference escapes the notice of many English readers.[5] We don't know to look it up because we don't realize we're misunderstanding the intent of the KJV translators at that place.

The first and second elements of a false friend are pretty objective. You can use various tools I'm going to show you to discover how we use a given word and how earlier English speakers used it.

But that third point depends on the reader. There are some skilled and experienced readers of the KJV out there, and there are some easy false friends that don't trip up all readers. Consider "The LORD is my shepherd, I shall not **want**" (Ps. 23:1). "Want" meant "lack," not "desire." I think a lot of KJV readers know this one.

But most false friends are simply not known or are known by very few. I feel quite confident that the fishing poles and lures I am about to hand you will help you catch more false friends than you knew before. I know this because I'm in the same fishing boat as you; none of us are native Elizabethan English speakers. I speak contemporary American English, not one from some other time or place. I thought I understood these words, but I didn't—because of language change.

Observing Language Change

Language change gets our attention mainly, I think, when it is controversial. Even openly non-Christian and self-confessedly liberal journalist Nicholas Kristof of *The New York Times* has expressed alarm at the ideological attempts at language change that

5. There is no International Olympic Committee for defining the standards here; I tend to think that if 15 percent of contemporary readers misunderstand a given KJV word *because of language change*, it should probably count as a false friend. Good people may set the number higher.

have been so divisive in recent years, writing, "Latino to Latinx. Women to people with uteruses. Homeless to houseless. LGBT to LGBTQIA2S+. Breastfeeding to chestfeeding. Asian American to AAPI. Ex-felon to returning citizen. Pro-choice to pro-decision. I inhabit the world of words, and even I'm a bit dizzy."[6]

Five of those eight attempts at language change are direct results of the sexual revolution, and that may be why language change has a bad name among my fellow conservative Christians. If indeed language change were all about affirming sexual sins, I'd be opposed to it. But language change is about far more than "gay" and "they."[7]

True language change—for a language as big as English—is far bigger than the latest list of so-called wokeisms. It's very rarely accomplished on purpose, whether by activists or anyone else. Language change is almost always, instead, natural. It's something God built into language. And I know that because it happens everywhere we look. It happens quietly in every language, and it happens all throughout each language.

Have you ever considered the fact that *every single word you ever think, speak, or write is the result of language change*? Go back far enough in history, and no resident of the British Isles would understand a single word you say (except "fish and chips," I'm pretty sure). Verbs change, nouns change, pronouns change, adjectives change, interjections change, sentence structures change,

6. Nicholas Kristof, "Inclusive or Alienating? The Language Wars Go On," *The New York Times*, February 1, 2023, www.nytimes.com/2023/02/01/opinion/inclusive-language-vocabulary.html.

7. Anne Curzan in the generally excellent *The Secret Life of Words: English Words and Their Origins* (The Teaching Company, 2012), lecture 28, makes the point that every developed community of language speakers will have those who police that language. And this policing isn't perpetrated only by progressives. Conservatives do it too. It seems that people who object to language policing are often objecting to their cultural enemies doing it; we're fine with it as long as we get to be the police! Here's what I suggest: Go ahead and have your word fights. Words are symbols of our common life. But once the fight is over, and "fireman" becomes "firefighter" (for example), remember that your kids or grandkids were born long after the dust settled and are just speaking the language as it's handed to them.

spellings change, pronunciations change. A few of these changes are rapid; most are not. In *Authorized*, I quoted Ammon Shea: "There are two things that have remained constant. The English language continues to change and a large number of people wish that it would not."[8]

In this book, I'm not cheering language change (though I do find it endlessly fascinating); I am merely acknowledging language changes. I don't think we should oppose language change in general, however—even if we must oppose specific changes. Here's Shea again, with some witty wisdom for us:

> There has never been an official governing body for the English language. For many people who think that English requires nightly baths and strict supervision, this is the linguistic equivalent of raising a child on a steady diet of potato chips and cupcakes, giving them no curfew, and always telling them that they are special, no matter what.[9]

And yet, he says this too (and I apologize for the way he makes light of eternal punishment; it's his overall point I'm trying to get across):

> According to those who sit up at night worrying about the state of our language, English has been headed to hell in a hand basket for a very long time. From the stubborn continuity of English, however, it seems clear that either (a) we are in an exceedingly slow hand basket or (b) the language will not break, no matter how willfully we mistreat it.[10]

People are often full of complaints about how (other) people are ruining the language and full of nostalgia for the golden era in which people used to speak and write English correctly—1950,

8. Ammon Shea, *Bad English: A History of Linguistic Aggravation* (Perigee, 2014), x.
9. Shea, *Bad English*, 174.
10. Shea, *Bad English*, ix–x.

say, or maybe 1611. But I'm convinced that they haven't reckoned with the God-given reality of language change.

Speaking Very Well English[11]

Too many critics of contemporary English have tied their linguistics to their eschatology (their expectations for the future): Language change, for them, can only wax worse and worse. But not one of those complainers speaks and writes like Eisenhower, let alone like King James. Changes have crept into their English unawares.

Now, my mother always said that people who don't have anything nice to say shouldn't say anything at all. I find it hard to trust the linguistic judgment of someone who finds nothing worth praising in contemporary English speech or writing. Where does my Christian faith or my Bible tell me that language change is always bad? Read the best, most sparkling English prose available in contemporary books and articles, and if your ear is tuned, you'll know it couldn't have been written fifty years ago or even thirty. When I sit down to read articles from the year I was born, 1980, I can tell they're as old as I am. I'm not saying writing was bad then. I am saying it can be good, very good, now. English has not gotten worse. Or better. Just different. Slowly. There have always been bad writers and good, bad speakers and good, in every version of our mother tongue.

I have my own pet peeves about contemporary language; all linguists do. It annoys me, for example, when interview subjects on the radio begin all their answers with "So . . ." and

11. Once upon a time, I was a graduate student who paid the bills by working at the university library. A young (American) student worker at the library stopped into my office and told me there was a Moldovan student looking for help with his homework. I asked her about his language proficiency. She said, "Oh, he speaks very well English." For some reason, this minor gaffe has delighted me for decades.

when they pepper their speech with "sort of."[12] That's faddish, infelicitous verbal clutter, in my humble opinion. But linguistic infelicities, too, have always existed.[13] They're not the special bane of our own time. And I'm willing to admit that the ugliness of "so" and "sort of" may be in the ear of this beholder. I even readily grant that they carry a conversation-smoothing function.

I simply think that complaints about contemporary English are often misdirected. Grumble about a screen-addled culture that doesn't sufficiently value beautiful language—fine. I do it too. But don't let yourself think that the English language itself is irretrievably damaged. There are countless people who haven't bowed the knee to banality. There are many very good English writers out there—people who write with clarity, insight, power, and verve.

It is an axiom—a first principle—of contemporary linguistics that every language is perfect to its speakers. Every language can be used to communicate everything its speakers or writers need to say. And this axiom fits rather well with the theology of a Bible in which God promised to bless all the families of the earth. *God can speak contemporary English.* He's not frustrated or limited by the changes that have occurred in it over time.

A tiny few attempted and actual changes in English are motivated by sin; I don't deny this. What I deny is that all language change is bad because a tiny bit of it is. Don't throw out the whole truckload of eggs because of three cracked eggs in the shipment. With that habit, you'll have nothing at all with which to make omelets.

---

12. One of my favorite writers—whose prose is simply excellent, whose mind is simply brilliant—Ross Douthat, says "sort of" about once a minute in every interview he does.

13. I find it interesting that in Britain they spell "um" as "erm," even though I think Americans hear it as "um."

Eight Ways Language Changes

I have observed that most people, if they ever think about language change beyond the controversies that make the news, think mainly of borrowings and coinages.

Borrowings are new words that are brought into the language from other languages, such as *karaoke* and *sudoku*, both of which happen to be from Japanese. Once those two things arrived on American and British shores, English needed labels for them. So, we "borrowed" the names for those things from their inventors, though I don't get any sense we're going to give them back. We're keeping them; they're English words now. This is indeed one way language changes. Languages grow as we need new words for new things. English has a glorious ability to beg, borrow, and steal from other languages.[14]

Coinages are another way words are added. It was Richard Dawkins in 1976 who invented the word "meme," meaning some element of culture—a tune, a fashion, a style of architecture—that gets copied and passed around among people. Since then, that word has changed, or expanded, to include internet memes—humorous images with accompanying text that are designed to be copied and passed around. I tend to think that only a tiny number of invented words ever get used by enough people to count as English. "Hangry," for example, is still more of a joke than a word. But who knows? We could look back one day and call it a coinage, a word invented by a specific person at a specific time and place.[15]

Borrowings and new coinages are, in my judgment, the second-best known elements of language change—second to

14. Anne Curzan once went through the whole alphabet and named a language starting with each letter from which English had borrowed at least one word. See her *Secret Life of Words*.

15. It could have been my wife, when she was pregnant with our first child in 2010, I think. When I read this sentence to my wife recently, she insisted that "hangry" *is* a word; sure enough, my favorite dictionary, NOAD, includes an entry for it. Perhaps I am behind the times.

whatever terms over which we are currently fighting a culture war. But borrowings and coinages and culture wars are far from the only ways language changes. Of the numerous ways in which languages morph over time, I'll mention just a few—and the units of this book will cover more. It is essential to understand language change if you wish to catch KJV words you don't know you don't know.

1. Deriving

Some words form by derivation from others. English speakers often add prefixes and suffixes to existing words to form new words. You can imagine the adjective "ethnic" becoming the noun "ethnicness." But it happened to use a different suffix and so became "ethnicity."[16]

2. Changing Part of Speech

Some words form by moving from one part of speech to another, such as from noun to verb. The noun "drill"—a tool most of us know—rather quickly became the verb "to drill," according to the *Oxford English Dictionary* (OED).[17]

Other words have moved from noun to adjective, like "fun." Consider "We had fun," and "That was fun." You could read "fun" in each as a noun (try it); but you can hear how "fun" in "That was fun" came from sounding like a thing (a noun) to sounding like a quality of a thing (an adjective modifying "that"). You can hear both meanings still, depending on how you cock your head. The OED suggests that "fun" was a noun for over a century before it started to be used as an adjective. Clearly, however, it's

16. Several of the labels and examples here are drawn from Joan Bybee, *Language Change* (Cambridge University Press, 2015), 2.

17. In fact, the noun first appears in 1611, of all years; the verb first appears eleven years later, in 1622. See OED, under "drill." (Note: The OED appears in many editions; I primarily quote the electronic version throughout this book, but I also have two different print editions.)

one now. If you object to language change, you can never have a fun time again.

3. Compounding

Some words are invented by joining other words together. English speakers once spoke of birds that were black, and they called them, quite naturally, "black birds." The stress was more on "birds" than on "black." English speakers likewise once wrote with chalk on boards that were black, and they called them "black boards." The stress, again, was on the second word (you can hear this kind of thing, depending on the compound, on very old radio recordings). But now, both "blackbird" and "blackboard" have become proper English words in their own rights, and a "backshift" has taken place in the stress: Now we speak of *black*birds and *black*boards.[18]

4. Narrowing

Some words narrow in meaning over time. "Hound" used to mean any dog; now it means only a certain kind of dog. "Meat" was once used to speak of all foods: "I have **meat** to eat that ye know not of," Jesus says in the KJV (John 4:32). But now the word "meat" has narrowed; it refers to only one kind of food, namely the edible flesh of animals.

5. Broadening

Some words broaden over time. "Decimate" is a famous example; you can see the Latin prefix for "a tenth" (*deci-*) in the word. Indeed, "decimate" used to be a very specific word that meant "killing one in every ten"[19]—one-tenth of the captured

18. I got the concept of the backshift from my favorite linguist, John McWhorter, who discusses many examples in his excellent podcast—of which I have listened to every episode—called *Lexicon Valley*.

19. "To punish every tenth man chosen by lot." P. G. W. Glare, ed., *Oxford Latin Dictionary* (Oxford University Press, 2012), under *decimō*.

enemy soldiers, say, or one-tenth of army deserters. But because that kind of decimation is not a thing people need to refer to very often, "decimate" came to mean something broader and more general: to severely or drastically reduce something, to almost destroy it. Along the way, the word has almost become the opposite of itself; it went from destroying only a tenth to destroying all but (approximately) a tenth.

You could make it your goal in life to get everyone to use "decimate" in its "correct" sense of one in every ten, but you won't succeed—and if you do, you'll have murdered the word.

6. Ameliorating (Getting Better)

Words in separate languages can follow similar paths. The words for "grab" in English and Spanish (*coger*) appear to me to have done just this. "Grab" used to mean something at least mildly evil: "to appropriate to oneself in a rapacious or unscrupulous manner" (OED). You grabbed land from a person or grabbed a person in an undesired way. That meaning persists to a degree today: Someone might "grab your seat" while you step away. But we also "grab" a bite to eat with no implication that we stole it. Our food does not feel ill-used from hearing that it was "grabbed." That word has, in most uses, gotten better than it once was.

Similarly, I was warned in Spanish classes that *coger* meant "to grab" or "to catch" (among other things) in some Spanish-speaking countries, but it's the equivalent of the F-word in Latin America—yikes!

So, you can't say to someone, "In Spanish, *coger* means 'to grab.'" You have to specify which region of the Spanish-speaking world you're talking about. Likewise, you can't say, "In English, 'grab' means 'to obtain something quickly, such as a coffee or a bit of food.'" You have to specify which era of English you're talking about. I don't know for sure which direction the word *coger* has gone in Spanish, but the word "grab" in English has ameliorated; it has gotten better.

7. Pejorating (Getting Worse)

Other words, over time, get worse. There is a well-known phenomenon in language called the "euphemism treadmill." It used to be that people who lived on the street were called "bums." The word ultimately came from the German word *bummeln*, meaning "to stroll" or "to loaf about." But so many negative connotations attached themselves to the word "bum" over time that it's more polite today—and not just among the politically correct—to say "the homeless." Almost certainly, the word "homeless" is picking up all those same negative connotations, because being a homeless person or a bum very frequently goes along with other dirty and risky and criminal behaviors. "Bum" got worse over time and "homeless" is already doing the same; it's now becoming more polite to say "those experiencing homelessness."

As with language change more generally, we tend to complain only about certain changes. Most others we just accept, often without even noticing them. For example, effectively no one in America today uses the phrase "colored people," even though the Black-run NAACP originally stood for the National Association for the Advancement of Colored People. That term has undergone pejoration. (Though "people of color" is currently culturally acceptable in an interesting twist of cultural and linguistic history.)

8. Metonymy (Moving Along a List of Related Concepts)

Some words change by moving from one idea to a related idea, a phenomenon in language called "metonymy." The word "bureau" was originally a French word for a piece of cloth, a *bure*, that was often placed on tables where people were working. So, how did the French word *bureau* become the "B" in FBI? Well, the word came to refer over time to the room in which people worked, not just the table. Then it ultimately came to refer to the work that was done in the room. It would be foolish, however, to tell the Washington Bureau Chief at CBS News that his title *really means* "head of the piece of cloth of the estate of the descendants of wheat sheaf." Every one of those three words in that title has changed meaning over time by the process of metonymy.[20] They simply no longer mean what they used to mean, and only the nerdiest nerds even know what they used to mean—or even stop to think that they once meant something other than what they mean now.

The Morality of Language Change

There are many more ways in which words change. I'm trying to demonstrate only that language change is natural, normal, inevitable, and widespread—and is, therefore, nothing to fear in itself. I give everybody permission to resist a few select instances of language change; I certainly don't like all changes that have occurred in English since I was born, especially when someone reminds me of my rapidly advancing age by using a slang term I don't know.

But you simply cannot oppose all language change, or you would be stuck having literally nothing to say—because we don't know the language Adam and Eve spoke, and we don't know the original forms of the various languages God invented at Babel.

20. Proper nouns like "Washington" are a special case, but indeed the name of the first president of the United States did not come from a town somewhere in England in which things were washed. *All* towns are places where things are washed, or they get dirty very quickly! "Washington" comes from "wheat sheaf," which probably became the name of a person or office, *Hwæsa;* plus *ing,* which meant something like "from" or "of"; plus *tun,* meaning "fenced-off estate" and, later, "town." "Chief" comes ultimately from the Latin word *caput,* meaning "head." A chief is like a head because he stands at the top of the organizational chart and directs the work of others—that's metonymy! Note: I draw the "bureau" example from Bybee, *Language Change,* 199. Also note: Take the evolved meaning of "bureau," add it to the Greek root for "power," which came to mean "rule," and you get yet another word, "bureaucracy"!

Every argument you make against language change has to be made using words whose meanings—and pronunciations, and spellings, and more—have changed over time.

It's illuminating to look at the changes to English that have annoyed or even infuriated previous generations. A common example is "balcony," which used to annoy some people who insisted it should be pronounced "ball-CONE-ee," with the stress on the second syllable—because that's the way it's pronounced in Italian. This doesn't even occur to us anymore.

Benjamin Franklin (himself a great writer) didn't like the word "colonize"; he thought it should be a noun only ("colony"), not a verb.[21] One obscure nineteenth-century elocutionist, William Henry P. Phyfe, left us a list of pronunciations he felt were unacceptable or low-class. "Isolate" had to be "IZ-zo-late"; "equable" had to be "EE-qua-ble"; "sacrilegious" had to be "sac-ri-LEE-jus." Presumably, those were acceptable pronunciations in his day. But clearly, they've all died out. Today, anyone who followed Phyfe's advice would, at best, appear odd. At worst, they'd be thrown off a ball-CONE-ee.[22]

When lexicographer (dictionary maker) Samuel Johnson began work on the world-famous *A Dictionary of the English Language* in 1746, he hoped that his work would end the messiness of language change "by enshrining the language in the frozen state of print."[23] He says this clearly in his preface. But by the publication of the work almost a decade later, he realized that he'd simply been wrong. The famously clever Johnson wrote in that same preface:

> When we see men grow old and die at a certain time, one after another, from century to century, we laugh at the elixir that promises

21. Curzan, *Secret Life of Words*, lecture 36.

22. I drew this example from the stupendous book that anyone interested in language change should read: John McWhorter, *Words on the Move: Why English Won't—and Can't—Sit Still (Like, Literally)* (Henry Holt, 2016).

23. McWhorter, *Words on the Move*, 2.

> to prolong life to a thousand years. With equal justice may the lexicographer be derided, who being able to produce no example of a nation that has preserved their words and phrases from mutability [changeableness], shall imagine that his dictionary can embalm his language, and secure it from corruption and decay—who shall image that it is in his power to change sublunary nature, or to clear the world at once from folly, vanity, and affectation. With this hope, however, academies have been instituted to guard the avenues of their languages, to retain fugitives, and to repulse intruders; but their vigilance and activity have hitherto been vain. Sounds are too volatile and subtile for legal restraints. To enchain syllables, and to tie down the wind, are equally the undertakings of pride.[24]

Clearly, English has changed since Johnson's day. We would say "imagine" where he said "image," for example. Language change is neither new nor bad, not in itself. Rejecting it wholesale is like insisting that your first ever Facebook profile pic, from 2007, is what you "really look like."[25]

And if you worry that accepting language change will cause meaning to fall apart, remember the handbasket. Language change may seem threatening, but after it happens, you can effectively see how it fits into stable patterns like those I've already mentioned: broadening, ameliorating, metonymy, and so on. McWhorter says, "The implications that pull a word's meaning in a new direction are ones that all speakers intuit, not the idiosyncratic fancies of single persons."[26] This is why, I think, different (Indo-European) languages experience similar changes.[27] This wouldn't happen if language change were unnatural, or entirely

24. Samuel Johnson, *Dictionary of the English Language* (London, 1755), 2. This quote has been lightly updated for contemporary legibility.

25. If that's actually true, well, more power to you. Or you are dead and the embalmers did their work rather well.

26. McWhorter, *Words on the Move*, 84.

27. See my chapter on "study" in this book, for example: In English and in Greek, the word went from meaning "be diligent" to meaning "hit the books" or "engage in academic research."

random, or caused only by linguistic lobbyists who are, like Big Brother in George Orwell's *1984*, trying to change reality by renaming it.

McWhorter acknowledges that watching your language change can be like watching your child date. It's not wholly pleasant; you don't want to think about it in too much detail. But both language change and puberty are natural. And without that growing maturity, there would be no grandchildren. We who worship a good God, the God of a created *order*, need to learn to love and live with the good things he placed in that order.

And, in case you were wondering, both the Hebrew of the Old Testament and the Greek of the New Testament were themselves results of language change. This is easier to see with the latter, because we have lots of Greek from previous eras to compare it to. But scholars have also carefully detailed grammatical and lexical (word-focused) changes in biblical Hebrew,[28] and the subsequent history of the language is fascinating—a language that died and was revived, like no other I've ever heard of, and one that has subsequently undergone change as modern Israelis have used it.[29] I myself have observed language change in Greek. I can read New Testament Greek, but I cannot piece together the older Homeric and classical Greek, and I can't follow today's Greek. The letters are basically the same, but it feels kind of like listening to someone who speaks with such a terribly thick accent that you're catching only one word in ten. In other words, I can't read modern Greek, but I can decimate it.

28. Cynthia L. Miller-Naudé and Ziony Zevit, eds., *Diachrony in Biblical Hebrew*, Linguistic Studies in Ancient West Semitic, vol. 8 (Eisenbrauns, 2012). "Diachrony" means language change over time (*dia* = through; *chrony* = time). The book lists several specific linguistic features—from spelling to the grammaticalization of certain words—that are used differently in the (apparently) later portions of the Old Testament than they are in the earlier parts.

29. I especially enjoyed Lewis Glinert, *The Story of Hebrew* (Princeton University Press, 2017).

All languages are on their way from being one thing to being something else. And that something else is not the final phase of the language, the state of perfection. Nor is it a state of complete degradation, in which all we're left with is the word "OK" and a variety of grunts and facial expressions. As Anne Curzan said,

> When people think about the history of English, . . . they want to make it have an endpoint toward which all the changes are heading. . . . Some think that this point toward which English . . . is heading is ultimate beauty or efficiency. Others may think it is the point of decay or ruin, and they often look back to some moment in the past when the language was more eloquent—1611, when the King James Bible was written; the time of the American Declaration of Independence; the time of Jane Austen or Charles Dickens or the time of Abe Lincoln. *That's when English was good, and that's when people knew how to use an apostrophe.*
>
> But language doesn't seem to have any specific endpoint. It is, of course, at the mercy of its speakers. And they are using the language to adapt to and talk about their worlds. Whatever they need the language to do, it will do. And if it can't, the speakers will borrow words, or make up words, or extend the meaning of words they already have, so that they can use the language to do what they need it to do.[30]

Individual English-speaking cultures might produce better or worse poetry, fiction, journalism, history, or other literary works over time. I think they do. Individual English writers may have more or less ability and talent. I think they do. But English itself isn't getting better or worse.

If language change exists everywhere, if it has given us the language we speak, if it gave us the languages in which God

30. Curzan, *Secret Life of Words*, lecture 35, emphasis mine.

chose to inspire his Word, if it neither perfects nor degrades our language—*then language change cannot be intrinsically evil.*[31]

Fishing for False Friends

Now back to false friends for a moment before we conclude this introduction. False friends are what happens when language changes. They are misunderstandings caused by the subtle shifts in word meaning that are abundantly natural to human language. False friends aren't the KJV translators' fault—or Shakespeare's fault, or Tyndale's, or any writers of English words from any period in history. And they aren't your fault. You are not dumb for missing the words in this book. If you are dumb, then so am I, because I myself misunderstood almost all of the false friends in this book for many years as a KJV reader.

I have been asked many times to provide a complete list of KJV false friends. For a good while, I thought this book might achieve that goal: I thought I might just write a chapter on every single KJV false friend. I got up to a manuscript that was 150,000 words long, with no clear end in sight. But my publisher wisely cautioned me against this plan. Instead of simply producing a false friends list that could create Bible study dependence, I'd rather teach people how to fish. As the classic saying goes, "Give a man a fish, and you'll feed him for a day; teach a man how to fish, and he'll be able to read the King James Version."

Plus, I don't have a full list. There are a fair number of edge cases; language interpretation is not a perfectly objective science. And more importantly to me, I can't bring myself to read

31. It is my personal opinion that multiple languages will be spoken on the new earth because Revelation speaks of the existence of "nations" in the eschaton, and language is often (though admittedly not always) a feature of nationhood. But this is mere speculation on my part. It is double speculation on my part—a rickety shack built on the back of an aging turtle—to then guess that language change itself will continue throughout eternity.

through the whole KJV for the purpose of looking for misleading archaisms. The Bible is God's Word, not a linguistic science experiment. All of my false friends—both in this book and on my YouTube channel—came to me naturally through my personal Bible study or were sent to me by commenters, friends, and viewers. *You* can read this book, learn my methods, and send me a false friend I may then make a video about. I'm certain there are more. Think of this book as trying to provide a representative sample of false friends—like one of those tasting plates at a seafood restaurant with all kinds of fish on them. If I inspire you to become a fisher, then you might someday add to the platter.

In this book, I've divvied up the false friends into loose categories by the kind of language change they exhibit. I don't present the categories as rigid, merely as (hopefully) helpful. And there's no particular order to them. You can loaf around, or you can stroll through. But I did front-load the book with fuller and more important examples. You might want to start with the first six—"study," "bruise," "science," "miserable," "sincere," and "hell"—before skipping ahead. "Miserable," for example, is the first word for which we'll use all five fishing steps rather than the more common four.

A note: As you read, I strongly, vehemently, ardently, fervidly, and earnestly encourage you to write out your answer to the simple question—"What does ___ mean?"—that is provided at the beginning of each chapter. I think you will get much more out of this book if you force yourself to describe your current understanding of each of my false friends before I discuss it. If you don't do this, I think your brain will do what my nine-year-old does when he gets something wrong on a test. It will say, "I knew the right answer the whole time!" I'm not here to trick you; I'm here to teach you. You'll learn better if you prove to yourself that you didn't know before.

Five Smooth Steps

It's time, then, for me to reveal the five steps we'll use to find, investigate, and verify the meaning of KJV words we don't know we don't know.

Five Steps for Fishing for False Friends

1. Notice a possible false friend, either . . .
   a. through contextual confilct or . . .
   b. through checking other translations.
2. Look up the relevant Hebrew or Greek word(s) in a responsible original-language lexicon.
3. Look up the English word in a contemporary dictionary to find out what it means today.
4. Look up the English word in the 20-volume OED to find out what it could mean in 1611.
5. Occasionally, when necessary, study the English word in a linguistic corpus.

The best way to learn what I mean by these steps really is just to jump in the water where the fish are.

Understandest what thou readest in the King James Version? Let me show you how.

Narrowing

I AM NOT USING RIGOROUS, scientific categories to organize this book—though I will sometimes borrow terminology that comes from those categories. "Semantic narrowing" is one of those, certainly. It refers to words whose meanings have specialized over time and become more restrictive. We'll start with a key example.

1. Study

> **Study** to shew thyself approved unto God, a workman that needeth not to be ashamed, rightly dividing the word of truth. (2 Tim. 2:15)

What do you think "study" means in this verse?

MOSTLY, I THINK WE do understand the KJV. I'm sure of it. Mostly, its English is our English. It's not hard to learn "thee" and "ye." And with only a little effort, we can learn some of the mildly more difficult words and constructions in the KJV.

Bible study is very, very important to me. I own tons of Bible study helps. I teach Bible study in church and on YouTube. I was the editor of *Bible Study Magazine* for two years. I'm pro–Bible study. And what's more, I study my Bible.

But I'm convinced there is a major Bible study tool that most KJV readers today are missing. It's the conceptual tool I mentioned in the preface and introduction: what I call false friends—or words we don't know we don't know.

"Study" is a perfect example, as we'll see. Notice how it's used in the commonly cited verse above. Indeed, what did "study" mean in 2 Timothy 2:15 in 1611?

Let's go through the four (sometimes five) steps. This first time, I'll list them out explicitly. In future chapters, they will be assumed.

1. Notice a possible false friend, either (a) through contextual conflict or (b) through checking other translations.

Our first step in the false friends process is simply noticing a possible false friend.

Empirically speaking, I don't think people today are noticing by careful reading that "study" in 2 Timothy 2:15 is a potential false friend. It is possible, however, that they might notice the word doesn't work well in its other New Testament occurrence:

> We beseech you, brethren, that ye . . . **study** to be quiet, and to do your own business, and to work with your own hands, as we commanded you. (1 Thess. 4:11)

Have you indeed noticed the apparent oddity of this use of the word "study"? Who takes courses or buys books that help them learn how to be quiet? (If anyone does, could they share these courses and books with me for use on my children during long car trips?)

If you are an exceptionally sharp and attentive reader, you may notice "study" in 1 Thessalonians 4:11 and remember it when you come to 2 Timothy 2:15.

But most likely, you will only notice this false friend if you read other English (and even non-English) translations. And this is true of translations that are based on the same Hebrew and Greek texts as the KJV.[1] The New King James Version, for example, reads this way:

> **Be diligent** to present yourself approved to God.

The old Reina-Valera Antigua Version of 1602 reads,

> **Procura** con diligencia presentarte a Dios aprovado.[2]

(Procura means "strive.") The KJV appears to be telling us to "hit the books," while other translations are more general: "be diligent," "strive." Are these other versions opposed to Bible study?

Don't be quick to conclude this; my concept of false friends will help show that some apparent contradictions between the

---

1. This book will studiously avoid the topics of Old and New Testament textual criticism, which are irrelevant to the purpose of this book. Readers are free never to check translations other than the KJV, or to check only those translations that are based on the Masoretic Hebrew text or Greek Textus Receptus, such as the KJVER, the Simplified KJV, the NKJV, and any of a large number of foreign language translations, such as older editions of the Reina-Valera in Spanish, the Luther Bible in German, and others.

2. *La biblia que es los sacros libros del Viejo y Nuevo Testamento* (en casa de Lorenc o Jacobi, 1602). The Reina-Valera Antigua was first translated and published in 1569 by Casiodoro de Reina, after twelve years of intensive work, and later put out in 1602 in revised form by Cipriano de Valera, who gave more than twenty years of his life to its revision and improvement.

KJV and other Bibles are due to totally reasonable misunderstandings modern readers have when we read the Elizabethan English of the KJV. They are due, in other words, to language change.

But we haven't confirmed this yet for "study" in 2 Timothy 2:15. On to step 2.

2. Look up the relevant Hebrew or Greek word(s) in a responsible original-language lexicon.

Our next step is to look up the original-language word in a responsible original-language lexicon (for what counts as "responsible," see appendix 1828). The standard Greek-English dictionary is BDAG.[3] And it says that the Greek word being translated here means

> to be especially conscientious in discharging an obligation, be zealous/eager, take pains, make every effort, be conscientious.

This word, BDAG tells us, is used when Paul responds to the Jerusalem council:

> They desired only that we should remember the poor, the very thing which I also **was eager** to do. (Gal. 2:10 NKJV)

3. Walter Bauer, Frederick W. Danker, William Arndt, and F. W. Gingrich, *A Greek-English Lexicon of the New Testament and Other Early Christian Literature*, 3rd ed. (University of Chicago Press, 2000). Some readers may wonder why I do not mention Strong's or Vine's, two resources I myself cut my lexicographical teeth on. I share some brief thoughts in appendix 1828, and I attempt to explain in greater detail in an article on the Logos Bible study blog, "How to Use Strong's Concordance and What to Use Instead," *Word by Word* (blog), March 30, 2023, https://logos.com/grow/min-strongs-concordance-and-what-to-use-instead/.

It's also used in Ephesians 4 when Paul tells the Ephesians they should be "**endeavoring** to keep the unity of the Spirit" (Eph. 4:3 NKJV).

This Greek word doesn't have anything necessarily to do with hitting the books. It is more general than our modern sense of the word "study."

3. Look up the English word in a contemporary dictionary to find out what it means today.

This leads to our next step: What is the modern sense? We've got to look at contemporary dictionaries—dictionaries whose job it is to describe English *as it is spoken and written today,* not as it was used in 1828, 1776, or 1611. Remember, English has a history going back into the mists of time. But contemporary dictionaries describe English as it is in the present.

I give more details on the dictionaries I use and don't use in appendix 1828. There are three contemporary English dictionaries that I have used extensively over many years. *Merriam-Webster Unabridged* (MW) I've used online and in Logos Bible Software; the *American Heritage Dictionary* (AHD) I've used online and in a beautiful (but aging) print edition. But in order to keep this book from being too detailed and confusing, I will be using (almost) only the *New Oxford American Dictionary* (NOAD). I give more details for this choice in that appendix, but NOAD is, in my judgment after intensive use, the best contemporary English dictionary for speakers of American English. I have consistently found that it stays up-to-date with the way educated Americans actually speak and write. And it happens to come stocked on every Mac computer, so it's easily accessible to many people.

Briefly, MW and AHD tend to hold on to senses that I have good reason to believe are no longer actively used by American (and usually other) English speakers—so they are absolutely useful for reading older literature. Those who are curious should read that appendix—and chapter 25, "Passenger," where I give an example of a word that I think NOAD gets right and other dictionaries get wrong.

So, what does NOAD tell me that "study" means?

> [To] devote time and attention to acquiring knowledge on (an academic subject), especially by means of books.

This kind of study surely involves diligence and effort, but it's more specific than the Greek word in 2 Timothy 2:15.

There *are* instances of this sense of the word "study" in the KJV. KJV translator Miles Smith warns us in the preface against failing to "studie" the Scriptures, and we see this sense (in the noun form) in Ecclesiastes:

> Of making many books there is no end; and much **study** is a weariness of the flesh. (12:12)

And there are other passages in the KJV where I am, frankly, not sure without checking the Hebrew what "study" means:

> Their heart **studieth** destruction, and their lips talk of mischief. (Prov. 24:2)

I poked around in the Hebrew to see what it means to "study destruction." It appears to mean to "devise" or "plot" destruction. (And don't forget "**study** to be quiet.")

What I'm hypothesizing at this point in the process is that "study" could have meant in 1611 what it means today, but it could also have meant something different. That is, it used to have more than one sense, and at least one of those senses is one we don't have anymore—though maybe one dictionary still includes it?

Let us turn, then, to step 4.

4. Look up the English word in the twenty-volume OED to find out what it could mean in 1611.

Now we must look at the fourth major English dictionary I constantly use, and I need to pause a bit to tell you about it. I am speaking of the world-famous OED, the *Oxford English Dictionary*. Oxford makes many dictionaries, including the NOAD that I've already praised. But the OED is the granddaddy of them all. It is massive, exhaustive, and expensive. If you buy it in print, you'll get twenty full volumes—or two large, heavy volumes in which the print is shrunk down so much that eight pages fit on one spread. It has to come with a magnifying glass.

Why is the OED so large?

A few reasons: First, it covers the whole English language—all the words and all the senses of the words. Second, it covers the whole *history* of the English language—all the words and senses that are still used along with all those that are no longer used. Lastly, it gives "citations," little snippets from English texts going far back into our history that illustrate the senses the OED editors see in the words.

The entry for "study" is available freely at the OED website at my request, and I believe it will remain open for at least a number of years.[4] I can't put the whole thing in a book, because it's too "tall." But I took a screenshot of the page online and edited it so that the entry comes in four columns instead of one, and the image below is what I got (I know the text is still too small to read).

4. Head to https://www.oed.com/dictionary/study_v.

You can see that there are numerous senses for the word "study" and numerous citations under each sense.

Do any of them help us in our quest to understand what the KJV translators meant by "**study** to shew thyself approved"? Yes. With the OED, the answer is always yes. The following image is the most relevant sense (this is just one of the twenty-eight senses and subsenses in the screenshot above).

I.1. † *intransitive*. With to, *for*, *after*, †*umbe*, etc.: to strive towards, direct one's efforts to, set one's mind on, devote oneself to. *Obsolete*. **late Old English–1816**

IOE Seo [*sc.* Martha] studdede emb þa uterlice þing [L. *circa exteriora occupatur*], þeos oðer þa inweardlice þing gemyndelice besceawode.
translation of R. d'Escures, *Sermo in Festis Sancte Marie Virginis* in R. D.-N. Warner, *Early Eng. Homilies* (1917) 136

***a*1382** Alle to auarice studien [Latin *omnes avaritiae student*].
Bible (Wycliffite, early version) (Douce MS. 369(1)) (1850) Jeremiah vi. 13

***c*1384** Forsothe grauntynge the trewthe of alle autours, bot we oure self studyinge to shortnesse [Latin *brevitati studentes*].
Bible (Wycliffite, early version) (Douce MS. 369(2)) (1850) 2 Maccabees ii. 29

***c*1450** Þou studiest aftir nyce aray.
W. Lichefeld, *Complaint of God* (Lambeth MS. 853) l. 205 in F. J. Furnivall, *Political, Religious, & Love Poems* (1903) 205

?1520 A great wytted man may sone be enrychyd That laboryth and studyeth for ryches only.
J. Rastell, *Nature .iiii. Element* sig. Aiij^{v}

1561 Certen thinges..I haue not set forth in these my sermons, studieng much, for breuitie.
J. Daus, translation of H. Bullinger, *Hundred Sermons vpon Apocalips* Preface sig. B.vi^{v}

1603 Their Prelates,.. studying for mony, omitted the punishment limitted by law.
J. Stow, *Suruay of London* (new edition) 191

1699 Surely a Giddiness hath seized on these Men, while they study for Subtilty.
T. Edwards, *Paraselene dismantled of her Cloud* 171/2

1759 The great men of the emperor's court..make it their chief amusement, when in disgrace or banishment, to study after some new improvement or discoveries in this and other curious arts and manufactures.
Modern Part of Universal History vol. IX. 102

1816 He does sigh and languish, and study for compliments.
J. Austen, *Emma* vol. I. vi. 100

Show fewer quotations

Notice a few things. We get a careful definition and then dated citations. The word "study" was used to mean "to strive toward" or "to devote oneself to" at least up until 1816.

And let's read one of those citations, specifically the one from J. Stow's *Survey of London* (which was then spelled *Suruay of London*) in 1603. He wrote,

> Their Prelates, . . . **studying** for mony, omitted the punishment limitted by law.

"Studying for money." In today's English, that would mean that these prelates were being paid to go to school, paid to learn. But the OED editors are saying that in that context, in that day—which was very near the work of the KJV translators (1604–11)—Stow meant that the prelates were striving for money, directing their efforts to it, setting their minds on it, devoting themselves to it.

That has to be what the KJV translators meant when they said, "Study to shew thyself approved." They read the Greek New Testament, knew the meaning of the operative Greek word there, and translated that Greek into *their* English. They were trying to communicate that Paul was telling Timothy to diligently do his best, to devote himself to and set his mind on demonstrating himself to be an approved workman—someone who doesn't need to be ashamed, a Bible teacher who rightly divides the word of truth.

And note something else about the OED, namely that it marks this sense as "obsolete" (the dagger symbol in the OED, †, means the same thing). This time around, I'll show you what the OED looks like; throughout the rest of the book, I'll just quote it.

I.1. **late Old English–1816**
† *intransitive.*
With *to*, *for*, *after*, †*umbe*, etc.: to strive towards, direct one's efforts to, set one's mind on, devote oneself to. *Obsolete.*

In the judgment of the OED editors, no English speaker uses "study" to mean this anymore. And though it's possible that you could have gotten this sense from MW, which still records it, this means that contemporary dictionaries are not a reliable and sufficient tool for reading the KJV well. If you'd even thought to look up the word, two of the major dictionaries out there would have been no help. This *also* means that today's readers are very unlikely to realize that "study" in 2 Timothy 2:15, in the KJV translators' day and in their minds, meant something different from what it means for us. We have landed a false friend.[5]

Complications

The OED reveals that there's *another* now-rare sense of "study" that has a slightly different nuance, one of "aiming" more so than of "striving," and for this one the OED editors select an example from the KJV: our "study to be quiet" (1 Thess. 4:11).

> **I.2.a.** *intransitive*. To aim, endeavour, or undertake deliberately to do something. Now *rare*. **1340–**
>
> **1526** We beseche you..that ye studdy to be quyet [so 1611 *King James*], and to medle with youre owne busynes.
> *Bible* (Tyndale) 1 Thessalonians iv. 11 ...

5. I did find this word in D. A. Waite's *Defined King James Bible*, where the footnote says that the relevant Greek word here in 2 Timothy 2:15 means "be diligent." This and several other KJV editions do a pretty good job of catching false friends, though they are basically putting fish in the margins rather than giving people fishhooks. None of them, to my knowledge, teaches KJV readers how to find and verify false friends as we are learning in this book.

The OED editors are being very good biblical exegetes here, because the nuance is different between 1 Thessalonians 4:11 and the verse we've been focusing on. You don't "be diligent to be quiet." You instead make it your aim. The Greek word in that passage is different too. The one in 2 Timothy 2:15 means "be diligent" and "set your mind," and that's the sense of "study" the KJV translators intended.

Irony

Some dedicated KJV readers get exasperated with me for arguing that there are words in the KJV that they don't know they don't know. I think they believe I am criticizing the KJV itself when I explain older words and senses found within it. In fact, 2 Timothy 2:15 is the very verse I hear most often from these brothers and sisters. Here's an actual comment I received: "Ever heard of a dictionary? That's something you use to study and learn what words that you don't know mean. 2 Timothy 2:15 Study to shew thyself approved unto God."

There is some sad irony here. It's just as Inigo Montoya once said: *They keep using that word "study"; but I do not think it means what they think it means.* It's a bit like my seven-year-old who, in an effort to taunt her little brother, wrote him this note:

This is called ironic self-incrimination. I've done it, too, friends—like the time I boldly volunteered to do math in my head in a room full of PhD-toting scientists and got it wrong. But I insist that I am *not* stuped; most readers today are misunderstanding the word "study" in 2 Timothy 2:15. Through no fault of the KJV translators, through no fault of our own (who could be expected to keep up with all the subtle changes in English over the centuries?), but solely due to the inevitable process of language change, "study" in several places in the KJV doesn't mean what most of us think it means. We don't know that we don't know it.

"Study" in 2 Timothy 2:15 is a false friend.

And you have at least one wriggling fish to eat for dinner tonight. Tell your family this one; they'll be sore amazed.

2. Bruise

> I will put enmity between thee and the woman, and between thy seed and her seed; it shall **bruise** thy head, and thou shalt **bruise** his heel. (Gen. 3:15)

What do you think "bruise" means in this verse?

____

____

THIS IS AN AMAZINGLY IMPORTANT VERSE, often called the "protoevangelium," because it is the first mention of the gospel, right there in Genesis 3. Given its importance, I was shocked and slightly embarrassed that I'd never thought to look this up, even though I noticed it was odd. And this false friend has some real theological significance to it.

The same word appears again in another theologically rich passage:

> He was wounded for our transgressions, he was **bruised** for our iniquities. (Isa. 53:5)

Have you ever noticed something off about the way "bruised" is used in these two verses?

Fishing for a False Friend

You will hear some intelligent people today saying the word "crushed" instead of "bruised" when they talk about this passage (and Gen. 3:15)—like the songs and theology books that speak of Jesus "crushing" the serpent's head. And this is a pretty big deal when it comes to both of these passages, because there's a big difference between the seed of the woman crushing the head of the serpent and merely bruising it; there's a big difference between the Father crushing the Suffering Servant of Isaiah 53 for our iniquities and merely bruising him.

But why does this difference exist between the KJV and this common way of talking about these passages? Has our understanding of Hebrew changed? Did the KJV translators commit an error? Do modern hymn writers try to make these verses more severe for some reason? Did the KJV translators try to make them less severe?

We've already gotten through step 1 of the false friends process: noticing a possible false friend. Now let's try step 2: looking up the relevant words in a responsible original-language lexicon.

This step is complicated this time, more than usual. The KJV translates multiple different Hebrew words with the English word "bruise." By my count, it's ten for Hebrew and two for Greek. Let's cover some of the less important words before getting back to the big ones used in Genesis 3 and Isaiah 53.

There are three places where the KJV translates one particular Hebrew word with the English word "bruised." Every one of them is in the brutal passage Ezekiel 23, which pictures Judah and Israel as two daughters, Aholah and Aholibah. These two daughters are up to no good, and both of them, the KJV says,

> commit whoredoms in Egypt. . . . There were their breasts pressed, and there they **bruised** the teats of their virginity. (Ezek. 23:3)

In this passage, it's breasts and teats that are "bruised." That's a little odd, because the picture is not of these two young women getting beaten up or physically abused but of committing whoredom. Let's hold on to that.

Another Hebrew verb is used to speak of "bread corn" being "bruised" (Isa. 28:28). "Bread corn" is an older way of saying "the kind of grain with which one can make bread"; it is itself a false friend. And, of course, grain doesn't get "bruised." Threshed, maybe; pulverized, maybe—but not "bruised," I think. Let's hold on to that.

Yet another Hebrew word gets translated "bruise" twice in the KJV. And this, too, yields some oddities. The two verses are very similar, so I'll just read one:

> Thus saith the LORD, Thy **bruise** is incurable, and thy wound is grievous. (Jer. 30:12; see also Nah. 3:19)

The reason this is odd is that bruises are, almost by definition, curable. They go away after a while—unless you die. In that case, the bruises stick around, which can help indicate cause and time of death (or so forensic pathologists on TV have told me). But that doesn't appear to be what this passage is talking about. Let's hold on to that too.

There are also several references in the Old and New Testaments to the "bruised reed." These also contain oddities.

> Now, behold, thou trustest upon the staff of this **bruised** reed, even upon Egypt, on which if a man lean, it will go into his hand, and pierce it. (2 Kings 18:21)

Did you ever think about this—what is a "bruised reed"? There are cattails down the street from my house in a little retention pond. If you whack one of them with a stick but don't break it, will it "bruise"? I went down the street with my kids and tried this. I'm not sure if it worked. I guess maybe it did? The result did not cause discoloration, just damage, I'd say. Apples can get bruised, and so can bananas—but reeds, I'm not so sure. And why would anyone want to rest on a reed anyway?

To make matters more complicated, the Bible also talks about a "bruised reed" as an image for the weak or suffering person that Jesus the Suffering Servant came to serve:

> A **bruised** reed shall he not break, and the smoking flax shall he not quench. (Isa. 42:3; see Matt. 12:20)

Again, let's hold on to that.

Let me also note that there are places where our modern sense of "bruise" seems to work just fine in the KJV.

> Ye shall not offer unto the LORD that which is **bruised**, or crushed, or broken, or cut. (Lev. 22:24)

> From the sole of the foot even unto the head there is no soundness in it; But wounds, and **bruises**, and putrifying sores: They have not been closed, neither bound up, neither mollified with ointment. (Isa. 1:6)

And let me tell you what's going to happen when you look up all these different Hebrew words. You'll get a bunch of different English words as possibilities: break, crush, pulverize, squeeze, grip hard, smash, squash, shatter—and, yes, bruise. It would get boring if I looked up every single one of these Hebrew words individually, though this is precisely what biblical scholars have to do if they want to translate the Bible carefully (and they do)! I just don't think you'd enjoy this chapter if we discovered the precise alloys used in all our metal fishing gear like this. It's enough to see that there are other options in English for pretty much all these words besides "bruise," and that "bruise" doesn't seem, on the face of it, to make great sense in all these passages. Again, did the KJV translators commit an error?

Let's move now to step 3 in the false friends process: What does the word "bruise" mean in the English of today? You won't be shocked by this. A bruise is

> an injury appearing as an area of discolored skin on the body, caused by a blow or impact rupturing underlying blood vessels: his body was a mass of bruises after he had been attacked. (NOAD)

It can also be

> a mark indicating an area of damage on a fruit, vegetable, or plant. (NOAD)

Thank you, lexicographers. You have done your job. Yes, this is the way I have heard the word "bruised" get used all my life.

So, what giveth? Why these oddities with the usage of "bruise" in the KJV? Why did I ask you to hold on to them? Because of step 4: looking up the word in the OED.

Before the big reveal, let me read just a few more "bruise" verses, this time from the New Testament rather than the Old.

> The Spirit of the Lord is upon me, because he hath anointed me to preach the gospel to the poor; he hath sent me to heal the brokenhearted, to preach deliverance to the captives, and recovering of sight to the blind, to set at liberty them that are **bruised**. (Luke 4:18)

This is odd, because when you think of captives, you don't primarily think of their bruises. It will be clear momentarily why I say this.

> And the God of peace shall **bruise** Satan under your feet shortly. The grace of our Lord Jesus Christ be with you. (Rom. 16:20)

This brings us full circle, back to the theme in Genesis 3:15. Does God merely "bruise" Satan's head under the feet of the seed of the woman? Does he indeed merely "bruise" Satan under our feet?

Look now at the *Oxford English Dictionary*. This is the first sense it offers under the verb "bruise":

> Originally: to injure, batter, or crush (a person, animal, body part, etc.) with a heavy weight or blow. Now usually: specifically to injure by a blow which discolours the skin but does not lacerate it or break any bones; to cause to develop bruising.

And here's sense 2:

> To break, to smash; to destroy or damage by breaking or smashing.

This sense they mark as obsolete.

Did the penny drop? Did the other shoe fall? Did the fish fry? *Did you catch it?*

In most—not quite all—of the places where the word "bruise" occurs in the KJV, the KJV translators were indeed intending to communicate something more serious than discoloration of the skin without laceration of that skin or breaking of the underlying bones. They were using their word for "crush." Now, they had that word "crush," but "bruise" back then could mean "crush." It's so clear once you see it.

Then the OED makes it even clearer. It gives example sentences. Let me tell you what to look for: impossible collocations—that is, word pairings that just feel wrong or don't fit, like "I saw a three-wheeled bicycle." If it has three wheels, it's not a bicycle. Listen for that kind of thing.

Here's the 1549 Book of Common Prayer:

> Thou shalt **bruise** them with a rod of yron:
> and breake them in pieces lyke a potters vessell.

I don't think the people who chose "bruise" meant "cause a blackish-yellowish patch to break out on the skin." Rods of iron do more than bruise; they shatter and crush. Or here's Shakespeare's *Richard III* in 1597:

> **Bruisd** vnderneath the yoake of tyrannie.

You don't get bruised underneath tyrannous yokes; you get crushed. A 1483 translation of a famous phrase from 1 Corinthians 11 will make this even clearer:

> He toke breed & **brosyd** and gaue it to his dyscyples.

And I love these last two from the OED: In 1590, R. Ferris in *Most Dangerous Aduenture* spoke of someone whose

> foote once slipped, . . . he would haue beene **brused** in peeces.

And then there was the poor man spoken of in the diary of J. Lamont:

> By the fall of a keap-stone his head was **bruised** in to peices.

You don't get bruised into pieces. You get crushed to pieces. "Bruised" in the English of the Elizabethans, in the English of the KJV translators, frequently meant "crushed."

Doesn't this just make so much more sense? It makes far more sense than imagining that the KJV translators committed an error. They didn't. But neither did you or I when, for decades, we've read about the "bruised reed" and the bruising of Satan and *we have misunderstood.* I misunderstood this one till years after I wrote *Authorized.* I've known for twenty years that modern versions often used "crushed" in Genesis 3:15 and in Isaiah 53:5, but the KJV got to me first. Its wording is still the default in my mind for so many Bible phrases. And I just never really put two and two together for some of them—especially the bruised reed. I never understood that (and it doesn't help that some modern translations such as the NKJV have stuck with tradition on this phrase; it's a rare false friend found in a few places in some modern versions).

Jesus wasn't bruised for our iniquities; he was crushed for them. This is what God meant and what the KJV translators meant.

And what about the bruised reed? It's a crushed reed; that's what the KJV translators meant. It's a splintered reed. It's a reed in the first place, which doesn't have much strength, and it's a dry reed that's been crushed and splintered.

It is "a crushed reed" that Jesus will not break in Isaiah 42:3 and Matthew 12:20. And it's the "crushed" or "oppressed" whom he will set free from their yoke in Luke 4:18.

The OED also explains why the KJV translators chose "bruised" to refer to what the Egyptians did to the breasts of Aholah and Aholibah. There is yet another sense of the word that can mean

> to apply pressure to; to push, press, squeeze.

There are places in the KJV where bruise means bruise, where modern translations like the NKJV stick with bruise, and it's clearly right. Isaiah 1:6 is one: Bruises definitely belong in a list with "wounds" and "putrifying sores."

But I'm glad to know that soon the God of peace will not merely bruise Satan under the feet of Christians; he will crush him (Rom. 16:20).

In every case where "bruised" doesn't make good sense in the KJV, a check of the Hebrew or Greek and, so importantly, the OED can solve the problem. It shows that the KJV translators did not commit errors when they used the word "bruised," and it shows what those translators intended to communicate—usually the concept of crushing or shattering. The OED is the key to unlocking the KJV reader's understanding, ultimately, in this case, of the sense intended by the Spirit of God.

That's always important, but especially so when we come to the weightier matters of the law. Genesis 3:15 and the crushing of the head of the serpent—that's important. Isaiah 53:4–5 and the crushing of the Suffering Servant under the hand of the Father—that's even more important.

Glorious Bruising

How glorious that God hasn't even told Adam and Eve what their punishments for sin are before he's giving them mercy and promising a redeemer. He will crush the serpent. How glorious that the act of the Father crushing the Son serves as a prelude to the act of the Son crushing that serpent!

I feel certain, however, that this glory was obscured for some of you till now—that you didn't know what you didn't know. This is a false friend I urge you to remember.

3. Science

> Children in whom was no blemish, but well favoured, and skilful in all wisdom, and cunning in knowledge, and understanding **science**, and such as had ability in them to stand in the king's palace, and whom they might teach the learning and the tongue of the Chaldeans. (Dan. 1:4)

What do you think "science" means in this verse?

"SCIENCE" SHOWS UP TWICE in the KJV. You just read one use above. Here's the second:

> O Timothy, keep that which is committed to thy trust, avoiding profane and vain babblings, and oppositions of **science** falsely so called. (1 Tim. 6:20)

In each case, the contemporary meaning of the word "science" makes perfect sense. Daniel and his three friends understood science—great. And Paul warned Timothy not to listen to evolutionists—whose work can't really be called "science" at all.

Right?

We'll go more quickly this time. I want to prove that the process of identifying false friends is not always a long, drawn-out one.

Fishing for a False Friend

Well . . . the ancients *did* have something we might call science in the Babylonian empire, centuries before Christ; they had sophisticated astronomy, for example. And the Greeks had systematic ways of thinking about nature, though they were substantially different from the empirical methods we call science. But still, was junk science a threat to Timothy's ministry? Doesn't that sound a little funny?

Contemporary English Bible translations such as the NKJV and SKJV use words like "knowledge" and "understanding" in the two passages I just quoted—not "science."

What's going on?

In our second step, we find that the Hebrew word translated "science" in Daniel 1:4 simply means "understanding" or "knowledge." The Greek word translated "science" in 1 Timothy 6:20 means the same thing: "knowledge." There is no mention of "science" in any of the major Hebrew and Greek dictionaries I check regularly—and not just for the words in Daniel 1:4 and 1 Timothy 6:20. In fact, there are literally no words in Scripture that my main Hebrew and Greek dictionaries think can be translated by the English word "science." It's the label for a particular grouping of concepts, a grouping that did not exist in the ancient world.

When we look up "science" in a contemporary dictionary, we find that grouping of concepts is this, as you surely already know:

> the systematic study of the structure and behavior of the physical and natural world through observation, experimentation, and the testing of theories against the evidence obtained. (NOAD)

Did the KJV translators commit an error, perhaps an anachronism akin to referring to the patriarch Jacob's smartphone?

No. And NOAD gives us a strong hint toward an explanation for what's going on with "science" in the KJV. It points to our next step by including a sense it labels as "archaic": "knowledge of any kind."

We've practically landed our fish, and the OED confirms that we don't need to throw it back. You can almost read a narrative of our word's development in the senses, though in actual history it didn't work out that neatly. The word seems to have originally meant—though the origins of effectively all old words are ultimately lost to us—"the state or fact of knowing." It came also to mean "knowledge or understanding acquired by study; acquaintance with or mastery of any branch of learning." It ultimately has come to mean "a branch of study that deals with a connected body of demonstrated truths or with observed facts systematically classified and more or less comprehended by general laws, and incorporating trustworthy methods" (OED).

In other words, we see the word narrowing. "Science" used to mean knowledge of all kinds; now it refers to knowledge of a specific kind.

Different Englishes

All this, quite obviously, explains why the KJV translators stuck with "science" in 1611 while modern translations such as the NKJV choose "knowledge." Neither is wrong. In fact, *both are saying the same thing*. They're not disagreeing. They're just speaking two different Englishes.

4. Miserable

> If in this life only we have hope in Christ, we are of all men most **miserable**. (1 Cor. 15:19)

What do you think "miserable" means in this verse?

____

____

I HAVE AN ELDERLY ACQUAINTANCE who loves the KJV, as I do. He was a preacher in his day, and his day was long. He's still a preacher, even from his wheelchair. He's an earnest, zealous Christian, whom I respect.

But he has trouble understanding why people like me feel the need to point out archaic and obsolete words in his beloved Bible. I talked about it with him once; he was 100 percent gracious. He told a story about hearing a man preach out of a version other than the KJV at a funeral—neither my friend nor I know which version it was. The man cited 1 Corinthians 15:19, but when he came to that memorable phrase—"If in this life only we have hope in Christ, we are of all men most **miserable**"—the preacher read, "We are of all men most **pitiable**."

My acquaintance heard that and thought, *That isn't right. It's "miserable," not "pitiable."* He said to himself, *I thought the modern versions were supposed to make reading easier, not harder—and "pitiable" isn't a word everyone knows, but "miserable" sure is.*

Why do modern English translators use the word "pitiable" when "miserable" is, arguably, easier—more common? It has nothing to do with copyrights or the underlying Greek.

No, it's because "miserable" in 1 Corinthians 15:19 in the KJV is a false friend. But it's a subtle one, so subtle that we're not likely to notice it through contextual conflict. There's simply nothing in the context of 1 Corinthians 15 to indicate that the word meant something different in 1611 than it does today. Our modern sense of "miserable" makes perfect sense in that context. The only way to notice this false friend is the way the elderly preacher did: through noticing that contemporary translations use a different word. Unwittingly, he stumbled into step 1 of our process for discerning false friends in the KJV. This leads us into the first false friend in this book that will go on to the little-used fifth step.

Fishing for a False Friend

This older preacher stopped here, however. He didn't realize he'd entered step 1. He assumed the KJV was right and didn't pursue it further. I say, humbly, that my brother should have gone on to step 2 once he discovered the mismatch. There's nothing like an apparent discrepancy between translations to set me on an interesting Bible study journey.

If my elder brother in Christ had continued, this is what he would have seen when he looked up the original Greek:

> pertaining to being deserving of sympathy for one's pathetic condition. (BDAG)

Here's the key: This Greek word focuses not on how I feel but on how others regard me. But BDAG gives both "miserable" and "pitiable" as possible translations of this word. So, are we left thinking that modern translators, for example, chose "pitiable" just to be different from the KJV, when they could have stuck with "miserable"?

Again, we need to go to the next step. Here's what we find that "miserable" means in our English:

> (of a person) wretchedly unhappy or uncomfortable. (NOAD)

"Miserable" focuses on how I feel: unhappy, uncomfortable. "Pitiable," on the other hand, focuses not on how I feel but on how others regard me—regardless of how I feel. "Pitiable" means this:

> deserving or arousing pity. (NOAD)

In other words, you can be pitiable and not know it. You can't be miserable without being fully aware of that fact. In contemporary English, a miserable person is a sad and dejected person. Whether they deserve our pity or not, the word "miserable" doesn't tell us.

We've got another KJV verse that suggests the word "miserable" meant something different in 1611 from what it means today:

> Thou sayest I am rich, and increased with goods, and have need of nothing; and knowest not that thou art wretched, and **miserable**, and poor, and blind, and naked. (Rev. 3:17)

In other words, there are rich people who are miserable but who are so unaware of their misery that they're boasting about their wealth. Doesn't that strike you as funny? Have you ever been miserable and not known it?

We're starting to get somewhere here. There is a difference in contemporary English between the two words "miserable" and "pitiable." Now we have to ask: Was there a difference between them in 1611 when the KJV was translated? Or did "miserable" indeed have a different sense that is not available or not used (same thing) in today's English? We have to look in the only dictionary that reliably tells us not only what English words mean now but *what they used to mean when the KJV translators were alive*. We need to go to step 4.

Here's what we find that "miserable" could have meant in 1611:

> 1.a. Living or existing in a state of external distress or misery; that is in a wretched condition. (OED)

Now, let me state clearly that though I respect the OED greatly, I do sometimes disagree with it. The OED is *not* wrong to name this as a sense of the word "miserable." It *is* wrong, I think, to fail to tell its readers that this sense is giving way (or, I'd argue, has given way) to another sense the OED records for "miserable":

> 1.c. Beset by a feeling of misery; feeling very unhappy; melancholy, depressed.

This just can't be what Paul is saying to the Corinthians. It is, again, subtle, but it's definite. Read it again: "If in this life only we have hope in Christ, we are of all men most miserable" (1 Cor. 15:19). His whole point is that our state of misery is unknown to us. Here we are hoping for resurrection, not realizing that our hopes will die when our brain activity does. We're in a pitiable state *and don't know it*. That's why the contemporary translation used by that preacher said "pitiable" and not "miserable."

I simply don't think today's readers are catching this meaning through the KJV—because of language change.

But where do I get off disagreeing with the august OED? I'll tell you where—by going to step 5, which I only tend to need when I do in fact disagree in some way with the OED—which is rare! But the OED isn't perfect, and I occasionally check up on it by doing my own homework.

So, step 5.

There is a famous picture of one of the early nineteenth-century editors of the OED, James Murray, standing in the OED "scriptorium."

Surrounding him are stacks upon stacks of paper, so large and numerous that they are bending the shelving on which they sit (see top right). These were citation slips recording quotations from all over English literature and illustrating the way given words were used. These are the sources for all the millions of citations in the massive OED.

Today, of course, computers are used to find and store the citations used by lexicographers. And there are other specialized tools for people who, like me, occasionally want to do their own lexicography. They're called "corpora."

Corpus was the Latin word for "body" (which is why in French, which is derived directly from Latin, "body wash" is *nettoyant pour le corps*—"cleanser for the corpse," or the body). A "body" of English texts that is easily searchable for students of English is called "a corpus." And there's a free one online called the NOW Corpus.

The NOW Corpus, as of this writing, has collected 18.2 billion English words from all over the English-speaking world. It has done so by grabbing articles from news sites (NOW stands for "News on the Web") that come from everywhere anyone speaks English. America and Britain and Australia predominate, of course, but there are many articles from Indian and African online newspapers as well.

The word "miserable" occurs almost ninety-five thousand times in the NOW Corpus. The image on the next page shows what the first page of the report looks like.

The job of the budding lexicographer at this point is to look at as many of these citations as possible—these slips weighing down the shelves of the internet—and see what kinds of things are said to be "miserable." Do English speakers today use "miserable" to focus on someone's internal unhappiness or on their pitiable external state, regardless of how they feel?

Look at some of the uses and decide for yourself:

"I used to be **miserable** about how selfish teenagers can be."

"Life has become **miserable** for us since Vedanta-Mythri arrived."

English-Corpora: NOW
english-corpora.org/now/

NOW Corpus (News on the Web)

SEARCH | FREQUENCY | CONTEXT | OVERVIEW

FIND SAMPLE: 100 200 500 1000
PAGE: 1 / 937

93630 ENTRIES: 84062 TEXTS
LIMITS: NONE
SORTING: DATE ▼-, COUNTRY

CLICK FOR MORE CONTEXT | SAVE | TRANSLATE | ANALYZE | HELP

1		The Mirror	possible five. Overall, Citizens Advice said parcel delivery firms were offering a " miserable " service for consumers. # A surge in online shoppin
2		The Mirror	a possible five # Citizens Advice has accused the delivery firms of providing a " miserable " service (# More than 13million people had to put up
3		The Mirror	came into the picture. He was doing everything to kind of make her life miserable. # " I saw what was going on from the outside and just said
4		London Evening Standard	. And when Princess Anne -- played by Claudia Harris -- notices that William looks miserable, she has a brilliant idea. # " Isn't it time? "
5	23-11-15 KE	tuko.co.ke	Dieter Ulrich, born in DDR Wednesday, 15 November 2023 11:54 AM # The miserable state of the people in China, Russia, Venezuela, Cuba is th
6	23-11-16 KE	lankaweb.com	The PDP has maligned and poured invectives on our judges at every turn since its miserable performance in the general elections. When it is ne
7	23-11-17 KE	theeastafrican.co.ke	Shah for ruining the Sri Lankan cricket, following the debacle over Sri Lanka's miserable World Cup campaign. # Because of the connection betv
8	23-11-16 NG	sports247.ng	children. He withdrew all of my children from school, and made their lives miserable, I wept when I saw my son yesterday after the police brou
9	23-11-14 ZA	all4women.co.za	to let parents share advice. Movi Inc. # " I used to be miserable about how selfish teenagers can be, " says Bowen. " They have last-minute
10	23-11-15 PH	ph.asiatatler.com	, swiftly took responsibility for the disastrous show by Jos Buttler-led side that finished a miserable seventh, the question is whether any stakeh
11	23-11-14 SG	prestigeonline.com	and OpenOffice to do everything. If MS wanted to they could really make life miserable for all who attack them, they should be congratulated fo
12	23-11-16 SG	eco-business.com	). # " I pray and hope that I will never see Johoreans as miserable as they were during that time ever again... the threat of climate change is
13	23-11-16 BD	unb.com.bd	sure who their fathers really are. Newington -- House Greyjoy # Basically a miserable bunch of p***ks Riverview -- House Tully # They've got so
14	23-11-14 PK	thenews.com.pk	sprawling shantytowns in major cities is enough to realize how the poor masses lead a miserable life year after year. The slums in the capital D
15	23-11-15 PK	tribune.com.pk	White Sox # HR # 1 # OPS+ # 60 # It took a truly miserable 2023 season from Anderson to convince the White Sox his once team-friendly $14 m
16	23-11-16 LK	ft.lk	The PDP has maligned and poured invectives on our judges at every turn since its miserable performance in the general elections. # " When it i
17	23-11-15 IN	livelaw.in	rule, will be thrown into the Arabian Sea with the Congress making their lives miserable again, " he said, addressing massive gatherings at Bodh
18	23-11-16 IN	timesofindia.indiatimes.com	bulk deal, because these are unlikely to grab any eyeballs even online given their miserable turn in theatres. # To be sure, several trade experts
19	23-11-16 IN	thewire.in	youth and elders from our village are hiding in the forests. Life has become miserable for us since Vedanta-Mythri arrived here. " # Photo: Raja
20	23-11-16 IN	saipantribune.com	) - If you regularly experience the symptoms of seasonal allergies, you know how miserable they can make you. The congestion, sneezing, runn
21	23-11-17 IN	businessinsider.in	harass his new tenant, as he decides to make his life more and more miserable everyday. # But not backing off, their car-parking fight turns pe
22	23-11-14 NZ	autocar.co.nz	lives and a new government will work for their betterment, bringing improvements in their miserable lives. # There is a general feeling among
23	23-11-15 AU	mumbrella.com.au	you successful, " he writes in his opening pages. " What I was miserable at was being myself... It's taken me fifty years to realize that there
24	23-11-17 AU	au.eurosport.com	of Forbes, Marshall and Spencer came on during the game. # With this miserable qualifying campaign behind them it leaves a question of if Mi
25	23-11-17 AU	honey.nine.com.au	Adult Emergency entrance at 300 Booth Drive. # It's a snapshot of the miserable, undignified and, at times, hopeless situation in the Grace Hos
26	23-11-17 AU	rugby.com.au	doesn't make robots any less depressing, and here we've collected the most miserable of them all. Scroll through this slideshow of automatic d
27	23-11-15 IE	independent.ie	the white stuff fall in November. # " November has gotten off to a miserable start as far as the weather is concerned and if the latest odds are
28	23-11-15 IE	irishexaminer.com	quick Google search, the version of what Irish food looks like is grey and miserable, " he laments. # Google is not our friend when it comes to
29	23-11-17 IE	echolive.ie	that can compete with the top sides in Europe. # It's been a miserable campaign for Stephen Kenny's side, who have earned just six points so f
30	23-11-14 GB	Metro	probably my last season, because of that one betrayal. # ' I was miserable the whole season.' # The presenter later shared the news of his exit
31	23-11-14 GB	The Guardian	into the future as we can see. # The people of Gaza face truly miserable lives, even by the standard of what they have suffered for so long.
32	23-11-16 GB	Daily Mail	faked her own death and she was' running away' to escape her' miserable' life. # The Duke said his 13-year-old self had wondered if it was
33	23-11-16 GB	Daily Mail	a' trick', writing in the book:' Her life's been miserable, she's been hounded, harassed, lied about, lied to. So
34	23-11-16 GB	Daily Mail	36 hours s***ging her off and doing everything in his power to make her life miserable. Pure evil #BBUK.' # Another said:' Tom is awful.
35	23-11-16 GB	Sky	the way to erasing Gaza City from the map. # They've witnessed utterly miserable scenes belonging to another century as Palestinians line up t
36	23-11-14 GB	standard.co.uk	people, making us poorer, causing more hostility to minority groups and generally more miserable. # Everyone behind this decision should be
37	23-11-14 GB	express.co.uk	to boost his libido and energy levels. # He has said he was " miserable " and if he misses any of his medication he goes " absolutely mental "
38	23-11-14 GB	express.co.uk	could barely be bothered leaving the house. My libido was gone and I was miserable. A routine blood test showed my testosterone levels were
39	23-11-14 GB	express.co.uk	out a stale relationship because that's the done thing. # Not being exactly miserable, maybe, but definitely not making the most out of their tim
40	23-11-14 GB	uk.news.yahoo.com	. " # Mr Forde added: " You can only imagine the terror and miserable existence that these children had. " # The fiends all denied any involveme
41	23-11-14 GB	uk.news.yahoo.com	# " Ooooh catching up on #bbuk and Tom and that little group are so miserable that they love to bully and critique everyone else and their frie
42	23-11-14 GB	dailyrecord.co.uk	another round of drinks and fleeing the scene. # For the latest updates on miserable towns from across the UK, click here. # CCTV footage shov
43	23-11-14 GB	dailyecho.co.uk	position that can relieve constipation fast # SUFFERING from constipation is surprisingly common and pretty miserable for everyone experienc
44	23-11-15 GB	scotsman.com	n't it? Robbing yourself of a bit of silly joy in this dark, miserable world. So I'm A celebrity will be watched by millions this year,
45	23-11-15 GB	scotsman.com	publicly declared she has no confidence in Mr Sunak, while plotters will make life miserable for the PM. 103485525 # U.S. President Joe Biden
46	23-11-15 GB	politico.eu	103486145 Thank you for subscribing! # Parcel firms have delivered a " miserable " service to consumers for the third year running, according
47	23-11-15 GB	liverpoolecho.co.uk	the Carabao Cup. For much of that match the Blues looked set for a miserable exit at the hands of the team that was then propping up the Foo
48	23-11-15 GB	cityam.com	anonymous Wikipedia editor, for bringing it to my attention. The game is truly miserable. I'm not even sure it's right to call it a game:
49	23-11-15 GB	sundaypost.com	Our marriage wasn't working. We could no longer pretend. We were both miserable and clearly something had to change. " 103488399
50	23-11-15 GB	sundaypost.com	former weather presenter revealed how the " debilitating " pain often leaves her feeling " miserable " and that sleepless nights can give her " br
51	23-11-15 GB	sundaypost.com	# " Nooo Matt don't compromise on a family, it will make you miserable, " said one fan. " Two lovely people BUT I feel for Matt
52	23-11-16 GB	dailyrecord.co.uk	the remote Atlantic island of St Helena, though he may have been even more miserable had he been subjected to Telford and its risible person
53	23-11-17 GB	metro.co.uk	So whether you love twinkling city lights at Christmas, or prefer to escape the miserable chills in search of warm and balmy climates, there's a c
54	23-11-17 GB	iwcp.co.uk	Miles arrives at Mars' so-called Happy Valley to discover that actually things are pretty Miserable Valley for people like him. # Miles steps off his
55	23-11-17 GB	uk.businessinsider.com	of 2024 but Save the Children UK warns the money is only " resetting the miserable status quo ". The charity says the support - designed to alle
56	23-11-17 GB	espn.co.uk	and unable to deal with the physical demands of English football, but despite three miserable years at United since arriving from Ajax, he is stil
57	23-11-17 GB	espn.co.uk	the rim down while scowling and screaming. # Westbrook's rediscovered joy following his miserable Lakers tenure could be felt on the other si
58	23-11-17 GB	eurogamer.net	More Related Articles # Dr Fernando explained: " Being unwell can be a miserable experience and, while illnesses such as the dreaded commo
59	23-11-17 GB	theargus.co.uk	they're having to learn quickly. " # The good news is that this miserable qualifying campaign is almost over, with only Monday's match at home
60	23-11-15 CA	psychologytoday.com	sheer pleasure in the doing. # Now think about another time when you were miserable. Take ten minutes and write in your journal, without sto
61	23-11-15 CA	psychologytoday.com	much, about a time when as a child you remember doing something that felt miserable. The chances are that you were doing something at sor
62	23-11-16 CA	princegeorgecitizen.com	ready for action. Reseal Windows and Doors # Drafty homes can make winter miserable and cost you a fortune on utility bills. In the early fall, s
63	23-11-17 CA	canadianinquirer.net	did. # Advertisement # I lied to Becca only once. " He looked miserable. " I textedafter watching her husband remarry. I knew her well enough t
64	23-11-14 US	Stereogum	everyone in attendance was far less inhibited than when they arrived. In an exceedingly miserable time to exist in the UK -- the reasons are too
65	23-11-14 US	The Boston Globe	# But if there's one silver lining that Patriots fans can draw from a miserable 2-8 start, it's that continued stretches of ineptitude should put Nev
66	23-11-14 US	Anime News Network	action. A whole episode of those two elements sounds like a recipe for a miserable episode. So I am very grateful this episode turns out pretty
67	23-11-15 US	The Economist	Israel may have dealt the group a fatal blow. But a long period of miserable displacement would ensure that something else rises in its stead.?
68	23-11-15 US	CBSSports.com	PPR Fantasy points. Finally came a blowout loss to the Cowboys when both were miserable. # That's four games for the trio with two smash ou

"The **miserable** state of the people in China, Russia, Venezuela, Cuba . . ."

"The version of what Irish food looks like is grey and **miserable**."

"Her life's been **miserable**, she's been hounded, harassed, lied about, lied to."

We could keep going and going and going through these citations. It's a lexicographer's job to do this. But we have to stop. You have to take my assessment for now—after which you are not just free but encouraged to go look at the evidence for yourself!

My assessment is this: It's complicated. "Miserable" can definitely still mean "deserving or arousing pity," but not when it applies to *people*. "States" and "foods" can be miserable without feeling it personally. But when people are miserable, they feel it—they're unhappy.

Most to Be Pitied

Did you notice the reference to "the miserable state of the people in" various Communist nations? The people in those nations might or might not know they're in a miserable state. The people described as being in a "miserable state" might not *feel* miserable. I've read of North Koreans, for example, who literally believed that their objectively miserable country was the best place on earth. All they knew was propaganda.

That's what Paul is saying we would be like if Christ had never risen from the dead. We would be North Koreans blithely going about our stunted lives, totally ignorant of the privileges and resources enjoyed by people in countless other nations around the world.

The KJV translators were not speaking of personal unhappiness in 1 Corinthians 15:19. Paul was not saying, "If Christ didn't really rise, we are the most unhappy and emotionally depressed of all people." And the KJV translators knew this. They chose a word that, in their day, meant what we mean by "pitiable."

I've always found this explanation of this verse to be compelling: If the dead don't rise, then we Christians who believe Jesus rose from the dead are most to be pitied *because we hoped the highest*. We hoped for the impossible miracle of resurrection.

I admit again that this is subtle linguistic stuff. The distinction is not massively important, but I'm convinced it's there. And language change is making it more difficult to see.

5. Sincere

> As newborn babes, desire the **sincere** milk of the word, that ye may grow thereby. (1 Pet. 2:2)

What do you think "sincere" means in this verse?

THERE ARE A GREAT MANY intelligent people who love the KJV, and not a few of them have reacted with at least initial rejection of my concept of false friends. I know how they feel: At first glance, it seems like I'm saying they don't understand a text that they've read for decades, a text they simply *know they do understand*. Of course, I'm not saying they don't understand the KJV. I'm saying something much more narrow, more targeted: namely, that today's readers are missing a certain number of individual words while still, probably, getting a generally good understanding of the passages they're reading. I've put years into my work on false friends, but I'm not saying they're a profound and terrible problem (you already bought this book, so I can admit this now). I'm not saying they will all necessarily cause false doctrine or massive misunderstandings. I am saying that true Christians ought to want to understand their Bibles, and today's readers will unwittingly misunderstand many KJV words if they don't learn how to fish for false friends.

One unnamed pastor, a man who has preached from the KJV for decades, encountered my work on false friends and had the understandable negative reaction I just described. He dismissed all my work, arguing that I was making a mountain out of a mole on a mole inside a molehill—and who's going to pay for cosmetic surgery for a rodent who lives in the dark most of the time anyway? I couldn't get real clarity on whether he thought that there were a few inconsequential false friends or whether he rejected the whole category. The conversation stopped there.

Fishing for a False Friend

But sometime later I happened to catch a sermon of his on 1 Peter 2:2. Here's the verse:

> As newborn babes, desire the **sincere** milk of the word, that ye may grow thereby.

And I heard him say this—almost automatically:

> Peter here calls God's Word "the sincere milk," which simply means "the pure milk."

Why did he add that last phrase? Why did he have to define a simple word like "sincere"?

Because he's a skillful preacher and Bible teacher, and he knows intuitively when his congregation won't understand an archaic word in the KJV—as long as, indeed, he himself is aware that it's an archaic word.

And that's my whole case right there. This brother, who explicitly rejected the idea of false friends, implicitly validated it with this quick little line. He froze the ugly mole off the poor, cute little mole.

The Greek word translated "sincere" in 1 Peter 2:2 means "unadulterated" (BDAG). In other words, it means "not mixed with anything else." Water down your milk and you may save a little money, but if the feds catch you selling it, they'll nail you for "adulterating" your product—for "rendering (something) poorer in quality by adding another substance, typically an inferior one" (NOAD).

But "sincere" in our English doesn't mean quite the same thing as the Greek word in 1 Peter 2:2. It means "free from pretense or deceit; proceeding from genuine feelings" (NOAD). To call the milk of the Word "sincere" is a little odd, maybe, because inanimate objects like milk don't have feelings or intentions.

But, of course, we do this in language. We anthropomorphize inanimate things, ascribing feelings to them and even putting words in their (nonexistent) mouths. For example, my wife, a flower farmer, frequently refers to individual plants as either "happy" or "not happy."

Perhaps, then, "the sincere milk of the word" is an arresting metaphor. It might mean "the unhypocritical truth of the Word that you're meant to drink in."

And yet . . . you probably already see where this is going. The OED gives this as one of the senses for "sincere":

> pure, unmixed; free from any foreign element or ingredient.

I must admit that the OED does not name this sense as obsolete, but listen to this sample sentence about wine from 1576. Can you imagine any English speaker saying this today?

> Is it a noate or token, that the spirit of the wyne was not **syncere** and pure.

No, we don't call substances "sincere" anymore, not when we're being literal. If you look up this word in the OED yourself—depending on when you're reading this line—you may see what I see: "First published 1911; not yet revised." In other words, the OED editors have been at their task since 1857, and they haven't yet gotten back around to editing this entry. Once they do, I feel certain they'll label this sense of "sincere" as obsolete.

Any time I disagree with the OED—in this case, not with their sense but with their failure to label it obsolete—I have to do a little more homework. I have to go to step 5 and check a corpus.

In the NOW Corpus, I looked at hundreds of examples of real-life uses of the word "sincere," and I found sincere gratitude, sincere efforts, sincere dialogue, and sincere commitments. I also found sincere people, appreciation, sympathies, apologies, words, condolences, plans to quit drugs, repentance, devotion, smiles, congratulations, interest, concern, and religious beliefs.

I found no sincere wine and no sincere milk.

Most certainly, we have hooked a false friend.

You can see how the two senses of "sincere" we've discussed are related. "Sincere" could once speak of purity of substances, not just of motives, but the word has narrowed, and it now means only the latter, not the former. Speakers of today's English cannot speak of "sincere milk" or "sincere wine" or "sincere tea tree oil" unless they sincerely wish to receive quizzical looks.

New Testament Greek had a word very much like our word "sincere" used to function—a word that could mean both "sincere" and "pure." There's one passage in the New Testament where this Greek word (not the same word as in 1 Peter 2:2) is still translated both ways by contemporary translations. Here it is in the KJV:

> That ye may approve things that are excellent; that ye may be **sincere** and without offence till the day of Christ. (Phil. 1:10)

Tyndale actually opted for "pure" here in the early 1500s. But the NKJV and SKJV still opt for "sincere." I'm not saying—with "sincere" or "study" or "hell" or "bruise"—that my false friends are necessarily false friends every time they appear. The truth is more complex than this.

Explaining the KJV

I learned many, many years ago to "translate" KJV English on the spot in encounters where I was witnessing to someone. There simply was no point in saying to a half-hungover woman on a rather run-down porch in a not-so-nice part of town, "But God commendeth his love toward us, in that, while we were yet sinners, Christ died for us" (Rom. 5:8). I instinctively and intuitively said instead, "God shows his love for us like this: Even when we were still sinners, Christ died for us." I didn't have to change everything, just a few key things I knew weren't part of her regular English: "commends," "yet." Even as a teenager I remember doing this.

For my whole life I've heard preachers do it too—instinctively and intuitively, while preaching from the KJV. They'll say, "The word of God is quick—that means 'alive,'" and "Be ye holy in all manner of conversation—that means 'conduct.'" Have you heard preachers do this?

I very much appreciate this practice because it's the fruit of a sincere desire (one I share) to understand and teach God's Word.

6. Hell

> For thou wilt not leave my soul in **hell**; Neither wilt thou suffer thine Holy One to see corruption. (Ps. 16:10)

What do you think "hell" means in this verse?

WHEN THERE EXISTS A STANDARD, time-tested, trusted Bible translation in any language, its decisions come to feel obvious, default, no longer in need of justification. Of course, that translation—no matter what it is, no matter what language it's made into—didn't always enjoy that trust.

If, let's say, leaders in the tiny group of Urdu Christians come to realize that their 1843 translation needs to be revised for various reasons, any alteration they make to the standard is going to be met with suspicion. Yet translators don't usually get much of a chance to explain their decisions. They just have to suffer in silence.

But not in complete silence. They can write prefaces, for example, in which they complain about the treatment they know they're about to receive from a skeptical public. One group of English Bible translators, whose work was finished in 1611 (guess who they were), did just this. These are the opening words of the KJV preface:

> Zeal to promote the common good, whether it be by devising anything ourselves, or revising that which hath been laboured by others, deserveth certainly much respect and esteem, but yet findeth but cold entertainment in the world. It is welcomed with suspicion in stead of love, and with emulation ["contention or

ill-will between rivals," OED] in stead of thanks: and if there be any hole left for cavil [petty objection] to enter (and cavil, if it do not find a hole, will make one), it is sure to be misconstrued, and in danger to be condemned.[6]

Little could Miles Smith, the author of this preface, know that his own work would one day be the standard against which future revisions would be judged.

Fishing for a False Friend

This brings us to "hell." "Hell" is used fifty-four times in the King James Version, but only fifty-two times in the SKJV and thirty-two times in the NKJV.

How did we get from fifty-four to thirty-two, and even less in other contemporary translations based on the Textus Receptus (TR)? Are the modern versions removing "hell" out of squeamishness toward the doctrine of eternal conscious torment? I've heard this charge—this cavil, it will prove to be—more than once. Modern translators don't really get to explain themselves. At most they get a few footnotes here and there or a journal article nobody reads.

I've read two autobiographies—one by C. S. Lewis and one by a former fellow church member named Larry—in which the writer seemed to have retained incredibly specific memories of minor things that happened in their childhood (Lewis) or of numerous specific meals they'd eaten in decades past (Larry). In my case, some of the memories I have retained are specific questions I had about KJV passages while I was growing up. I don't know whether these questions came during childhood or during my teenage years, but I remember having them.

6. David Norton, ed., *The New Cambridge Paragraph Bible with the Apocrypha: King James Version*, rev. ed., vol. 1 (Cambridge University Press, 2011), xvii.

Indeed, aren't there some uses of "hell" in the KJV that have simply struck you as odd? I remember wondering why the psalmist would say, "Thou wilt not leave my soul in **hell**" in Psalm 16:10. Even if this statement is fully Messianic, many or most Bible-focused Protestants like me have felt squeamish about saying that Jesus "descended into hell," as some of the ancient creeds do.[7]

I remember loving Psalm 139 as a kid or teen, but I was puzzled by this statement: "If I ascend up into heaven, thou art there: If I make my bed in **hell**, behold, thou art there" (v. 8). I thought, *What would it mean for David to make his bed in the lake of fire? And what in red blazes would it mean for God to be "in" that lake of fire?* I concluded that it must simply be hyperbole: *Even a place God would never go, he'd go there to protect me.*

It seemed clear enough to me as a young Bible reader that "hell" meant "the fiery place of eternal conscious torment," because Jesus spoke of "hell fire" in one of my favorite passages, the Sermon on the Mount:

> But I say unto you, That whosoever is angry with his brother without a cause shall be in danger of the judgment: and whosoever shall say to his brother, Raca, shall be in danger of the council: but whosoever shall say, Thou fool, shall be in danger of **hell fire**. (Matt. 5:22)

He spoke, too, of "hell" as a "fire that never shall be quenched" (Mark 9:43). And he told the story of the rich man and Lazarus:

> And in **hell** he lift up his eyes, being in torments, and seeth Abraham afar off, and Lazarus in his bosom. (Luke 16:23)

I also found it confusing that at the end of the Bible, we are told that "death and **hell** were cast into the lake of fire" (Rev. 20:14).

7. I believe this chapter will help explain why this traditional language has been used.

If hell *is* the lake of fire, what does it mean that hell was thrown into the lake of fire?

I have had some YouTube viewers so taken with my concept of false friends that they want to call every archaism or interpretive difficulty in the KJV a false friend. But false friends are something specific, and they always involve language change. Outside the tiny bubble of nerds who listen to my nerdy ramblings on YouTube, I find that the role of language change in interpreting the KJV isn't so much little understood as it is completely ignored. People just assume that a common word like "hell" must mean what it has always meant.

I've learned to question that, to at least try language change as a possible source of solutions to uncertainties and confusions KJV readers face.

For nine years I worked for Logos, the makers of the premiere (in my opinion!) Bible study app, which I have used nonstop for almost two decades. One of the reasons I love Logos is its powerful Bible Word Study tool. With a click, I can see all the Hebrew and Greek words that are translated by the English word "hell" in the KJV.

There are three such Greek words—words naming places we can call Gehenna, Tartarus, and Hades.

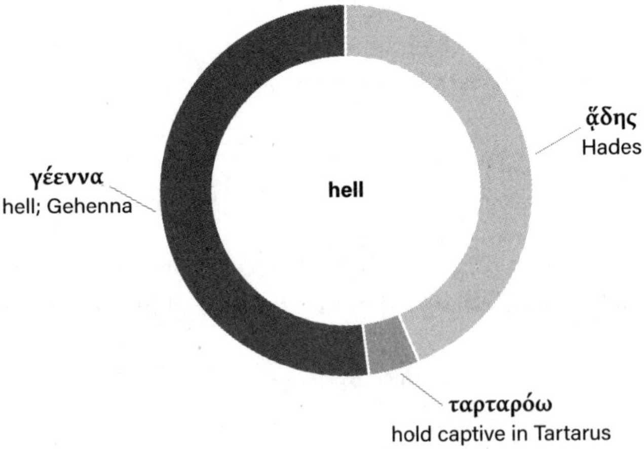

There's just one such Hebrew word, and it's the somewhat commonly known word Sheol.

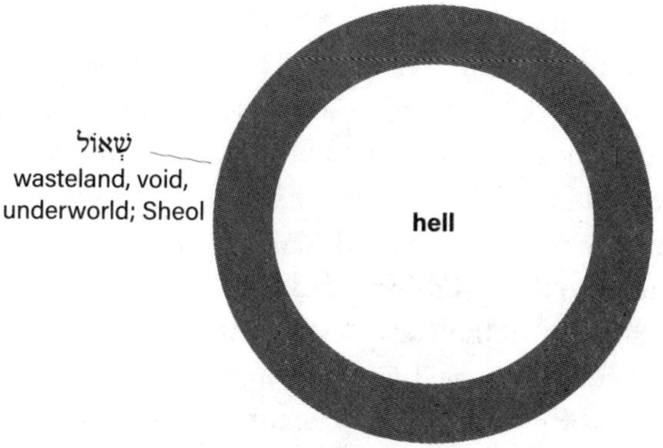

This makes four different words—with, obviously, four different definitions.

Gehenna is a transliteration of the Hebrew phrase "Valley of Hinnom," which meant "the place of punishment in the next life" (BDAG). Tartarus, which shows up just once in the New Testament (2 Pet. 2:4), referred to a location that was "thought of by the Greeks as a subterranean place lower than Hades where divine punishment was meted out, and so regarded in Israelite apocalyptic [literature] as well" (BDAG). Hades, likewise, meant "the nether world," or was considered a "place of the dead" (BDAG). Sheol similarly meant "wasteland, void, underworld"—the realm of the dead (HALOT).[8]

The KJV translators always translated the three Greek words above with "hell"—except just once, in the phrase, "O death, where is thy sting? O **grave** [*hades*], where is thy victory?" (1 Cor. 15:55). With the Hebrew word *sheol*, the picture is different. There, the KJV translators chose "hell" about half the time and "the grave" about half the time ("the pit" also shows up three times).

8. Ludwig Koehler, Walter Baumgartner, and Johann Jakob Stamm, *The Hebrew and Aramaic Lexicon of the Old Testament*, 5 vols., trans. and ed. M. E. J. Richardson (Brill, 1994–2000).

If you noticed, there was a mixture of pagan and Judeo-Christian ideas found in those Greek and Hebrew words. What did the various biblical authors who used them mean by them?

It's complicated. I'm not sure how deep to dive into the details. And I can't say I myself have them all perfectly sorted out. As with many matters of eschatology, God has not chosen to provide in Scripture all the details we might possibly wish to have. Nowhere does the Bible tell us what Tartarus is, for example; all we have to go on is the one passage in which it's used, the overall teaching of Scripture on the last things, and uses of that word outside the Bible at the time of the New Testament.

Let me punt this time by just saying that I take what I believe to be the classic evangelical Protestant viewpoint on eschatology: There is an intermediate state in which all the dead, both small and great, await a resurrection of the just and the unjust, followed by eternal conscious torment in the lake of fire for the wicked and eternal life in the presence of God on a new earth for the righteous. It appears to me that the three major biblical words for (something like) "hell"—Sheol, Gehenna, and Hades—all name different locations in the narrative I've just told and not always the same ones. Sometimes Sheol and Hades, particularly, refer to "the grave" into which even the righteous go (1 Cor. 15:55), and sometimes they refer to a place of torment. Gehenna, however, always refers (all twelve times it appears) to a place of torment for the wicked.

When matters are this complex, it's understandable that Bible translators might also wish to punt by transliterating instead of translating. I defend this practice: "Gehenna," "Hades," "Sheol," and even little-used "Tartarus" have effectively become English words among Bible-focused Christians who study Scripture carefully. But, on balance, if it were up to me, I'd probably *translate* "Sheol" and "Hades" more often than modern Bible translators in my experience tend to want to do. I'd probably use "grave" more often, in particular (some contemporary translations do, in fact, do this).

Let us now, however, return to the question of whether language change is playing any role that KJV readers may not have yet noticed.

NOAD sees "hell" as meaning always and only a place of torment for the wicked:

> a place regarded in various religions as a spiritual realm of evil and suffering, often traditionally depicted as a place of perpetual fire beneath the earth where the wicked are punished after death: *irreligious children were assumed to have passed straight to the eternal fires of hell.*

This is what I expected to find: "Hell" in modern English, it seems to me, means this and only this. We find the same major senses for "hell" in the OED that we saw in NOAD. Here's the place-of-eternal-punishment sense:

> the infernal regions regarded in various religions as a place of suffering and evil; the dwelling place of devils and condemned spirits; the place or state of punishment of the wicked after death.

The OED does also include, however, a sense of the word "hell" that fits the concepts we saw expressed in Scripture. I might call it the abode-of-the-dead sense:

> the dwelling place of the dead; the abode of departed spirits; the infernal regions regarded as a place of existence after death; the underworld; the grave; Hades.

Neither sense is marked as archaic or obsolete. But I'm not satisfied. I remember being a young KJV reader and puzzling over this verse:

> For thou wilt not leave my soul in **hell**; neither wilt thou suffer thine Holy One to see corruption. (Ps. 16:10)

What in the world could David mean here? I wondered, even as a kid. To "leave" David's soul in hell implies that David's soul might go there in the first place. How could this man after God's own heart, a man inspired to write a large portion of Scripture, say such a thing?

I've answered that question: That's not what David meant. He meant the abode of the dead, or the grave, not the place of eternal punishment. But this raises another question: Did I misunderstand this verse because I was an ignorant kid and this topic is complicated, or did language change have something to do with my puzzlement? (Or maybe both?)

I find it very instructive that NOAD doesn't even mention the abode-of-the-dead sense. (Neither does the *Collins English Dictionary*, which I use only here in this book, though I do recommend it; it works hard to describe English as it really is written and spoken now.)

I also checked the NOW Corpus, and as you can imagine, "hell" in the mouths (and keyboards) of contemporary English speakers is almost always either (a) some kind of reference to the place of eternal punishment believed in by Christians or (b) some kind of phrase or idiom ultimately derived from the former sense. You can have a "hell of a" something; you can be "hell-bent" on something; you can go "through" hell or "to" hell. I did not see anyone using "hell" to speak of an abode of the dead that was distinct from the place of eternal punishment.

I sort of take that back. I did see this citation:

> The pair are attacked by Thor, setting them on a journey through hell and across the many treacherous lands of Norse mythology.

That was the closest I came to the abode-of-the-dead sense. But I had to look up Norse views of hell to confirm that their goddess Hel presided over both the good and the evil dead.

I think it's too many leaps to ask English readers to make it from Thor in a movie to David in a psalm. And the corpus (along with NOAD and Collins) suggests that I have good reason to see language change as playing a role.

I'm certain people today are misunderstanding the word "hell" in certain places in the KJV. I am not absolutely certain that language change is the major reason, but I do believe this can fairly be called a false friend. Modern English speakers, even lifelong Christians, read "hell" in the KJV and hear "place of fiery eternal torment," but that's not what the KJV translators meant by it in their English in every instance.[9]

Changing Hell?

All of this difficult, complex discussion doesn't tell us exactly how to translate the four Hebrew and Greek words at issue. But it explains, I think, why so many modern Bibles have not used the word "hell" as much as did the KJV but have reached instead for transliterations like "Sheol" and "Hades." They are trying

---

9. This distinction between "hell" as a place of punishment and "hell" as an abode of all the dead may also be helpful in untangling what ancient Christians meant when they confessed that Christ "descended into hell." They looked at passages such as Psalm 16:8–11 (quoted and applied to Christ in Acts 2:25–28); Ephesians 4:9; Romans 10:7; Revelation 1:18; and 1 Peter 3:18–22, and they concluded that Christ proclaimed his victory over death to all the dead. As Matthew Emerson argues, he did not "suffer in 'hell'"; no, his descent into the abode of the dead was "part of his exaltation, not his humiliation." (Matthew Emerson, *"He Descended to the Dead": An Evangelical Theology of Holy Saturday* [IVP Academic, 2019], 64–65.) However, Emerson's is not the only view. The great Dutch theologian Herman Bavinck looks at the variety of views on the clause and concludes, "The wide difference of opinion in this matter proves that the original meaning of the words descended into hell has been lost. We do not know the source of this clause in the creed, nor what it was really intended to say. Scripture says nothing about any literal, actual, spatial descent into hell." (Herman Bavinck, *Our Reasonable Faith*, trans. Henry Zylstra [Eerdmans, 2016], 346.)

to respect the distinctions among the original-language words we've been discussing; they are putting some onus on the reader to do some study.

But this has not satisfied everyone. I've heard critics of the NKJV in particular worry that the NKJV was softening or confusing the Bible's teaching on hell by choosing so often to use the word "Hades" where the KJV had "hell." They ask, "Why did they have to change this simple word everyone knows?"

Here's at least part of the answer: because "hell" doesn't mean in contemporary English exactly what it meant in the English of the KJV translators.

Here's another part: "Hell" itself was a pagan word before it was a Christian one. Hel was indeed the goddess of the Norse underworld.[10] "Hell" has been used by English speakers to refer to similar concepts in Christian theology, in Greek and Latin mythology, and in Scandinavian legend. It isn't a specifically Christian word.

It is perhaps an uncomfortable truth, at first, to discover that the Bible used "pagan words" like "hell" or "Hades." Even *logos* ("word") in John 1 was a thoroughly un-Christian concept until John plundered the pagans and made it refer to Jesus. But it's true.

Without endorsing all of the then-current pagan beliefs about Hades found in Greek culture—or all the then-current pagan beliefs about Sheol in ancient Near Eastern culture—the Spirit used labels that were generally familiar to people.

Sheol and Hades and Gehenna are no longer familiar, at least not to most contemporary Western people. These words will have to do what a respected Bible translator friend of mine who works in Southeast Asia described: "acquire meaning" over time as English Bible readers study their Bibles.

"Hell" may be a false friend as much because of the complexity of the Bible's teaching on the topic—and because of theological

10. OED, under "Hel."

ignorance—as because of language change. But the KJV translators felt that their readers would understand "thou wilt not leave my soul in hell," and today we don't. And we don't *know* we're misunderstanding. I think language change is playing a role here, and I think we have a false friend.

7. Bowels

> Yea, brother, let me have joy of thee in the Lord: refresh my **bowels** in the Lord. (Philem. 20)

What do you think "bowels" means in this verse?

ONE ACID TEST for whether people judge a given KJV word to have changed in meaning is whether or not they're willing to use it in public in mixed company.

Give "bowels" the acid test with me: Would your pastor use the word in the normal course of a sermon without referring to its use in the KJV? Would you cringe as, looking ahead while reading out loud to the teens, your peripheral vision encountered it? Would you have to glare at the class clown as you read to make sure they didn't crack a joke?

"Bowels" fails these acid tests. And yet there it is, in black and white, on the pages of the KJV, thirty-nine times.[11]

11. I use Logos for effectively all my KJV searches, but there are countless free tools online for searching the KJV. I recommend using Logos—and it comes in a free version—because it provides room to grow in Bible study ability.

Fishing for a False Friend

The tittering by itself may be enough to suggest that "bowels" in the KJV is a false friend. But the word still appears in the SKJV (though not the NKJV). Despite the snickers that might result, at least one modern Bible still uses the word "bowels." Why?

Let's look at one of the places in the KJV where "bowels" is a false friend. There's a one-chapter book in the New Testament in which it appears three times: Philemon. Listen to those three verses.

> We have great joy and consolation in thy love, because the **bowels** of the saints are refreshed by thee, brother. (v. 7)

> Receive him [Onesimus], that is, mine own **bowels**. (v. 12)

> Yea, brother, let me have joy of thee in the Lord: refresh my **bowels** in the Lord. (v. 20)

Clearly, we don't talk like this. If you ever were to need to mention your bowels feeling refreshed, it would only ever be at the doctor's office, most certainly not in church. And not a couple times in a short letter to a friend. I'm pretty fastidious with my speech; I feel confident that I have never once used the word "bowels" in my entire life—outside of reading and discussing the KJV.[12]

The Greek word here is *splanchna*, which kind of sounds like a doughnut falling into your digestive juices—*splanch*; sorry, but it's true. BDAG defines it as "the inward parts of a body, including esp. the viscera, inward parts, entrails." And that's clearly the way we use the word today, though I just don't want to give an example or spend any more time on this word than I have to. But

12. I also believe I have used the word "disemboweled," though I can't remember why. I hope no one got hurt.

this word, in this sense of entrails or viscera or small intestine, does occur in the Bible—and that's why it gets used in contemporary translations a few times. When Judas fell from the tree on which he had hanged himself, Peter says in Acts 1:18, "All his bowels gushed out." That was *splanchna*.

Modern dictionaries tell us that "bowels" in contemporary English means

> the part of the alimentary canal below the stomach; the intestine. (NOAD)

I'm not a medical doctor and do not generally need to refer to this portion of my or others' anatomy. Yet this is why the SKJV includes the word in Numbers 5:22—because that portion of the body is being referred to.

But how in the world did Philemon refresh the part of the alimentary canal below Paul's stomach? How exactly does Onesimus count as Paul's own intestine?

My Greek-English dictionary has another comment that will explain why this word is used in the emotional letter of Paul to Philemon, who owned the runaway slave Onesimus who had then become a close friend of Paul:

> as often in the ancient world, inner body parts served as referents for psychological aspects: . . . of the seat of the emotions, in our usage a transference is made to the rendering heart. (BDAG)

Now here's the question: Did the original readers of the KJV understand "bowels" in Philemon to mean "the inner seat of the emotions"? I'd say that the OED speaks with an uncertain sound here. They suggest that, yes, such readers would have understood what's going on. They have a sense for this word that is now "somewhat archaic":

> considered as the seat of the tender and sympathetic emotions, hence: . . . pity, compassion, feeling, "heart."

This sense appears first in the Wycliffe Bible, where I'm going to have to guess that he translated literally and therefore invented a new sense for this word. My best guess as to what's happening in English at the period of the KJV is that long custom had made Christian people aware of what "bowels" meant in biblical times. So, I'm going to guess the KJV translators felt safe in assuming that they would not cause teens to titter. Although now the word does cause precisely this, leading me to call it a false friend, I could see someone disagreeing with me here; I really could. But, on balance, and taking one thing with another, as I am often wont to do, it's a false friend.

"Bowels" in English Bibles

English Bible translators have a problem: They can be literally accurate and force modern readers to travel into the biblical thought world, but choosing to use the word "bowels" will most likely confuse those readers if they lack a study Bible or an expository preacher (or at least a footnote). Or translators can use the modern equivalent—probably "heart," our culture's main word for the seat of the emotions—and everybody will get the meaning on the first go-round.

Both of these strategies are, in my judgment, legitimate in many places in the Bible. It can be a good thing to make modern readers scratch their heads and look for a helpful footnote. This is why many translations go for "Sheol"—it's a hard word, because we don't really have the concept it names in our culture. People are going to have to do some study to understand it anyway, so you might as well tip them off to that fact by using a word they don't know. Over time, they'll come to know it.

But the potential for confusion with this particular word, "bowels," is so great, and the demand on tittering teens so towering, that translators today nearly always choose the latter option. I could see some translation going for "Receive Onesimus, that is, my own viscera." We still use "visceral" as a word naming the seat of emotions. But in my judgment, "viscera" would still be confusing and distracting and gross. On balance, BDAG's suggestion is best. I like the idea used by some biblical scholars today: "I am sending back to you Onesimus, my very heart." That gets Paul's intended meaning across immediately.

The role of language change in this one is a little less clear. But I generally presume that the KJV translators wanted to be understood, and the OED does not, at least, contradict my best guess as to whether the original KJV readers understood "bowels." Another acid test: I'll bet you wouldn't give yourself an A-plus on the answer you wrote in the blank at the beginning of the chapter. I believe we have yet another false friend.

8. Holy Ghost

> Now the birth of Jesus Christ was on this wise: When as his mother Mary was espoused to Joseph, before they came together, she was found with child of the **Holy Ghost**. (Matt. 1:18)

What do you think "Ghost" means in this verse?

____

____

WHY DOES THE KING JAMES VERSION call the Holy Spirit the "Holy Ghost" ninety times? "Holy Spirit" was fully available in Elizabethan English; that phrase, in fact, appears seven times in the KJV. So, why did the KJV translators vastly prefer "Ghost" to "Spirit"?

We who grew up in church and are of a certain age are probably used to the phrase "Holy Ghost." "We're going to have a Holy Ghost revival" is just one of the pieces of churchy jargon learned, depending on where one grew up. Kind of like "I have an unspoken," or "God laid it on my heart," except this jargon falls within the Bible. Or, that is, in certain translations of the Bible.

The English translations that use the phrase "Holy Ghost" are all rather old, and none are widely and actively used today, except for the KJV. These include the Douay-Rheims Catholic Bible of 1899, the never-popular English Revised Version of 1885, and, going back further, the Geneva Bible of 1599 and the Bishops' Bible of 1568.

Once you're equipped with the elegant fishing hat provided by this book—you know, the wavy-brimmed one with all the lures stuffed into the little loops around the top—you might be able to guess that language change is playing a role in the obvious move away from "Holy Ghost" in Christian speech and toward "Holy Spirit."

Fishing for a False Friend

The Hebrew and Greek words for "Holy Spirit"—as in "take not thy holy spirit from me" (Ps. 51:11) and "grieve not the holy Spirit of God" (Eph. 4:30)—do indeed mean "holy" and "spirit." As in English, so in Hebrew and Greek; the word for "spirit" (many Christians know these: *ruach* in Hebrew and *pneuma* in Greek) ultimately comes from using breath or air as a metaphor for the interior, nonphysical "part" of a person.

Let me pontificate about language a little bit here. It does feel like the concept of "breath" properly precedes the concept of "spirit," that the former word must have developed to have the latter sense. Air and breath and wind feel more elemental—surely a word for these things came first? And as people developed complexity in their descriptions of the world, maybe they realized that "air" would be a suitable metaphor for the interior life?

I'm not so sure. I wonder now if the just-so stories of evolution are making this seem like the right story. The Christian story doesn't demand that more complex concepts develop from less complex ones. Perhaps "spirit" was a metaphor based on breath in the language of Adam and Eve.

Indeed, what I have found when I have tried to push back into the earliest histories of some of the major languages I've studied—English, Spanish, Hebrew, Greek, Latin—is that there never was a time when the literal sense of "spirit" as air or breath existed by itself. What humans have ever not needed to refer to a "spirit"? The senses of the Latin word *spiritus* read very like the senses of the modern English word "spirit" (which we, of course, drew from the Latin). You can have a spirit of the age, a human spirit, even a team spirit. It's all there in the ancient language of the Italian peninsula. The main thing Latin speakers and writers had that we don't is a word that combines the immaterial and material senses. We don't use "spirit" to speak of literal breath anymore; it's just the immaterial stuff for us.

I cannot give other examples, but I am certain I have encountered this sort of thing over and over, especially within English itself. It wasn't as if primitive Celts knew only of physical things and only developed sophisticated metaphysical terminology in due time. It sure seems that, most of the places I look, their language was just as sophisticated as ours.

Just a thought for you.

In contemporary English, "ghost" means

> an apparition of a dead person which is believed to appear or become manifest to the living, typically as a nebulous image. (NOAD)

As I've said, "spirit" means

> the nonphysical part of a person which is the seat of emotions and character; the soul. (NOAD)

These are, of course, not the same thing. But those of you who are used to "Holy Ghost" (like me) probably can't experience the visceral feeling of what "Holy Ghost" sounds like to the uninitiated, to people who know contemporary English but not church-speak.

Consider this: What if some Christians started calling the Holy Spirit "the Holy Soul"? That would be jarring—wouldn't it? We'd suspect they were off into some heresy we hadn't heard of yet.

I do think that's how some folks hear "the Holy Ghost." *The holy what?!*

I can't prove this; I don't even think this misunderstanding is common. I would guess from long experience that most adults figure out quickly that "Holy Ghost" in the KJV (and in preaching and other Christian talk) doesn't mean "holy apparition of a dead person which becomes manifest as a nebulous image." But I'd bet that there are lots of children who do think this, and who probably need to be asked by their parents right now what they're thinking so that their misunderstanding can be cleared up.

Because, of course, "Holy Ghost" is just the older way of saying "Holy Spirit." And the OED confirms this, if we even need to look it up. The first sense of "ghost" that it gives is

> the soul or spirit, as the principle of life.

Then it carefully notes that this sense is "obsolete except in [the] phrase to give up . . . the . . . ghost." We just don't use "ghost" to mean "the soul or spirit as the principle of life" except in that one phrase.

Going back much further in the history of English, the OED will tell you that *holigost* was the standard Middle English term for Holy Spirit, and *se hálga gást* was the Old English way of saying it before that. This isn't far from the contemporary German *Heiliger Geist*. Anybody who knows their etymologies will know that that G + [vowel] + ST makes the Germanic word for "spirit." You can still see this in the word "zeitgeist," which has come over into English and means "spirit of the age."

Today, though, English is different. All ghosts are spirits in today's English. We can say, "The spirits of the dead were haunting the cemetery at night." We can also say, "The ghosts were haunting the cemetery at night." But in our English, not all spirits are ghosts. The cheerleaders can say, "We have school spirit!" but they cannot say, "We have school ghost!" And more to the point, when the Bible speaks of "the spirit of man that is within him," or says that "the spirits of the prophets are subject to the prophets," it's not talking about ghosts. "Spirit" is one of several words we use for the interior part of someone. Synonyms in English and in the Bible (and that overlap is not an accident) include, especially, "soul." But you couldn't say, "all is vanity and vexation of ghost," in Ecclesiastes 1:14. That just doesn't work in our English.

"Spirit" in English has held pretty steady for a long time in a number of senses. But "ghost" has been a victim of semantic narrowing. It used to be—like its still-existing Germanic ancestor, *Geist*—the English word for "spirit." But Latin *spiritus* came in and ruined everything for "ghost," knocking it off its pedestal and forcing it into a narrow slot in the language. Few people today really believe in ghosts, and if they do, they kind of know to be embarrassed about it in polite company.

Let's follow this rabbit trail for just a few seconds; it'll teach us a little something. "Give up the ghost" or "yield up the ghost" appears eighteen times in the KJV. And we still have the phrase "give up the ghost" today, even though that sense of "ghost" is otherwise obsolete, according to the OED. This happens so often in language: A word dies or shifts, but it sticks around in idiomatic phrases anyway.

You can *wend your way*, but you can't *wend* your anything else.

You can *ride* or *run roughshod* over someone, but you can't *walk roughshod* or *jump roughshod* over them.

You can be *dead as a doornail*, but you can't buy a *doornail* at Home Depot.

Why did "give up the ghost" stick around after "ghost" gave up its standard meaning? Like several of these phrases that include otherwise dead words, it sticks because it's alliterated; it trips easily off the tongue. Why do you think I chose the label "false friend" for the central concept in my work on the KJV? Alliteration helps make something memorable.

Linguistic Reflections on "Holy Ghost"

OK, the rabbit is in the hedge and we can go back to the main trail. Where does all this leave us when it comes to the phrase "the Holy Ghost"? Well, it leaves us in a place where we risk trivializing the Third Person of the Trinity. Whenever we hold on to traditional language even after our spoken language has shifted, we risk creating a situation in which some kids and uninitiated adults will be unnecessarily confused. We're thinking "invisible person," and they're thinking "Casper and Halloween." This makes "Holy Ghost" a false friend—a misleading mismatch between the English of the KJV and the English of today.

But let me speak very carefully here. I personally have never met anyone who was confused by this false friend. I'm pretty sure it never confused me, even as a small kid. So how does this count as a false friend?

The answer to this question will defend the KJV and perhaps teach you something about Bible translation.

The fact is that the Bible creates, on its own, enough context to make it clear that "Holy Ghost" can't mean "a dead, translucent person floating around in a sheet with dark eyeholes." There's the biblical context itself, and there's the church context it creates. Nobody in my church context ever acted as if "Holy Ghost" referred to a divine apparition glimpsed late at night in the attic, and once I started reading the Bible on my own as a kid, the biblical context showed me quickly that that meaning didn't work—if it ever even occurred to me. The Holy Ghost baptized people (Matt. 3:11); he was named among the members of the Trinity (Matt. 28:19); he was given as a comforter and guide to the disciples (John 20:22). Ghosts don't do these things.

So, yes, it is possible—especially for the uninitiated—to misunderstand "Holy Ghost." It's another bump in the readability sidewalk. I definitely think that "Holy Ghost" is a false friend for some people. But even a mildly attentive KJV reader will know quickly that the Holy Ghost isn't a ghost. The KJV certainly made no error here, and I don't think it's causing much of a problem even today. "Holy Ghost" is likely to be one of the first pieces of churchy jargon into which a new Christian is initiated. The KJV isn't causing a big problem.

This little sword I've picked up to defend the KJV cuts both ways, however. Sometimes KJV readers encounter any and all updates to the KJV, even minor ones, as maximally suspect. As I mentioned in the chapter on "hell," one such brother was deeply concerned that readers of the NKJV would think that its use of "Hades" referred not to the Christian concept of hell but to the Greek concept of the underworld.

We might point out that if this is a problem for us, it was surely a worse problem for the original readers—who lived among people who sincerely believed in that Greek concept. But even more importantly, we can say that careful reading of the whole Bible will eliminate some possible misunderstandings. If "Holy Ghost" doesn't make all contemporary readers think of the modern sense of "ghost," then "Hades," at least over time, probably won't make them think of the musical *Hadestown*, the Disney movie *Hercules*, or the Greek mythology they had to read in college.

So, "Holy Ghost" is a fairly minor, commonly known false friend. It's probably just good to remind ourselves that four-year-olds and first-time visitors (1 Cor. 14:24–25) might not realize they're misunderstanding the phrase.

9. Communicate

> But to do good and to **communicate** forget not: for with such sacrifices God is well pleased. (Heb. 13:16)

What do you think "communicate" means in this verse?

____

____

There are some husbands out there who really don't like to talk in more than monosyllables when they come home from work. Sometimes my wife wishes I were one of them; she, an introvert, usually has the opposite problem with me. I'm kind of a words guy. But for talked-out men, to communicate is a sacrifice that they must forget not when they come home from work.

Right?

Some preachers of this passage have thought so. They take "communicate" to mean what it would today rather than what it meant in 1611. One preacher at a Bible church in the American Midwest did just this. Now that so many sermons are online, and so many are transcribed, it's fairly easy to find examples such as his—and I will not footnote this example, lest I embarrass this poor brother. He said in his sermon,

> All right, "to do good and . . . communicate." Communication, it's talking and sharing with each other the real things, the real things of our life. The true things. You know, there's people who absolutely share everything. Social media has exacerbated this matter to the maximum, because now you know what everybody's having for supper, you know what kind of food they like to eat, you know what kind of cookies they like, you know where their favorite restaurant is.

There are these people, he said, and then there are others for whom communication is a sacrifice. He continued, "There's sacrifice involved in communicating, if you'd be willing to not forget it. There's a price you'll pay for communicating."

So, to communicate forget not.

But isn't this just a funny thing to say? Who forgets to communicate and needs to be encouraged to do so? We've got at least a potential contextual conflict—one that very good readers will notice. How many people who read this statement in the KJV are this kind of good reader? I really don't know. But I feel reasonably sure that I myself did not pick up on this one when I first read it, probably in my late teens. I think I was a pretty good reader, but I don't think I got this one.

Fishing for a False Friend

The word "communicate" here in the original Greek is a noun, though the KJV rendered it as a verb (which is just fine—it's something you have to do sometimes to produce natural English). BDAG says that this noun here means an "attitude of good will that manifests an interest in a close relationship." It offers these possible translations: "generosity, fellow-feeling, altruism." I'm thinking "generosity" is the sense here, because most translators today go with "share."

> But do not forget to do good and to **share**, for with such sacrifices God is well pleased. (Heb. 13:16 NKJV)

Tyndale and the Geneva Bible—both written before the KJV—use "distribute."

In today's English, "communicate" can't mean "share your stuff" or "be generous." It's intransitive in this verse, meaning it has no object. The KJV in this verse doesn't tell people *what* to communicate. And the only commonsense meaning of "communicate" that is intransitive is to "share or exchange information, news, or ideas" (NOAD). NOAD gives the example sentence "A politician must have the ability to **communicate**."

Very few KJV readers, in my experience, are aware that the twenty-volume OED is the only reference work that covers the whole history of English and therefore is the only truly reliable source for looking up KJV words as apparently simple as "communicate." And sure enough, there's an intransitive sense of "communicate" that fits the Greek word and this context perfectly.

> To have a common part or share; to partake, participate, share (with another person). Frequently with in (the thing shared; also with, [occasionally] of).

And wouldn't ya know it: The OED marks this sense as obsolete.

Now, there are, I would say, two verses in the KJV New Testament that use the word "communicate" in such a way as to show that, back then, it could mean "share physical goods or money." Context provides good clues in those places that the KJV translators intended to use this obsolete sense:

> Let him that is taught in the word **communicate** unto him that teacheth in all good things. (Gal. 6:6)

That's a little obscure and will trip up some readers, but in context it can only mean "communicating" money or food—that is, sharing *things*, not words.

Then there's the Pauline epistle where the apostle says this:

> Now ye Philippians know also, that in the beginning of the gospel, when I departed from Macedonia, no church **communicated** with me as concerning giving and receiving, but ye only. (Phil. 4:15)

I'd say that's also a bit obscure: "Communicated with me as concerning giving and receiving" will definitely make some people think the Philippians talked to Paul about giving and receiving. But some sharp readers will, I think, get what the KJV translators intended.

But then there are other places where I think you'd have to be a pretty amazing Englisher to understand what "communicate" meant in 1611. Like the prior verse in Philippians.

> Notwithstanding ye have well done, that ye did **communicate** with my affliction. (v. 14)

Even knowing that "communicate" can mean "share"—or, here, I think, "share in"—I have a hard time making my brain understand this to mean anything other than the Philippians talking back and forth . . . with Paul's affliction. The modern sense of "communicate" is just so well ingrained in my brain after decades of use.

I think we have precisely the same kind of false friend in 1 Timothy 6:18 as we have in Hebrews 13:16:

> That they do good, that they be rich in good works, ready to distribute, willing to **communicate**. (1 Tim. 6:18)

Now that we know "communicate" is a potential false friend, the meaning is obvious here. But I daresay that if you ask ten people in your church and ten people on the street, all of those people will assume that it means "willing to share their thoughts with others."

The NKJV renders the last few verses I've talked about this way:

> Let him who is taught the word **share in** all good things with him who teaches. (Gal. 6:6 NKJV)

> Now you Philippians know also that in the beginning of the gospel, when I departed from Macedonia, no church **shared** with me concerning giving and receiving but you only. (Phil. 4:15 NKJV)

> Nevertheless you have done well that you **shared** in my distress. (v. 14 NKJV)

> Let them do good, that they be rich in good works, ready to give, willing to **share**. (1 Tim. 6:18 NKJV)

Once again, "communicate" was not wrong in 1611, and the NKJV is not disagreeing with the KJV to revise that word.

Look It Up, Dear!

Some of the places where "communicate" gets used in the KJV will probably make some readers confused enough that they'll look it up. But most, I think, won't. Who looks up words they already know when the senses they know work well enough in context? Not most people. And that's what makes "communicate" in Hebrews 13:16—and several other passages in the KJV—a false friend.

10. Honesty

> [Pray] for kings, and for all that are in authority; that we may lead a quiet and peaceable life in all godliness and **honesty**. (1 Tim. 2:2)

What do you think "honesty" means in this verse?

I GET TRIPPED UP by false friends in the KJV to this day, even after thousands of hours of working with them. With "honesty," my best friend caught me misunderstanding it while he was looking over something I wrote for publication!

Here's the story. Not long ago, I wrote a Bible textbook as a freelancer for a Christian textbook publisher where I used to work and where my best friend still works. The book is about biblical worldview, and it's written for sixth graders. I loved working for that ministry for nine years as a Bible textbook author, and when they offered me the chance to write the new book, I jumped at it. I cleared my schedule and wrote two thousand words a week with basically no breaks for a little over a year. I managed this by working every day on the bus, a forty-five-minute trip to my office and back. My friends at the publisher did an excellent job forming an outline and lesson objectives for the book. My main job was to communicate the truths engagingly to sixth graders.

I was asked to use the King James Version for this book. I worked hard to put explanatory words in brackets anytime I felt a given KJV word wouldn't make sense to kids born in 2010 or later—the intended audience for my work. I don't have very many quotations of any length from the KJV in that book without brackets because I'm manic about making sure kids can understand Bible quotations.

I like to get specific, so here are some actual examples from the book.

It's simple things sometimes, like that pesky word "of":

> After that he was seen of above [that is, by more than] five hundred brethren at once. (1 Cor. 15:6)

Or just one key word that I sense will need explanation:

> The wrath of God is revealed from heaven against all ungodliness and unrighteousness of men who hold [suppress] the truth in unrighteousness. (Rom. 1:18)

There was one place, though, where I should have added brackets but didn't.

Fishing for a False Friend

Months after I finished, that friend, who is a high-level theological editor and expert biblical consultant, was looking over the material, and he noticed something in my work. He sent me this note:

> I'm working on the Teachers Edition for Bible 6, and you quote the KJV of 1 Timothy 2: "that we may lead a quiet and peaceable life in all godliness and honesty." I'd bet that most readers . . . won't recognize that "honesty" means something different from our contemporary usage here. However, a comparison of BDAG and the OED led me to conclude that the sense that the KJV translators had in mind is . . .

But wait. We're not there yet. Hang on. In this case, it wasn't (a) contextual conflict or (b) checking other translations that led me to see "honest" as a false friend; it was secret option (c): someone telling me I was wrong.

As usual, he was right. The Greek word means "dignity" or "holiness":

> manner or mode of behavior that indicates one is above what is ordinary and therefore worthy of special respect . . . *dignity, seriousness, probity, holiness.* (BDAG)

According to BDAG, Paul is telling Timothy to teach people to live a life of the more general dignity or holiness, not of the more specific "telling the truth."

Because, of course, "honesty" in today's English is clearly something more specific than "dignity" and "holiness." I hardly need to look this up for you; "honesty" is such a common word. But contemporary dictionaries do tell me that it can mean "the quality of being honest" (NOAD). And "honest," in turn, means "free of deceit and untruthfulness; sincere" (NOAD).

Ask ten KJV readers—or two, how about just two?—what "honesty" means in the phrase, "all godliness and honesty," and I think ten out of two of them will say that it means "telling the truth."

The OED has a number of obsolete senses for "honesty" that fit the Greek word in 1 Timothy 2:2. This is the one I think the KJV translators intended:

> Exemplary or honourable moral behaviour; virtue, rectitude. *Obsolete.*

This is a false friend. The KJV translators used a word that for them could mean what the Greek word means but for us means "telling the truth."

One of the acid tests here for a shift as subtle as this (obviously, honorable behavior includes honesty—that's why this chapter is the last in the "narrowing" category) is to read the citations collected by the OED. Could you imagine contemporary English speakers saying these things?

Consider this citation I found from 1682:

> When it is once understood that the Law is made for publick **Honesty's** sake, the Superstition is now taken away.

I found the original book on Google Books—and you can go look at it for yourself there with the link in this footnote.[13] The language is a bit obscure, but the context favors the OED editors' assessment[14] that this word was being used to speak of the broader concept of public virtue, not the specific concept of public truth-telling.

13. You can see it for yourself here: https://bit.ly/oed-honesty-citation.

14. Note that I found this citation under a slightly different sense but one that is also possible for "honesty" in 1 Timothy 2:2 in the KJV—and one that is also marked obsolete in the OED.

The End of the Matter

As I mentioned above, when I quoted 1 Timothy 2:2 in the student textbook I wrote, I gave no explanatory bracket for "honesty." I also repeated the word later as I was explaining the passage. I gave no indication this word meant something different in 1611. I, the self-crowned King of False Friends, got tripped up by a false friend in the KJV. Yet again.

Everywhere the words "honest" or "honesty" or "honestly" appear in the KJV, they mean something bigger and more general than telling the truth. And a few of the contexts suggest this. A very perceptive reader might notice that it's a little odd, for example, to contrast something as general as "evil" with something as specific as "honesty":

> Now I pray to God that ye do no evil; not that we should appear approved, but that ye should do that which is **honest**. (2 Cor. 13:7)

Same with this passage:

> Recompense to no man evil for evil. Provide things **honest** in the sight of all men. (Rom. 12:17)

And this one:

> Let us walk **honestly**, as in the day; not in rioting and drunkenness, not in chambering and wantonness, not in strife and envying. (13:13)

It's also a little odd for Paul to tell people to think about things that are "true" and then to follow that up with "honest." Aren't "honest" things "true" things?

> Finally, brethren, whatsoever things are true, whatsoever things are **honest**, whatsoever things are just, whatsoever things are pure, whatsoever things are lovely, whatsoever things are of good report; if there be any virtue, and if there be any praise, think on these things. (Phil. 4:8)

In the places where the KJV has "honest" or "honesty," the NKJV tends to have the word "honorable" or "noble." The NKJV does use "honest" to speak of scales and weights (Lev. 19:36; Prov. 16:11); it also uses the word to speak of truth telling. The NKJV translators were not changing the KJV when they used "honorable"; they were saying what Paul meant—and what the King James translators meant when they chose the word "honest."

I missed all this completely when I wrote that textbook.

But I know this: I have worked very hard over many years to read the King James Bible with care and attention, and I have devoted more time than most mortals to uncovering the false friends created during the four centuries in which Elizabethan English evolved into our English. I was working extra hard while writing that textbook to look for words that today's sixth-grade students would not understand. I had my guard up and my thinking cap on. *I actually wrote about this false friend—"honest"—in my prequel to this book.* And I still didn't notice it when I was doing Bible teaching as a Bible textbook writer. How embarrassing!

It is difficult to keep your guard up sufficiently to catch all the minor differences that occur between KJV English and ours. It takes readerly dedication. When we see a word, our minds will go with the dominant sense we've given it. If that produces nonsense—a sentence that doesn't work, like "There's a married bachelor riding a one-wheeled bicycle!"—we realize what's going on and go back to the beginning of the sentence and start over. But if it makes tolerable sense, we tend to go merrily on. C. S.

Lewis, himself a master reader of old books, writes about this and believed that contemporary readers are often deceived. He calls these "dangerous senses."[15] I call them false friends.

And now—or at least, *for* now—you know another one. Maybe now you and I will remember it!

15. See C. S. Lewis, *Studies in Words*, 2nd ed. (HarperOne, 2013), 11.

Broadening

In Scottish English to this day, a "grice" is a pig, especially a young pig. "Grice" has what linguistics calls "intension": Its meaning is clear and specific. But it has little "extension": It doesn't refer to a very large number of objects in the real world. When a word or phrase "broadens," it typically loses intension and gains extension. It loses some of its specific meaning and becomes more general, but it gains the ability to refer to more entities in the world.[1] One could easily imagine a world in which "grice" goes from meaning "young pig" to meaning "pig" to meaning "any kind of farm animal in the swine family." That hasn't happened with "grice," but it is the kind of thing that has happened with the words in this section.

11. Watchings

In all things approving ourselves as the ministers of God, in much patience, in afflictions, in necessities, in distresses, in

1. I draw this specific example from Vern Poythress's excellent chapter, "Words and Precision," a reading I assign to my seminary students. The book in which the chapter appears, *Symphonic Theology: The Validity of Multiple Perspectives in Theology* (P&R, 1987), is available for free at frame-poythress.org/ebooks.

> stripes, in imprisonments, in tumults, in labours, in **watchings**, in fastings. (2 Cor. 6:4–5)

What do you think "watchings" means in this verse?

IN 2 CORINTHIANS 6, Paul is in self-defense mode, as he regularly is with the Corinthians. He's describing all the difficulties he has endured that tend to validate his sincerity as an apostle, a messenger of God. He suffered "afflictions," and he found himself "in distresses" and "in imprisonments"—and "in watchings" (v. 5).

The KJV uses this word just one other time, only a few chapters later. Here Paul is again talking about difficulties he's endured as one of God's ministers:

> Thrice was I beaten with rods, once was I stoned, thrice I suffered shipwreck, a night and a day I have been in the deep; in journeyings often, in perils of waters, in perils of robbers, in perils by mine own countrymen, in perils by the heathen, in perils in the city, in perils in the wilderness, in perils in the sea, in perils among false brethren; in weariness and painfulness, in **watchings** often, in hunger and thirst, in fastings often, in cold and nakedness. (11:25–27)

I'm going to tell you what I always thought this word meant: I pictured Paul maybe hiding out on the side of the road in some brush as he watched that passel of Jewish men who conspired to kill him pass by. I pictured him meeting secretly in a back room and looking out the window into the alleyway and cocking his ears every few minutes, watching for signs that his enemies had discovered his hiding place. Perils, perils everywhere. And he had to watch for them.

There was nothing in either of these contexts to tell me I was wrong, but I was.

Fishing for a False Friend

The New King James Version doesn't ever use the word "watchings." In both of the places where the KJV uses this word, the NKJV (translating exactly the same Greek text as the KJV here) says "sleeplessness."

Huh. That doesn't sound the same as "watchings" to my mind. Let's check the Greek. Sure enough, our responsible original-language lexicon, BDAG, says the word means "the state of remaining awake because one is unable to go to sleep, sleeplessness."

Watching out for danger might be the reason that you can't sleep, but that's not communicated by the Greek word Paul used in these two passages.

But NOAD doesn't give this sense of "watchings."[2] There is a military sense of the verb "watch" that involves staying awake to be on guard duty. But when I hear "watchings," my mind pictures someone's eyes scanning the area alertly. Yes, of course, they must be awake to do this. Their heart has to be beating too. And their retinas can't be detached. But those other concomitant ideas are not what I picture. It's "alert looking" that the word "watchings" brings to mind.

Sense 1 of this word in the OED is, I believe, what the KJV translators intended:

> to be or remain awake.

2. MW does, but it names that sense as obsolete.

The OED marks this sense as obsolete. No one says "watchings" and means this anymore. Sure, we have "the night watchman"; and, yes, an implication of watching is that the guard must remain awake. But the point in our minds, I think, is the looking, not the not-sleeping.

I believe we have caught a false friend.

Other Watchings in the KJV

I quoted for you at the beginning of this chapter the only two times in the KJV that this sense of "watchings" appears. Elsewhere "watching" is a gerund, a verbal form, that means just what we mean by it today.

> And when he came, lo, Eli sat upon a seat by the wayside **watching**: for his heart trembled for the ark of God. (1 Sam. 4:13)

> Blessed is the man that heareth me, **watching** daily at my gates, waiting at the posts of my doors. (Prov. 8:34)

These instances of "watching" happened during the day: The idea of being sleepless is clearly not included.

We also have in the KJV the various "watches" of the night being mentioned—like when Jesus came walking on the water toward his disciples in the "fourth watch of the night" (Matt. 14:25). And now I know why it's called that: A watch is a time of wakefulness. But I didn't know that before I went scurrying around underneath English to see what was in its crawl space.

Before I looked up its etymology, I did guess that the word "watch" was part of the Germanic, Anglo-Saxon stock of English words. Super common one-syllable words with thick consonant clusters like "tch" often are very old and very much Germanic. "Watch" didn't come in from Latin or Greek, or from Latin through Old French via the Norman invasion as so many words did. I can just tell by looking at it. This is an ancient word. And its ancient etymology is a clue to its meaning in these two passages in the KJV. "Watch" does come from the early Indo-European word for "wake." But the two ideas split a long, long time ago. "Watch" and "wake" are related but distinct—which is why we have two different words in contemporary English.

The only way I could imagine someone possibly understanding all this without a dictionary is by a process of deduction that would make them approximately four watches of the night smarter than I am.

12. Moderation

Let your **moderation** be known unto all men. (Phil. 4:5)

What do you think "moderation" means in this verse?

I ALWAYS THOUGHT "moderation" meant avoiding extremes. Don't be a die-hard leftist or a die-hard right-winger; don't eat too much or too little; do everything in moderation. And I have most certainly heard many Christians cite this phrase in just this way.

I don't think "moderation" in this verse means that, but there isn't enough context here to tip me off that it is a false friend. Paul is just kind of rattling off some final exhortations before he winds up his letter:

Rejoice in the Lord.
Let your "moderation" be known to everybody.

Don't be anxious about anything.

Pray instead.

Think about true and honorable things.

So, if there's nothing in the surrounding sentences to indicate that the KJV translators meant something different by "moderation" than we would in a context like this, how did I notice it?

Fishing for a False Friend

The reason I noticed that this might be a false friend is that I happened to check other translations, which use something like "gentleness" (NKJV). This is not the same as "avoidance of extremes."

The Greek word here, according to the most responsible lexicon, doesn't mean "avoidance of extremes" either. It means "not insisting on every right of letter of law or custom: *yielding, gentle, kind, courteous, tolerant*" (BDAG). The word also shows up in Titus 3:2, which urges elders "to speak evil of no one, to be peaceable, **gentle**, showing all humility to all men" (NKJV). One commentator suggested "meeting someone halfway" as a good way to understand Philippians 4:5.[3] I like that, and I'll bring it up again in a minute.

If you check NOAD, you get what I always thought the word meant in this verse:

> the avoidance of excess or extremes, especially in one's behavior or political opinions: he urged the police to show moderation.

3. Ben Witherington III, *Paul's Letter to the Philippians: A Socio-Rhetorical Commentary* (Eerdmans, 2011), 243.

This clearly does not match the meaning of the Greek word. Did the KJV get this one wrong?

Do you realize by now that the answer to this question is always going to be no in this book? This book will not and does not criticize the KJV or its translators. Frankly, I hold them in awe.

Indeed, if you check the OED, you'll see a sense that matches the Greek word well:

> originally: the quality of being moderate in harshness or intensity; mildness, clemency.

This is subtle, but think with me here. The OED says that this precise sense of the word is obsolete, no longer used, but that it later developed into the more general quality of being moderate in conduct or opinion—the "avoidance of extremes" sense that we now use. The OED sees an evolution here in the word. If the Greek word the KJV translators were translating means "not insisting on every right of letter of law or custom," then "clemency," in particular, fits. Paul is saying not to be harsh or strict with people when they cross you. Instead yield to them, be gentle to them, and be kind, courteous, and tolerant—as much as lieth in you. Tyndale went for "softness" here; the Bishops' Bible the KJV translators were revising went for "patient mind."

Paul isn't saying in this verse, "Don't take extreme views," or "Avoid gluttony," or "Always look for the golden mean between two parties."

Sure enough, no contemporary English translation translates the Greek word here with the English word "moderation." It simply doesn't mean what it once did. The relevant sense is obsolete. Unless KJV readers regularly check the Greek and Hebrew or check multiple English translations, they will misunderstand this verse—through no fault of their own, because English has simply changed in the last four-hundred-plus years; and through no fault of the KJV translators, because they couldn't predict the many subtle ways in which their English would change on its way to becoming our English.

Peroration

My whole life, till after I wrote *Authorized*, I quoted Philippians 4:5 and did not realize what Paul intended.

And if KJV readers miss the meaning here, they miss a verse I find very helpful and instructive—and convicting—for my interactions with others, especially online. It has struck me so many times how much more convincing someone is *when they meet their opponents halfway*. Some issues are truly binary; don't get me wrong. I'm not going to be half LGBTQ-affirming or half pro-choice.

But how many major issues that divide people, that divide Christians, are really like those two examples? I have a close friend who is divided from me over the Calvinism-Arminianism debate; I have another respected friend who thinks it's wrong for Christians to sell Christian books—to him that's like selling prayer. I grant that both of these brothers make important points. I also grant that I don't have answers for all their hard questions. I assume the best about their motives, even when I can't bring myself to agree. I listen. In other words, I meet them halfway.

A few times in my life (just a few . . .), I have gotten very bitter online comments on articles I've written or videos I've published. Occasionally, I can feel my own dander rising when these folks say provocative and insulting things. Am I the only one who experiences this?

In these times, I often think of the parable of the unforgiving servant. He was shown incredible clemency—the forgiveness of a ten-thousand-talent debt. I did the math once, and I concluded that Jesus was, I'm not kidding, saying something like "450 gazillion dollars." The impossibly massive size of the debt was his whole point, because Jesus was picturing our sin debt to God. And, of course, this man goes right out and chokes someone who owes him a measly couple thousand bucks. He showed no clemency, no mercy, no willingness to moderate his supposedly righteous demands.

All this, to me, is what it means to let love cover others' offenses. Jesus's payment of my terrible sin debt is what fuels my ability to give soft answers that turn away online wrath.

All this is what enables me to search for a charitable interpretation of someone else's words.

All this is what it means to show moderation—gentleness, graciousness, reasonableness—to all people.

Semantic Reversal

SEMANTIC REVERSAL MEANS that a given word comes to mean the opposite of what it once did. Does this sound impossible?

Not only is it possible, but there are instances of words that hold on to both contradictory meanings. There aren't many, but here's one: "peruse." This word has for many years been used to speak both of light reading and of deep reading—of skimming and of diving. You can casually "peruse" the new titles at the bookstore with a latte in your hand (this is what sounds more natural to me), or you can "peruse" someone's dissertation for hours. You know by context which sense is intended. I presume that "peruse" will one day come to mean only one of those things; I don't know how long this contradiction can last.

Likewise, there are words and phrases in the KJV that have come to mean their opposite over time. The difference is that they no longer mean both A and not-A. They've simply shifted to mean not-A.

I don't discuss it in this book, but "he who now letteth will let" (2 Thess. 2:7) provides an example. "Let" today, in a context like that one, would most naturally mean "permit" or "allow." But in 1611 it meant to "hinder" or "obstruct" or "prevent" (OED).

Speaking of "prevent," that's a false friend you'll find in this section, and the others are some of my favorite false friends. That's because they are so clear and because they were sent to me by a dear brother and a respected teacher.

13. So That

> Therefore now, LORD God of Israel, keep with thy servant David my father that thou promisedst him, saying, There shall not fail thee a man in my sight to sit on the throne of Israel; **so that** thy children take heed to their way, that they walk before me as thou hast walked before me. (1 Kings 8:25)

What do you think "so that" means in this verse? This verse is complex. Read carefully.

ONE OF THE PROBLEMS with my work on false friends is that once I alert people to the presence of a false friend somewhere in the KJV, I can no longer observe what they "really think" that word means. They get nervous, like I'm trying to trick them. They start racking their brains. I see almost no way around this.

What would you have assumed "so that" means in 1 Kings 8:25 if I hadn't just told you it's a false friend?

It's been nothing short of absolute delight to have just a few people really catch on to the idea of false friends and the methodology for finding them. People assume I have a master list; I don't. So, I'm very happy when they are sent to me. This one was sent to me by an especially important friend. I had never noticed it.

Fishing for a False Friend

This friend noticed one day that there was a place in the KJV that said "so that" where the NKJV had something so different that it really seemed like the opposite. The NKJV renders 1 Kings 8:25 like this, and I'll bold the relevant words:

> Therefore, LORD God of Israel, now keep what You promised Your servant David my father, saying, "You shall not fail to have a man sit before Me on the throne of Israel, **only if** your sons take heed to their way, that they walk before Me as you have walked before Me."

Where the KJV has "so that," the NKJV has "only if." The KJV appears to make living holy lives the *result* of God's choice of David's line to sit on the throne: He put them on the throne *so that* they would lead holy lives. The NKJV makes living holy lives a *condition* for David's sons to sit on that throne: He will continue to put them on the throne *only if* they will lead holy lives.

If you're a really, really attentive reader, you might have picked this up through contextual conflict instead of noticing it in different translations. I wasn't that reader. And neither was my diligent, intelligent friend. It would take a superhumanly good reader to notice that, indeed, it's a little strange for Solomon to say "so that" here—if "so that" means what *we* mean by "so that." "You will never fail to have a son of David sitting on the throne . . . *in order that* your sons will live holy lives"? How does that follow? It didn't, in fact. The sons of David did not live holy lives, and they had to be cast from that throne. *The* son of David now sits on it,[1] but only because he's divine and undid the failures of all his merely human predecessors.

The Hebrew here is a two-word phrase meaning literally "only if"—or in contemporary English word order, "if only." The main Hebrew-English lexicon I use gives this definition:

> given that, if only. (HALOT)

This lexicon gives three example verses, one of which is 1 Kings 8:25. Let's look at the other two for some help, to see how the phrase is used.

The first is in the Pentateuch:

> There shall be no poor among you; for the Lord shall greatly bless thee in the land which the LORD thy God giveth thee for an inheritance to possess it: **only if** thou carefully hearken unto the voice of the LORD thy God, to observe to do all these commandments which I command thee this day. (Deut. 15:4–5)

Here the KJV translators translate the very same phrase as 1 Kings 8:25, but they do it far differently. They agree with my lexicon, using "only if." And, clearly, that's what it has to mean. Carefully hearkening to God's voice and observing all his commandments is the *condition* for retaining title to their God-given land.

This verse in 2 Kings is pretty much the same:

> Neither will I make the feet of Israel move any more out of the land which I gave their fathers; **only if** they will observe to do according to all that I have commanded them. (21:8)

1. Depending on your eschatological viewpoint—some believe that he is not yet on that throne but will one day be.

To be clear, the KJV translators translated the relevant Hebrew phrase as "so that" in 1 Kings 8:25 but as "only if" in these two other places. To be even clearer, as usual, I think they made no error. But it remains for me to explain how that could be the case when "only if" and "so that" sure seem to be opposites.

Step 3 in our process is to look up the words in a contemporary dictionary, specifically NOAD, which gives the sense, "with the result that." This is precisely what I expected. It's the only way I've ever used or heard the phrase "so that." It's the only way you have ever used or heard the phrase, too, I would guess.

The OED most certainly records the same sense for this phrase that we saw in our contemporary dictionaries, the ones that describe our language as it now is. The OED says the phrase can "denote result or logical consequence," that it is equivalent to "in order that." And it says this use of the phrase is very, very old, going back to the Old English days. It cites *Beowulf*, in fact. English speakers have been saying "so that" to indicate result for a long, long time.

Indeed, it's important to point out that "so that" could mean in 1611 what it means today: result, purpose, consequence. It usually means this in the KJV, including in its very first appearance in Genesis:

> And the land was not able to bear them, that they might dwell together: for their substance was great, **so that** they could not dwell together. (13:6)

Here's the second instance:

> And I will make thy seed as the dust of the earth: **so that** if a man can number the dust of the earth, then shall thy seed also be numbered. (v. 16)

But the OED also records a sense of the phrase "so that" that will solve our dilemma and reveal (you guessed it) a false friend:

> so (that), in limiting sense: On condition that, provided that, so long as, if only.

This is perfect. It fits the Hebrew. It fits the context. And yet, I would argue, we don't use this sense of the phrase "so that" anymore. It doesn't show up in any of the three contemporary dictionaries I checked.

I also couldn't find it in the NOW Corpus, though I admit I wearied of that task quickly as I saw that, over and over again, "so that" meant "in order that."

I will also admit that the OED does *not* mark this sense as archaic or obsolete, but the last use it records comes from 1859—and I took my nerdiness to extreme levels by checking the first edition of the OED, published back in 1913, over one hundred years ago. The entry for this sense is essentially unchanged in the most recent edition—and the entry notes this. A few citation dates have been corrected in the OED edition I have now, but all the citations are exactly the same. None are added; none are missing. I would argue that the OED lexicographers, when they next get around to revising this sense of the phrase "so that," will need to mark it as obsolete. I don't think anyone will get the intended meaning of the KJV translators unless they happen to use some of our false friends fishing tools.

Conditional Promises

If people check the Hebrew, they may think the KJV translators made a mistake when they didn't. This is a false friend that materially changes the meaning of the verses in which it appears and makes them close to nonsensical. Again, it isn't the KJV translators' fault. It's the "fault" of language change over the last four centuries. We don't have that sense of "so that" anymore.

Elsewhere the KJV reads,

> Neither will I any more remove the foot of Israel from out of the land which I have appointed for your fathers; **so that** they will take heed to do all that I have commanded them, according to the whole law and the statutes and the ordinances by the hand of Moses. (2 Chron. 33:8)

This is a specific kind of covenantal promise, a conditional one. And that's important to the theology of the Old Testament. The people will remain in their land *if only*—provided that—they obey. This is the old covenant, not the new. There was grace in that old covenant: God picked these people alone among all the nations of the earth to be recipients of his special blessing. But that covenant did not provide the power to obey, as our new covenant does—a covenant enacted on better promises through the death of our Great Mediator.

Within the new covenant there is still an expectation of holiness—holiness without which no one will see the Lord. We ought to look at these conditional promises God made to the Israelites and fear, lest we ourselves come up short of the promise. But we can also rest in the assurance that not only do we have an Advocate with the Father when we sin, but we have the Paraclete, the Comforter, who abides in us and produces holiness in us. This is something the members of the old covenant couldn't bank on.

All this is clear enough in the KJV as a whole, certainly. People who read the KJV can still see these things outside these particular "so that" passages, and they have done so and will continue to do so. But the little phrase "so that" is like static being played at key moments during an audiobook. It's like a sign that was hit by a truck and got swiveled around, pointing in the wrong direction. It is, in short, a false friend.

14. Choose Your Own Adventure!

> Yet hath he not root in himself, but dureth for a while: for when tribulation or persecution ariseth because of the word, by and by he is offended. (Matt. 13:21)

For this chapter, I'm not going to put the false friend in bold in the quoted passage. Where do you think the false friend is, and what does it mean?

UNDERSTANDEST THOU WHAT thou readest in the King James Version? This time, I bet you don't. I didn't. It never occurred to me that this particular false friend was a false friend at all—not until it was brought to my attention by an old professor of mine several years after I wrote *Authorized*. Matthew has always been my favorite Gospel, so I had read this verse many, many times over many years. I'd gone right past this false friend without realizing I was misunderstanding the KJV English. In fact, this false friend is sort of like a contronym between the two Englishes. In 1611, it meant the opposite of what we mean by it today.

But this time, I'm not going to tell you what the false friend is. You have to figure out the mystery. You have to relive the series from my childhood: Choose Your Own Adventure. *Will Parsley save Rosemary in time?* Make the right choice, and you'll find out.

I will make this multiple choice. Do you think the false friend is "root," "dureth," "tribulation," "by and by," or "offended"? Make your selection, then read on to confirm your guess.

"Root" "Tribulation" "Offended"
"Dureth" "By and by"

Go ahead! Be bold! I promise I won't make fun of you if you get this wrong. Remember: I didn't realize this was a false friend until well after I had a 401(k).

Root

Nope. "Root" isn't it. Sorry! "Root" in 1611 meant "root," just like it does today: the part of the plant that goes underground to get nutrients and stabilize the plant.

However, as our hero, Parsley, dies a slow death at the hand of the evil Queen Paprika, who has Rosemary locked away in the dungeon, I have a funny philological story to tell about "root."

"Root" is a false friend between American English and Australian English, if used in just the wrong way. I preached in Australia for a week one summer—I had a wonderful time getting to know some precious brothers and sisters there at a Christian camp in North Queensland. But I made the mistake of using the word "root" in a sermon to talk about "rooting" for a particular sports team.

Only subsequently did I learn that "root" is a rather bad word there. Thankfully, my audience was aware that American English speakers use the word differently, and no one gasped.

Goodbye, Parsley.

You're going to have to choose a different adventure.

Dureth

Nope. "Dureth" isn't it. Sorry!

I find that some people want to call any and all KJV archaisms false friends. But "dureth" is not a false friend, because (a) we don't use it, and (b) it isn't misleading. It falls into an awkward gray area: I'm tempted to call "dureth" a dead word,[2] but it's so close to "durable" and "endure" (and the much less common and highfalutin "perdure") and the context is so clear as to what word needs to go in this slot, that I think most readers today understand what the KJV means here. It means "the root *endures* for a little while."

Choose a different adventure.

Tribulation

Nope. The false friend is not "tribulation," either.

The OED does label this word as archaic, and "affliction" and "trouble" and "distress" could feasibly be used today instead. Those are indeed more commonly known words among the plow boys of today. They don't have the old-timey whiff about them "tribulation" does.

But it's only a whiff, not a big deal. The word hangs on in the phrase "trials and tribulations." And I sense that, unlike "doornail," which is kept alive solely by the phrase "dead as a doornail," "tribulation" still carries meaning to most English speakers. And the NKJV and SKJV still choose "tribulation" in Matthew 13:21.

Choose another adventure.

Offended

OK, I was a little tricky. I admit it. I chose Matthew 13:21 as my example passage in part to give you this misdirection. You're going to have to choose a different adventure.

But I will point out that if you paid careful attention to the instructions, I said that the false friend in Matthew 13:21 is a

2. The OED and MW label the relevant sense of "dureth" as "archaic," but the word doesn't even occur in AHD and NOAD, nor could I find it in the NOW Corpus.

contronym of sorts; it now means the opposite of what it meant in 1611. "Offended" is not a contronym between the two Englishes. Its meaning has shifted, but it hasn't shifted to the opposite of what it once was. I won't dig into this word now because chapter 21 is coming apace.

By and By

DING DING DING DING! You got it! You are either really smart or really lucky. Or you tried all the other options and now you're here.

This false friend is a real backstabber, isn't it? It's the kind of false friend that talks a great talk to your face but goes and says the very opposite thing to someone else the next minute. Or not the next minute—it said the opposite thing to someone else over two hundred million minutes ago. English has changed in a lot of subtle ways since then.

What I mean is that in 1611, "by and by" in this context—and in all four places where it shows up in the KJV—meant the exact opposite of what it means today. It is indeed a kind of contronym between the two Englishes. Like "let." To "let" today means to "permit" or "allow" someone to do something. Back in 1611 it could mean the opposite: "hinder." Paul says, "He that now letteth will let" (2 Thess. 2:7), and the KJV translators did not mean, "He who now permits will permit."

Here are the four places the KJV uses the phrase "by and by":

> Yet hath he not root in himself, but dureth for a while: for when tribulation or persecution ariseth because of the word, **by and by** he is offended. (Matt. 13:21)

> And she came in straightway with haste unto the king, and asked, saying, I will that thou give me **by and by** in a charger the head of John the Baptist. (Mark 6:25)

> But which of you, having a servant plowing or feeding cattle, will say unto him **by and by**, when he is come from the field, Go and sit down to meat? (Luke 17:7)

> But when ye shall hear of wars and commotions, be not terrified: for these things must first come to pass; but the end is not **by and by**. (Luke 21:9)

The one that got my professor wondering was the second one. Why in the world would Salome ask Herod to bring her John the Baptist's head "by and by"? Does that strike you as odd? Wouldn't she want it right away? Who says to the king, "Please behead that man in prison after a while, when you're good and ready"?

There are three different Greek words (though two are very similar) being translated as "by and by" in these four passages. BDAG says they all mean "immediately" or "at once."

In fact, elsewhere the KJV translates all three of these words with "immediately" or "straightway," an older spelling of our word "straightaway." For reasons we do not know, these four times, the KJV translators chose instead to use the phrase "by and by."

"By and by" now, of course, means "after a while." NOAD gives "before long, eventually."

To me, the phrase feels a little quaint. I associate it with older folks sitting on rocking chairs on porches in the Georgia pines, humming "In the Sweet By and By," and saying to one another, "I'll get down to the store by and by." "By and by" is noncommittal, indefinite. I don't know that I've ever said this phrase. I always get down to the store right away. But I certainly know it.

Sure enough, the OED reveals that there once was a sense of "by and by" that fits the Greek perfectly:

> of sequence of events: straightway, immediately, directly, at once. *Obsolete.*

One OED sample sentence is right from the KJV, Luke 21:9 (which we'll cover in a moment). We have a clear and definitive false friend.

Immediate Stumbling

When Jesus said that certain soils don't have good roots but last only until tribulation or persecution arise, he meant that such people *immediately* stumble when those pressures come. "By and by he is offended," in 1611, meant "Right away he falls."

Other English translations don't say "by and by" in Matthew 13:21. The NKJV says "immediately."[3]

> Yet he has no root in himself, but endures only for a while. For when tribulation or persecution arises because of the word, **immediately** he stumbles. (Matt. 13:21 NKJV)

In the other three places where this phrase occurs, really good KJV readers may pick up on the possibility of a false friend even without checking the NKJV, because our modern sense of "by and by" doesn't work well. I do have some vivid memories of the ways in which I understood various KJV passages as a kid. I believe I was puzzled by this use of "by and by":

> Which of you, having a servant plowing or feeding cattle, will say unto him **by and by**, when he is come from the field, Go and sit down to meat? (Luke 17:7)

To me that always meant, "Which of you will say to your servant, **after a while**, when he comes back from working in

---

3. The Modern English Version, which is based on the Textus Receptus, stumbled embarrassingly here. The MEV translator who worked on Matthew has, "For when tribulation or persecution arises because of the word, **eventually** he falls away." This revisor almost certainly went by his gut-level understanding of KJV English without checking the Greek. That's unpardonable. Translators shouldn't get tripped up by false friends, because they should be reading the originals.

the field . . ." That just didn't make sense to me. The NKJV has "at once" and the SKJV has "right away" here. That clears it up.

> And which of you, having a servant plowing or tending sheep, will say to him when he has come in from the field, "Come **at once** and sit down to eat"? (Luke 17:7 NKJV)

Nobody does this, Jesus is saying. If you have a servant, you ask him to feed you before you invite him to eat.

I find Luke 21:9 confusing too—given my modern feel for what "by and by" means:

> But when ye shall hear of wars and commotions, be not terrified: for these things must first come to pass; but the end is not **by and by**.

I can't make sense of that contextually. Clearly Jesus has to mean "the end is not yet" or "is not soon." But I read right past this many times, picking up the overall gist from context, and didn't stop to realize that "by and by" was a funny thing to say here.

Let me repeat something important: The KJV translators did not make a mistake in any of the four instances in which they used the phrase "by and by." All they did was fail to predict the future, which isn't a fault. They didn't know that, after a while, "by and by" would come to mean "after a while."

Through no fault of the KJV translators nor of my own ignorance, but solely because of the inevitable process of language change, I misunderstood for most of my life what Jesus meant by this phrase.

Question

I have a question: Now that you do know what "by and by" meant in 1611, do you think you'll remember it four and half years from now, when you come across the phrase in the KJV again? You might; you might not. Our English is such a powerful force in our minds. It's hard to remember to doubt our reflexive understanding when reading older English.

I don't want to forget. I want to understand the Bible when I read it—every word. I want to get the right picture in Jesus's parable of the soils. I want to see that person falling away from the Word the instant persecution or tribulation arises. They don't *eventually* fall away; they get knocked over at the first blow. What a powerful picture. A picture obscured not by the KJV translators and not by our failure to be good readers but by the inevitable process of language change.

We must be on guard, because false friends lurk in unexpected places, threatening to keep Parsley from saving Rosemary in time.

15. Prevent

> We which are alive and remain unto the coming of the Lord shall not **prevent** them which are asleep. (1 Thess. 4:15)

What do you think "prevent" means in this verse?

"PREVENT" IS ANOTHER false friend many KJV readers know. Do you? I think many readers know that "prevent" in the verse quoted above means "come before" or "precede." This is a famous verse, and our current sense of "prevent" makes poor sense there.

But here's what I believe to be an important question: Does knowledge of this famous false friend (for those who possess it) help KJV readers in the other places in which it appears?

> All the sinners of my people shall die by the sword, which say, The evil shall not overtake nor **prevent** us. (Amos 9:10)

If you have learned that "prevent" in 1 Thessalonians meant "precede" in 1611, will that help you in Amos 9:10? First, will you remember to doubt your intuitive understanding of the word "prevent"? And if you do, will that help?

Let's try it: "The evil shall not overtake nor precede us." Does that make sense? I don't think it does. What would it even mean for people to boast that evil would not "precede" them?

Or take Job 3:11–12:

> Why died I not from the womb? Why did I not give up the ghost when I came out of the belly?
> Why did the knees **prevent** me? Or why the breasts that I should suck?

If "prevent" in the KJV means "precede" or "come before," what would this mean? Job is asking why he didn't die in the womb or in childbirth. Why did his mother's knees not "precede" him? What would that mean?

I could mention others, but I think the point is already clear: Even if you know what "prevent" means in 1 Thessalonians, this knowledge will not necessarily help you in many of the other places where the word occurs.

Fishing for a False Friend

Let's pick two passages—one in the Old Testament and one in the New Testament—and go through our process. I myself am curious about these passages; as of the moment in which I'm writing this paragraph, I don't really understand what "prevent" means in them.

Here they are:

> The sorrows of hell compassed me about: the snares of death **prevented** me. (Ps. 18:5)

> And when he [Peter] was come into the house, Jesus **prevented** him, saying, What thinkest thou, Simon? Of whom do the kings of the earth take custom or tribute? Of their own children, or of strangers? (Matt. 17:25)

The Hebrew word translated "prevented" in Psalm 18:5 means "to go up to someone" or to "meet" them (HALOT). In other words, the snares of death "met" David or, perhaps, "confronted" him. That's what he was saying (in Hebrew). The Greek word translated "prevented" in Matthew 17:25 means "to be ahead of someone in some activity," and some ways to translate it might be "[to] be ahead of, come before, anticipate" (BDAG). In other words, Jesus was the first to speak, not Peter. Jesus "spoke to him first."

But as you must know, "prevent" doesn't mean "meet" or "come before" in contemporary English. It means "keep (something) from happening or arising" (NOAD). When the snares of death "prevent" you, they're stopping you from something—like, well, living. When you "prevent" people from coming into the house, it doesn't mean you're speaking first; it means you're barring the door.

Interestingly, NOAD does include an archaic sense of "prevent":

> *archaic* (of God) go before (someone) with spiritual guidance and help.

But this doesn't help me in either of our passages. Was David saying that the snares of death were "going before" him with spiritual guidance? Was Jesus "going before" Peter into the house with spiritual help?

I turn now to the OED, hoping for more than one sense of "prevent" that will help me understand the intent of the KJV translators. I just don't see (yet) how "come before" is going to help me in every passage I've mentioned.

The very first sense in the OED nails the Matthew 17 passage. This just *has* to be the sense the KJV translators intended:

> *transitive*. To act before or more quickly than (a person or agent); to anticipate in action; to act in advance of. *Obsolete*.

Jesus acted in advance of Peter: He spoke first. This is just what Tyndale thought the word meant.

> And when he was come into the housse / Jesus **spake fyrst** to him saying . . . (Matt. 17:25 Tyndale)

However, this sense doesn't work in Psalm 18:5 . . . or not well. The snares of death "acted in advance of" me? I'm struggling to make that work.

But if we keep looking down the list of senses of "prevent," we find this:

> *transitive*. To come, arrive, or appear before. . . . *Obsolete*.

That's it. It fits the Hebrew, and it fits the meaning of Psalm 18:5. The snares of death "appear before" David. They face or confront him.

We have a false friend. Or two, depending on how we count it.

Or more—you be the judge. Perhaps it's time you did some of your own fishing, after all. I've trained you. Now go and fish likewise. Look up the other uses of "prevent" in the KJV. Maybe try that one from Job:

> Why did the knees **prevent** me? Or why the breasts that I should suck? (3:12)

Look up the Hebrew word in the best dictionary you've got (I recommend the site Marble.Bible), then go to your local library and find their copy of the OED. They'll have one. Ideally, they'll help you get set up with electronic access.

Cast out. Reel in. You can do this. Write me if you catch something!

Metonymy/ Synecdoche

"Metonymy" is naming something by using a related thing. When a British citizen dishonors "the crown," it's not really a piece of bejeweled, golden headwear that is being disrespected but the wearer of it. "Skirt-chasers" are not usually interested in fabric, and "The White House said today" doesn't mean that a building somehow spoke.

"Synecdoche" is naming something by using a part of that thing. When someone gets a "hired hand," they usually want the whole body.

The type of language change of the words in this section is sometimes difficult to pin down. I won't die on the hill of how these words are categorized.

16. Coasts

> And the locusts went up over all the land of Egypt, and rested in all the **coasts** of Egypt: very grievous were they; before them there were no such locusts as they, neither after them shall be such. (Exod. 10:14)

What do you think "coasts" means in this verse?

HAVE YOU EVER NOTICED that in a few places in the KJV "coast" doesn't make great sense? Something is odd. Like when Numbers 13:29 talks about the Canaanites who dwell "by the **coast** of Jordan." Rivers don't have "coasts" in contemporary English. Only seas and oceans do. This might pique the reader's interest.

In Numbers 34:3, if you really know your geography, you might catch the oddity. This verse talks about a border of the promised land that runs "from the wilderness of Zin along by the **coast** of Edom"—Edom, a tiny, almost landlocked country with only a tiny, tiny bit of land on the ocean. That's odd. Right? I can't really make sense of this verse in the KJV if it's saying that the southern border of the promised land runs from the wilderness of Zin along that tiny spit of land. That would seem to me to eat up Edom entirely.

Or consider Joshua 18:11, which is describing the small territory allotted to the tribe of Benjamin. It speaks of the "coast of their lot" as going between that of Judah and that of Joseph. You can see this on the map on the following page. Notice that while Edom is not quite landlocked, Benjamin is entirely landlocked. How can it have a coast?

Fishing for a False Friend

Logos is able to tell me through its Bible Word Study that "coast" in the KJV is used to translate *fourteen different Hebrew words.* One Hebrew word predominates in the Old Testament, however, and, likewise, one Greek word predominates in the New.

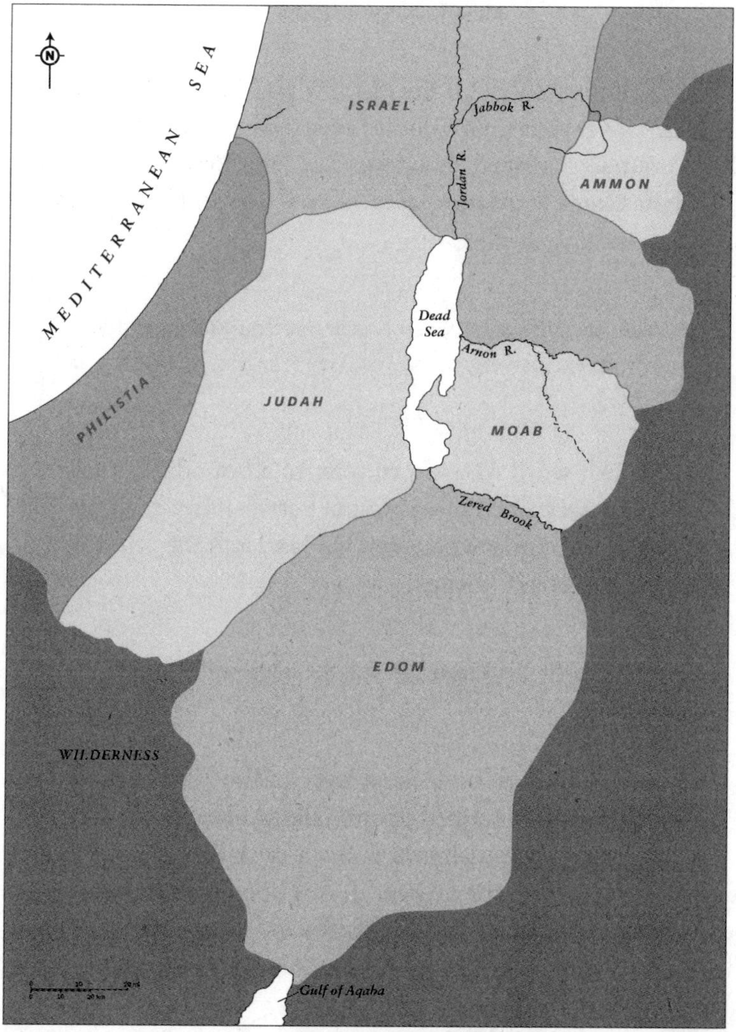
MEDITERRANEAN SEA
ISRAEL
Jabbok R.
Jordan R.
AMMON
Dead Sea
Arnon R.
JUDAH
PHILISTIA
MOAB
Zered Brook
EDOM
WILDERNESS
Gulf of Aqaba

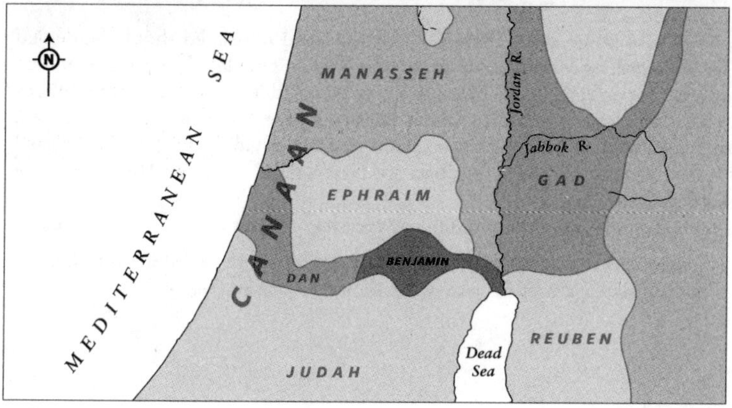
MEDITERRANEAN SEA
MANASSEH
Jordan R.
CANAAN
Jabbok R.
GAD
EPHRAIM
BENJAMIN
DAN
REUBEN
Dead Sea
JUDAH

The dictionary entry for the Hebrew word translated "coasts" most often (over sixty times) doesn't even include the word "coasts." The word means instead "boundary" or "territory" (HALOT).

And the Greek word translated "coasts" most often (ten times) means something similar:

> marker of division between two areas, boundary mostly, in our lit. exclusively, pl. boundaries = region, district. (BDAG)

The English word "coast" *can* refer to a boundary, a marker of division between two areas but not between two regions. The coast is only a boundary between the land and the sea. Right?

Here's what "coast" means:

> the part of the land near the sea; the edge of the land. (NOAD)

A coast is a kind of boundary, but not the kind the Hebrew and Greek words we looked up are talking about.

So, did the KJV translators make a mistake? If you haven't realized this by now, the answer in this book is always going to be no. The KJV translators specifically mention in their preface that they are not above mistakes,[1] but I do not charge them with a single one in this book.

---

1. "[There is] no cause therefore why the word translated should be denied to be the word, or forbidden to be current [that is, circulated], notwithstanding that some imperfections and blemishes may be noted in the setting forth of it. For [we ask:] whatever was perfect under the sun, where Apostles or apostolic men, that is, men endued with an extraordinary measure of God's Spirit, and privileged with the privilege of infallibility, had not their hand?" (Norton, *New Cambridge Paragraph Bible*, xxviii.)

Summarized (and shortened) in contemporary English:

> There is no reason why the word of God stops being the word of God when it's translated simply because some imperfections and blemishes occur in

All three of the English dictionaries we haven't checked yet provide the answer for this one. MW, AHD, and the venerable and august OED all say the same thing: There was once a sense of "coasts" that meant precisely what the Hebrew word in Joshua 18:11 means: "border" or "frontier."

The OED says the word used to mean

> the border, bound, or limit, of a country; territory on or near a boundary or frontier, borderland.

All three of these dictionaries also list this sense as obsolete. We have definitely caught a false friend.

In 1611, the word "coasts" often meant "borders." Today, it means "the edge of the sea," which is generally a border marker, but it is a more specific word than "border." Pretty much all seacoasts may be borders, but not all borders are coasts. English has shifted. The last use the OED records for this older sense of "coasts" comes from 1618. The OED also records a sense of "coasts" to mean "territory," which we also see in Exodus, when the Lord sends locusts to the "coasts" of Egypt. He didn't just send the locusts to the coastal areas. He sent them to the whole territory. The OED also dutifully records that "coast" used to be used, rarely, to refer to the edge of a pond or river—just like the KJV does at least once.

(A little tidbit: the phrase "the coast is clear" comes from this older sense of the word "coast." It pictures armies amassed at a border, not at the seaside—and not a navy. If the armies have marched off and are no longer stationed at the border, we can say, "The coast is clear." The phrase has stuck around because of the nice alliteration—coast and clear—but the meaning of "coast" has changed.)

---

that translation. Was there ever anything perfect in this world aside from those things that were done by apostles?

Bethlehem Beaches?

"Coasts" is another false friend that experienced and careful KJV readers will probably learn after a while. It's just hard to make sense of certain passages if "coasts" means "seacoasts." When Herod "slew all the children that were in Bethlehem, and in all the coasts thereof" (Matt. 2:16), that just doesn't work since Bethlehem has no beaches.

In one interesting verse, the KJV translators rendered the very same Hebrew word as "coast" and as "border" within the same sentence:

> From thence they removed, and pitched on the other side of Arnon, which is in the wilderness that cometh out of the **coasts** of the Amorites: for Arnon is the **border** of Moab, between Moab and the Amorites. (Num. 21:13)

They had the word "border." I'm not entirely sure why they didn't use it more than "coasts."

But I do know that when people today read, "He restored the **coast** of Israel from the entering of Hamath unto the sea of the plain" (2 Kings 14:25), they are likely to think the Bible is talking about the seacoast. It will be hard to make an accurate mental map in that case.

In Mark 7:31, when Jesus is "departing from the **coasts** of Tyre and Sidon," readers might assume he was on the seaside edges of these small coastal areas, when what the KJV translators meant—using their English—was that Jesus was in the "regions" of Tyre and Sidon. (The Greek word here means "regions," not "seacoasts.") Sometimes "coasts" in the KJV does mean what we mean by it; they had that sense too. In Acts 27:2 Paul and Luke were "meaning to sail by the coasts of Asia."[2]

---

2. "Asia" itself is a kind of false friend. In New Testament times that word referred to a different part of the world than it does today.

But most of the 113 times the KJV translators used the word "coasts," they meant "borders" or "territory," not "the part of the land touching the sea."

Warning: If you ever go back in time to the early 1600s, and if you're involved in a naval disaster and put out a distress call to the Coast Guard, it will be border guards that come, meaning they probably won't have boats.

Or radios. So, there are multiple reasons they will not come.

17. Counsel

> The **counsel** of the LORD standeth for ever, the thoughts of his heart to all generations. (Ps. 33:11)

What do you think "counsel" means in this verse?

IF YOU DON'T UNDERSTAND the concept of false friends, certain revisions in contemporary English Bible translations will look random, needless, or wrong. Look at the bolded words in the KJV and NKJV below (and remember that the NKJV translators were translating exactly the same Greek words). Here's the KJV:

> For of a truth against thy holy child Jesus, whom thou hast anointed, both Herod, and Pontius Pilate, with the Gentiles, and the people of Israel, were gathered together, for to do whatsoever thy hand and thy **counsel** determined before to be done. (Acts 4:27–28)

Here's the NKJV:

> For truly against Your holy Servant Jesus, whom You anointed, both Herod and Pontius Pilate, with the Gentiles and the people of Israel, were gathered together to do whatever Your hand and Your **purpose** determined before to be done.

Why did the NKJV change "counsel" to "purpose"? Who doesn't know what "counsel" means? Well, me, apparently. "Counsel" is—often, not always, as we'll see—a false friend in the KJV. I now realize that I at least partially misunderstood multiple verses in which it's used, and some of them are pretty important, like the ones above.

Fishing for a False Friend

I don't remember what got me to notice that "counsel" seems odd sometimes in the KJV. But take a look for yourself at the following verses. What do you notice? (Hint: Hebrew poetry is built on parallel lines; it rhymes thoughts rather than words. The second line in a couplet, the "rhyming" one, adds to or intensifies the first line. What words does the Old Testament "rhyme" with "counsel"?)

> And it came to pass, when our enemies heard that it was known unto us, and God had brought their **counsel** to nought, that we returned all of us to the wall, every one unto his work. (Neh. 4:15)

> Lord, thou knowest all their **counsel** against me to slay me: forgive not their iniquity, neither blot out their sin from thy sight. (Jer. 18:23)

> He taketh the wise in their own craftiness: and the **counsel** of the froward is carried headlong. (Job 5:13)

> Ye have shamed the **counsel** of the poor, because the LORD is his refuge. (Ps. 14:6)

> The LORD bringeth the **counsel** of the heathen to nought: he maketh the devices of the people of none effect. (33:10)

> Hide me from the secret **counsel** of the wicked; from the insurrection of the workers of iniquity. (64:2)

> And the land of Judah shall be a terror unto Egypt, every one that maketh mention thereof shall be afraid in himself, Because of the **counsel** of the LORD of hosts, which he hath determined against it. (Isa. 19:17)

> O LORD, thou art my God; I will exalt thee, I will praise thy name; for thou hast done wonderful things; thy **counsels** of old are faithfulness and truth. (25:1)

I'm going to give you some more blanks. We're in chapter 17, and by now you should be able to spot some things. What do you notice that is odd, even a little bit, about these uses of the word "counsel" or "counsels"?

____

____

____

____

____

____

____

Assuming that "counsel" means "advice" (usually good advice—but see step 3), I'll list a few things I noticed:

"Counsel" is parallel to "devices," which means "schemes," in Psalm 33:10. In what way is "advice" a synonym of "schemes"?

The "counsel" in these verses seems often to be more definite than advice. The Lord brings the "counsel" of the heathen to nothing; that's what you say about a plan, not a piece of advice—right?

Likewise, Jeremiah complains that his enemies had "counsel" against him to slay him—doesn't that sound a little odd?

The KJV uses the English word "counsel" to translate about six different Greek words and a dozen or so Hebrew ones. To do full justice to this KJV word, I would need to look at every single one, but we don't have the necessary time and space. Instead, I'll pick one Hebrew word and one Greek word, both of which are commonly translated "counsel" in the KJV.

The Hebrew word that is most commonly translated as "counsel" in the KJV can mean "advice," just as we might expect; but it can also mean "plan" or even "God's plan decision" (HALOT)—in other words, something like "God's definitive plan." The first sample passage listed for this last sense is Jeremiah 49:20, and sure enough, the KJV uses the word "counsel" to translate it. But read this carefully, in light of what you've just heard that the Hebrew means. And note, again, the parallelism:

> Therefore hear the **counsel** of the LORD, that he hath taken against Edom; and his purposes, that he hath purposed against the inhabitants of Teman. (Jer. 49:20)

"Counsel" is set in parallel with "purpose," not a word like "advice." The "counsel of the Lord" here, according to my Hebrew dictionary, means "plan" and not "advice."

It's similar but not the same with New Testament Greek. The Greek word that is most commonly translated as "counsel" in the KJV means "that which one thinks about as possibility for action," and it can be translated as "plan, purpose, [or] intention" (BDAG). There is no note of "advice" in this word.

This is the word Peter used in Acts 2:23 when he said that Jesus, "being delivered by the determinate **counsel** and foreknowledge of God, ye have taken, and by wicked hands have crucified and slain."

BDAG is saying that the Greek word here does not mean "counsel"; it means "plan." And doesn't that make sense? Jesus was given up to be crucified by the predetermined plan of God. If you're unsure about whether you can say that, read Isaiah 53. It was the will of the Father to crush the Son, to make him bear the iniquity of us all.

So, why does the KJV say "counsel" instead of "plan"? NOAD tells me that "counsel" means what we already know it means: "advice, especially that given formally."

We haven't solved this one yet.

And before we do, let me stop to make something else clear: There are many places in the KJV where "counsel" is *not* a false friend—not at all. It is used just the way we use it. The very first instance of the word in the KJV, for example, is in a passage in which Moses's father-in-law, Jethro, is giving him advice:

> Hearken now unto my voice, I will give thee **counsel**, and God shall be with thee. (Exod. 18:19)

Or consider this famous verse that says that the blessed don't take advice from the wicked:

> Blessed is the man that walketh not in the **counsel** of the ungodly, nor standeth in the way of sinners, nor sitteth in the seat of the scornful. (Ps. 1:1)

It would be easier to tell KJV readers that "counsel" is always a false friend in the KJV. But it wouldn't be true. Not without qualification. We'll talk more about this in a bit.

The mighty OED also says that "counsel" could be used in the past to mean

> resolve or intent as to a course of action; purpose, intention; (also) an instance of this; a resolution. Now rare and chiefly in religious contexts.

In other words, "counsel" used to (often) mean "plan." Is this making sense to you? And notice that last line: "Counsel" is now rare but hangs on in religious contexts, the OED says. But the final citation the OED gives is from 1970, and it's actually just a quotation from the KJV.[3] I checked hundreds of lines in the NOW Corpus for this word, and I couldn't find any use of "counsel" to mean "plan" outside of quotations from the KJV.

That isn't the way English used to be. The OED reveals that "counsel" used to be able to mean "plan" even outside religious contexts. It lists this now as an obsolete sense:

> a person's private, confidential, or secret intention, purpose, aim, etc.; a plan, a design. *Obsolete.*

Often our false friends are not a one-eighty from what modern readers are already seeing in a word in a given context. And that's

3. "It was Paul that told us that everything works after the counsel of God's will" (The OED cites "*Life Line Freedom Talk* [Dallas] 20 September 3/2"). This is clearly quoting Ephesians 1:11.

true with "counsel." There is not a massive difference between "counsel" and "plan." When people give counsel, they're often expressing a plan. And plans often derive from counsel or advice. But I want to understand whatever the KJV translators intended, because I want to understand what God intended. I invite you to go back and read the long list of verses at the beginning of this chapter. Don't they make better sense now that you understand what the KJV translators intended by the word "counsel"?

Or how about these well-known verses?

> The **counsel** of the Lord standeth for ever, the thoughts of his heart to all generations. (Ps. 33:11)

> There is no wisdom nor understanding nor **counsel** against the LORD. (Prov. 21:30)

"Counsel" in 1611 equals "plan" today. Right?

And to "declare unto you all the counsel of God" (Acts 20:27; I usually hear this as "preaching the whole counsel of God") means to explain God's *plan*. Doesn't that help? I love this false friend, because I love to understand God's Word.

Maps of Meaning

An extra tidbit for you; maybe this will help.

Languages "map" meaning differently. Spanish, for example, observes a careful distinction between two kinds of knowing and two kinds of being: *conocer* versus *saber* and *ser* versus *estar*. I've taken years of Spanish, and I don't truly understand these distinctions. When it comes to "knowing," the rule of thumb I've picked up is that you *conocer* people and *saber* things. But there are exceptions, and English doesn't make that distinction—so I'm certain that I sometimes use the wrong word. When it comes to "being," the rule of thumb is that *ser* is a permanent state and *estar* is a temporary one. But there are exceptions, and English doesn't make that distinction either—so I'm certain that I sometimes sound like a dummy to native Spanish speakers. (I find speaking Spanish to be very humbling.)

Likewise, Elizabethan English maps meaning in a way that is different—at many points—from contemporary English. Elizabethan English speakers did not draw a distinction between the concept of "advice" and the concept of "plan"; they relied on context to make that distinction. They used the same word for both concepts: "counsel."[4] But our modern map has changed; it requires different words be used for these two different concepts. In this place Elizabethan English is less precise than modern English. In fact—and this may shock you as it did me—*the word "plan" did not exist in English in 1611.* It was not available to the KJV translators. Its first recorded use in English comes from 1635. So, of course, the KJV uses the word "plan" precisely zero times.

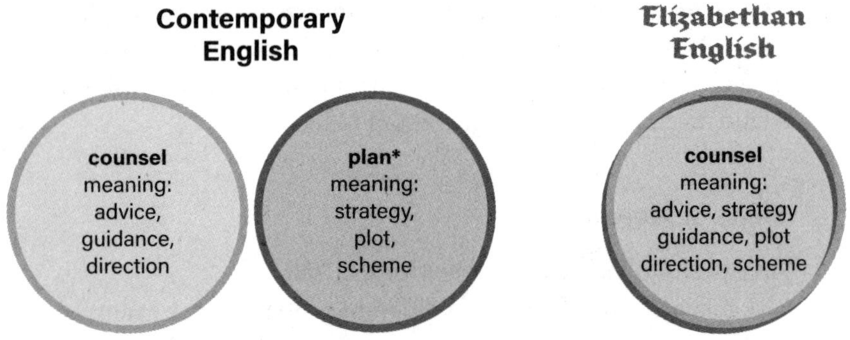

*The word "plan" did not exist in 1611.

If you didn't find that interesting, yea, even fascinating, put down this book and go watch TV. That's my counsel.

(Though not my plan.)

4. They did have other words for "plan," such as "devices": "He disappointeth the **devices** of the crafty, so that their hands cannot perform their enterprise" (Job 5:12). "Devices" were evil or mischievous or crafty plans.

18. Sodden

> Eat not of it raw, nor **sodden** at all with water, but roast with fire; his head with his legs, and with the purtenance thereof. (Exod. 12:9)

What do you think "sodden" means in this verse?

SOME PEOPLE WHO LOVE the KJV get truly exasperated with me. They just can't fathom why I go on and on about KJV archaisms when they are all so easily resolved. They tell me that it's a good thing the KJV contains archaisms; the older words make them slow down, stop, and think. They are forced to study.

One very courteous man—he was only a little exasperated—gave me an example from his Bible reading that day. He said, "This morning I ran across the word 'sodden' in Exodus 12:9. All I had to do was look it up online, and I found within seconds that it means 'saturated.'"

That was a nice way of saying, "Why is this so hard for you? Why do you have to make the KJV so complicated?"

When this brother first sent me the word "sodden," I was pretty fuzzy on whether it was a live word or a dead one. I leaned toward the latter as I looked up the verse he referenced. I wasn't sure if we say "sodden" anymore. If it was still a current word, it was on the edge of my vocabulary.

But several neurons in my brain fired at that exact moment. They came running out of their offices, screaming: *Go through your normal false friends process and see what happens!* That's what they said.

Fishing for a False Friend

Hmm, funny, other neurons in other offices in my brain said when I looked up the Hebrew word translated "sodden" in Exodus 12:9. *The Hebrew word translated "sodden" doesn't mean "saturated" at all.*

My hardworking neurons were correct. All the Hebrew-English dictionaries say the Hebrew word here means "boiled." That does make a lot more sense in Exodus 12:9. This is the passage in which the Lord is instructing the Israelites, still in Egypt, how to eat the Passover lamb. You can imagine people eating lamb raw, or roasted with fire—but who eats meat "saturated with water"?

Sodden *is* a current word that means "saturated." My mildly exasperated acquaintance's Googling was successful:

> saturated with liquid, especially water; soaked through: *his clothes were sodden.* (NOAD)

So, did the KJV translators get it wrong?

As I've said several times, this book doesn't question a single translation choice made by the KJV translators. They did excellent work. In fact, I believe the KJV got every one of the false friends in this book right. But at this point in my research, some of my neurons genuinely thought that *maybe the KJV translators have finally gotten it wrong this time.* I really thought that.

Enter the OED to save the day yet again. The OED reveals that there is a no longer used sense of "sodden" that fits the Hebrew and the context of Exodus 12:9 perfectly.

> Boiled; cooked or prepared by boiling. *Now rare or obsolete.*

I told you that you would find something interesting, said my self-satisfied neurons.

We have another false friend. "Sodden," in the six times it appears in the KJV, means "boiled," not "saturated" like it means today. Read the four verses we haven't looked at to see for yourself.

> But the earthen vessel wherein it is **sodden** shall be broken: and if it be **sodden** in a brasen pot, it shall be both scoured, and rinsed in water. (Lev. 6:28)

> And the priest shall take the **sodden** shoulder of the ram, and one unleavened cake out of the basket, and one unleavened wafer, and shall put them upon the hands of the Nazarite, after the hair of his separation is shaven. (Num. 6:19)

> Also before they burnt the fat, the priest's servant came, and said to the man that sacrificed, Give flesh to roast for the priest; for he will not have **sodden** flesh of thee, but raw. (1 Sam. 2:15)

> The hands of the pitiful women have **sodden** their own children: They were their meat in the destruction of the daughter of my people. (Lam. 4:10)

Send Your Neurons to School

This word provides a good example of why the OED figures so prominently in my KJV study methods. It simply isn't the job of contemporary dictionaries to describe the English of earlier eras. They sometimes do it anyway—but not always, not reliably. This is a place where the diligent student of the KJV *will be misled* by following the standard advice given to all KJV readers: "Look it up, dear!"

All regular KJV readers should make sure to buy or (better yet) get online access to the OED. Your neurons will thank you for the education.

19. Judgment

> He shall not fail nor be discouraged, till he have set **judgment** in the earth. (Isa. 42:4)

What do you think "judgment" means in this verse?

THERE ARE A FEW Hebrew and Greek words that lots of both Christians and non-Christians know. Some of these have become full-fledged English words—such as "amen" and "hallelujah." Some have become English words common within the Christian community—such as "agape" and "Hosanna" and even "Yahweh."

Some you don't tend to learn until you've been in church a little longer. They don't get used often enough to count as English words, but a fair number of Christians know them. In this category I'd put words like *hesed*, which the KJV tends to translate as "mercy," "kindness," or "lovingkindness." Another Hebrew word that some Christians will know is *mishpat*. Do you know it? This word occurs hundreds of times in the Hebrew Bible, and the KJV tends to translate it with the English word "judgment."

Fishing for a False Friend

The very first use of *mishpat* in the KJV is odd. Have you ever noticed this? It's part of a divine soliloquy—one of the only times in Scripture I can think of where God is speaking to himself. He is pontificating about Abraham's morality after discussing with

Abraham the fate of Sodom. The Lord says this about the first Jewish patriarch:

> I know him, that he will command his children and his household after him, and they shall keep the way of the LORD, to do justice and **judgment**. (Gen. 18:19)

The Lord is saying that Abraham will teach God's ways to his children; that much is obvious. But then he explains what those divine ways are with two words: "justice and judgment."

It makes perfect sense to think of Abraham teaching his children "to do justice." I teach it to my children literally every day, even if I don't use the word. I teach them to act justly and fairly.

Here's what I do *not* teach them: "to do . . . **judgment**." My children are all too eager to enact judgment upon one another after the slightest (or even imagined) infraction. One of my children is the rules child. This child remembers Mom's and Dad's rules even better than Mom and Dad do. This child also notices everyone else's failures to live up to Mom's and Dad's stated will. And we have noticed that this child tends to exercise judgment without mercy.

Were ancient times vastly different? Did Abraham teach his children to do judgment? Or maybe to do judgment on the nations? But God told Abraham that he wanted to bless all the families of the earth through Abraham's seed. So, why would Abraham need to teach his children to do judgment?

The very next use of the word "judgment" in the KJV does *not* sound funny to my ears, not in the least. It is deadly serious.

> For I will pass through the land of Egypt this night, and will smite all the firstborn in the land of Egypt, both man and beast; and against all the gods of Egypt I will execute **judgment**: I am the LORD. (Exod. 12:12)

If "judgment" means what I think it means, Exodus 12:12 makes sense, but Genesis 18:19 does not.

One more Old Testament passage, this time from Isaiah. Notice how "judgment" in this context just has to be something good, something parallel to "righteousness":

> How is the faithful city become an harlot! It was full of **judgment**; righteousness lodged in it; but now murderers. (Isa. 1:21)

Let's turn in our mental Bibles to the New Testament, to the amazing passage in which Jesus issues withering rebukes to the Pharisees. Here, he uses (in the KJV) the word "judgment." As in the Isaiah passage we just read, "judgment" in this context just has to be something good:

> Woe unto you, scribes and Pharisees, hypocrites! for ye pay tithe of mint and anise and cummin, and have omitted the weightier matters of the law, **judgment**, mercy, and faith: these ought ye to have done, and not to leave the other undone. (Matt. 23:23)

But "judgment" is precisely the thing the Pharisees did *not* omit. They had it in spades; they went around judging others as a sort of pastime. What could Jesus mean here? Why would he tell the Pharisees that they had omitted this good thing the law commands called "judgment"?

The Hebrew word most commonly translated "judgment" in the KJV is, again, *mishpat*. It was used in all the Old Testament passages quoted since the beginning of this chapter, and it can indeed mean "decision" or "judgment" (HALOT). It can also refer to a "dispute" or a legal "case" (HALOT). Another little word, though, that keeps popping up in the Hebrew-English dictionaries in entries for this word is "justice."

The Greek word Jesus uses for "judgment" when he says the Pharisees are missing it is similar to the Hebrew word. That is, it can mean the following:

> legal process of judgment, judging, judgment. (BDAG)

But it can also mean "justice":

> administration of what is right and fair, right in the sense of justice/righteousness. (BDAG)

The relevant Hebrew and Greek words can both mean either "judgment" or "justice." The two concepts are related, of course. It has always been true that judgments from a judge (any judge, even the rule-following child in my family) should yield justice. Those judgments should be right and fair, and they should satisfy every good conscience.

"Judgment" doesn't mean "justice" today. This is what it means:

> a misfortune or calamity viewed as a divine punishment: *the crash had been a judgment on the parents for wickedness.* (NOAD)

Does this sense of "judgment" make sense in the Old and New Testament passages we've looked at in this chapter? Could Jesus be excoriating the Pharisees for failing to issue divine punishments? Did God praise Abraham for teaching his children to send divine misfortunes? These questions themselves are almost incoherent. I hope the answer to them is obvious.

So, what saith the OED? The OED, as always, gives a definition that fits contemporary English, but it also solves our difficulties in the Bible passages we examined. The OED tells us that "judgment" could, at one time, mean this:

> the right or proper administering of justice; justice, righteousness, equity. . . . *Obsolete.*

Any place where the word "judgment" occurs in the KJV but "judging people" or "rendering divine punishments" does *not* make good sense in context, "justice" is probably what is meant. Indeed, the NKJV uses "justice" and not "judgment" in a lot of these places.

> For I have known him, in order that he may command his children and his household after him, that they keep the way of the LORD, to do righteousness and **justice**, that the LORD may bring to Abraham what He has spoken to him. (Gen. 18:19 NKJV)

> How the faithful city has become a harlot!
> It was full of **justice**;
> Righteousness lodged in it,
> But now murderers. (Isa. 1:21 NKJV)

It is utterly key we understand two things. One, the KJV translators *did not make a mistake* when they chose the word "judgment" in these passages. Two, the NKJV translators *did not disagree* with the KJV translators when they chose "justice" instead of "judgment" in these places.

No, the KJV translators chose a word that could do double duty—it could communicate the concepts of judgment or justice—but it no longer can. We've caught a false friend.

Doctrinal Error?

Now that you know what "judgment" can mean, try to forget it.

Now read this phrase:

> For I the LORD love **judgment**. (Isa. 61:8)

What does that mean?

If you've successfully forgotten what you read above, it sounds like God is saying he loves to judge people. And the context doesn't make the problem go away.

> For I the Lord love **judgment**. I hate robbery for burnt offering; and I will direct their work in truth, and I will make an everlasting covenant with them. (Isa. 61:8)

This could easily be read—and surely has been by at least some KJV readers (wouldn't you agree?)—to mean that God loves to judge people, such as the robbers he hates. Of course, what this meant in 1611 is that the Lord loves *justice*.

Is "I the Lord love judgment" a doctrinal error? I mean, if you understand it the way it sounds in contemporary English? We need to think carefully about this as we close this chapter.

On the one hand, yes: Clearly this false friend ends up giving readers the wrong picture of God. Nowhere in Scripture does he say that he loves to judge others. One could even call this a contradiction, because the book of James says that "mercy triumphs over judgment" (2:13 NKJV), and when the Lord chooses to describe himself in his closest encounter with Moses, he focuses on his grace:

> And the Lord passed by before him, and proclaimed, The Lord, The Lord God, merciful and gracious, longsuffering, and abundant in goodness and truth,
>
> Keeping mercy for thousands, forgiving iniquity and transgression and sin. (Exod. 34:6–7)

We must be careful not to set mercy and judgment against one another, of course, as if they cannot coexist in one person; for God follows this up with a description of his wrath against sinners:

> And that will by no means clear the guilty; visiting the iniquity of the fathers upon the children, and upon the children's children, unto the third and to the fourth generation. (v. 7)

Indeed, the God of the Bible both loves and has anger: "God so loved the world" (John 3:16) and "God is angry with the wicked every day" (Ps. 7:11).

But the Bible doesn't say, "God is wrath," while it does so clearly say, "God is love." There is something off, biblically speaking, with saying that God loves judging.

On the other hand, I do not honestly think that KJV readers are going to let one somewhat obscure phrase in Isaiah 61 override all that the Bible says elsewhere about God's grace, mercy, and love. I do not think my false friends cause doctrinal error so much as static, obscuring God's Word at numerous—typically minor, but occasionally less minor—points.

I teach you how to fish because I'm not happy about a situation in which a lot of KJV readers might misunderstand—might get even one pixel askew in their picture of God. This false friend, "judgment," is one that many, many more KJV readers need to know about.

20. Suffer

> Thou shalt not hate thy brother in thine heart: thou shalt in any wise rebuke thy neighbour, and not **suffer** sin upon him. (Lev. 19:17)

What do you think "suffer" means in this verse?

____

____

Writers of lengthy, complicated texts simply cannot make certain that all readers will understand those texts. Translators of such texts have an even harder job. They have to bring meaning across lines of geography and culture to an audience that the authors may not have been thinking of. Translators of *ancient* texts have an even more difficult job. They have to bring meaning across lines not only of geography and culture but also of time.

Some people will misunderstand, no matter how good a writer or translator is.

But some misunderstandings I find particularly regrettable—those that are caused by language change. Consider the story told by a female speaker at a women's conference: She had a woman come up to her after an evening session and say, "I have a question. I don't understand why God would allow children to suffer." And then this woman pointed to the famous KJV verse, "Suffer the little children to come unto me." It turns out she was the pastor's wife. So why did she come at night like Nicodemus to ask her question privately? The speaker observed, "She couldn't afford for people to know what she didn't know."[5]

Using a contemporary English translation of the Bible in church or personal study will not erase all silly misunderstandings of the Bible. These can and will happen with the NKJV and SKJV. No translator can stop all readers from arriving at misunderstandings.

But, clearly, the false friend "suffer" played a role here.

Would this reader have misunderstood Matthew 19:14 in the NKJV or SKJV? Maybe. The NKJV reads,

> **Let** the little children come to Me, and do not forbid them.

5. See "Know Your Bible," YouTube video, 1:51:54, uploaded by The Village Church—Flower Mound, July 14, 2017, https://youtu.be/Moulqq-h-d8.

The SKJV reads,

> **Allow** little children to come to Me, and do not forbid them.

I suppose people can always misunderstand. People are pretty adept at twisting God's words. But here's what they couldn't do: They couldn't be tripped up by language change, because this is all clearly our English.

Fishing for a False Friend

Now, let's talk about this comparatively easy false friend, "suffer." This false friend is *not* one that tripped me up as a KJV reader. Or not that I recall. It was, honestly, so obvious to me through context that it had to mean "permit" or "allow" that I have a hard time, even now, making my brain take this word as, apparently, some modern people do. "Suffer the little children to come unto me" makes zero sense if "suffer" means "endure pain and hardship."

Anybody who has read their whole King James Bible with attention will have observed that "suffer" just has to mean "permit."

> Her father would not **suffer** him to go in. (Judg. 15:1)

> The goodman of the house . . . would not have **suffered** his house to be broken up. (Matt. 24:43)

> God **suffered** him not to hurt me. (Gen. 31:7)

There are a few places where I could imagine a new reader of the KJV being tripped up:

> **Suffer** me that I may speak. (Job 21:3)

I could see a newbie thinking, vaguely, as some do when they read an exotic-to-them book like the Bible, that this means "Make me suffer so that I can speak."

Or . . .

> How long shall I be with you, and **suffer** you? (Luke 9:41)

I could see someone thinking that that meant "to cause you to suffer."

Or . . .

> He humbled thee, and **suffered** thee to hunger. (Deut. 8:3)

I can sort of see how KJV beginners could read that to mean he caused them to suffer through hunger. It doesn't help matters that the word "suffer" is also used in the KJV just the way we use it:

> An idle soul shall **suffer** hunger. (Prov. 19:15)

> From that time forth began Jesus to shew unto his disciples, how that he must go unto Jerusalem, and **suffer** many things of the elders and chief priests and scribes. (Matt. 16:21)

But when you read, "Suffer the little children to come unto me," hopefully, even if it's day one of reading KJV English for you, you'll realize that our modern sense of "suffer" just doesn't work. There's a contextual conflict. So, though you probably won't be doing this on your first day reading the KJV, ideally, you would go to step 1 in our process. We've already done that here, so let's move on to step 2.

The Greek word translated "suffer" in all three of the places in the Gospels where "suffer the little children" appears (Matt. 19:14; Mark 10:14; Luke 18:16) means

> to convey a sense of distancing through an allowable margin of freedom, leave it to someone to do something, let, let go, allow, tolerate. (BDAG)

NOAD does provide a sense of "suffer" that matches the Greek here.

> *Archaic* **tolerate**: he severely reprimanded him for his conduct thus far, and declared to him that he would **suffer** it no longer.

The sense is labeled as archaic, but its appearance in NOAD means that a significant number of people still understand it—even if it sounds a bit highfalutin.

I have to admit that the OED, though it certainly lists the relevant sense (and notes that a few other senses of this word that are present in the KJV are obsolete), does not mark this particular sense of "suffer" as obsolete or even archaic.

So, for the third official time in this book, we're going to have to go to the little-used step 5 in my false friends fishing process. We'll use a linguistic corpus to check up on the work of the dictionaries.[6]

Sure enough, after looking at five hundred uses of this word, I found precisely zero instances of it being used to mean "permit." And zero out of five hundred tells me something, especially when my gut as an English speaker says the same thing: We just don't use "suffer" to mean "permit" anymore, at least not in common speech and writing. That's why the dictionary sample sentences sounded so highfalutin to me.

If I were a lexicographer, I would at least mark this sense of "suffer" as archaic or literary. I might even do extra homework

6. The reason I don't use this step often is precisely because dictionaries usually get it right. I don't need to check up on their work.

to satisfy myself that it is fully obsolete. But right now, my gut tells me that well-educated people probably do know this sense of the word, and that many others will pick it up from context if they read the KJV enough.

The Question

There's something really beautiful and majestic about KJV language. I feel the pull of its grandeur. I do. I love the phrase "Suffer the little children to come unto me." And it's precisely when KJV English differs from our day-to-day English that it is likely to convey that sense of otherworldly eloquence. I went to a church recently in which the whole congregation read a written prayer of confession together, and to me it felt funny that the prayer was in contemporary English rather than King James-y English.

Alternately, when KJV English differs from our English, we're also likely to see readers stumble and misunderstand. In other words, we've got two genuinely valuable things that are in tension with the word "suffer": grandeur and understanding. As I mention in the conclusion, in this book I am leaving the weighing of those things to you.

One more quick thought: I've heard stories like the one that started this chapter my whole life—stories of people misunderstanding KJV verbiage. For a while, they're just funny. People are funny. We misread things. We have foibles—I surely do. But after a certain number of these stories, I see a pattern: A lot of them are happening because language change makes reading the KJV difficult in many places for many modern readers.

What percentage of KJV readers have to misunderstand "suffer" for it to count as a false friend? My proposed number is 15 percent, though you might want to go higher or lower. There's no International Olympic Committee for false friends. Whatever number you'd pick, I don't know if we're there or not with "suffer"; I haven't done a study using this word.

So, suffer me to continue writing this book.

(My word processor flagged "suffer me to continue" as a grammatical error, and suggested instead, "I will continue to suffer." That's true too.)

Metaphorical Extension

I ADMIT THAT I NEEDED something of a catch-all category, and "metaphorical extension" is it. I almost called it "semantic shift," which is just another way of saying, "language change"—or to return to my controlling metaphor for the book, "This fish that used to swim in that current now swims in this one." A metaphorical extension takes a literal sense and builds it into a picture of an invisible, intangible reality. For example, when someone speaks of spending time, wasting time, saving time, and budgeting time, we are so accustomed to the metaphorical idea that time equals money that we don't even think of "spending," "wasting," "saving," and "budgeting" as metaphors at all.

21. Offend

And if thy right eye **offend** thee, pluck it out, and cast it from thee: for it is profitable for thee that one of thy members should

> perish, and not that thy whole body should be cast into hell. (Matt. 5:29)

What do you think "offend" means in this verse?

I'VE SPENT THIRTY YEARS considering the teaching of Jesus's Sermon on the Mount, initially (from age ten or so) because Matthew 5–7 seemed to be the longest stretch of unbroken red letters in my Bible, and I thought that was cool. The message of Jesus's famous sermon came to be very important to my young life, because I wanted my house to be built on the rock.

There were things I didn't understand in the Sermon on the Mount as a child and teenager, but I worked at it—slowly, intermittently, but steadily. There were also things I understood all too well—because they revealed my sins of anger, lust, and hypocrisy.

Fishing for a False Friend

Then there were things I thought I understood but didn't. Like the word "offend."

In his famous sermon, Jesus uses the word "offend" twice in the KJV. One of these is the verse at the top of this chapter:

> And if thy right eye **offend** thee, pluck it out, and cast it from thee: for it is profitable for thee that one of thy members should perish, and not that thy whole body should be cast into hell. (Matt. 5:29)

When has your right eye ever offended you? When have you ever said, "I cannot *believe* my stupid eye just said that about me—its owner! How could it do that?"

Or should we understand this as: "Seeing that advertisement on TV was offensive to me"? In that case, the eye isn't causing the offense, just recording it. That's how I think I took it as a young reader. The first meaning was clearly bizarre, even though I had to do some mental contortions to get to the second.

What is Jesus saying here really? It would be nice to know, because it's clearly serious. Whatever it means for an eye to offend, the result, Jesus says, is that I should pluck that eye out.

Or take this use of the word "offend" from later in Matthew:

> But whoso shall **offend** one of these little ones which believe in me, it were better for him that a millstone were hanged about his neck, and that he were drowned in the depth of the sea. (18:6)

Do little ones even get offended? In my experience, they get hurt or angry at being teased, but I can't really think of times when my kids have been "offended"—that feels like a word used to describe adults or at least teens. I could be wrong about this.

Here's another one—this is Jesus speaking to his disciples at the Last Supper:

> All ye shall be **offended** because of me this night. (26:31)

Doesn't that seem a little weird? The disciples were scared, and they fled Jesus in cowardly betrayal—but at what point were they "offended" because of Jesus? At what point did they say, "I can't believe he just said that about us"?

And here's one that causes some problems. Paul writes in Romans,

> It is good neither to eat flesh, nor to drink wine, nor any thing whereby thy brother stumbleth, or is **offended**, or is made weak. (14:21)

If the Bible tells me I have to avoid doing anything that offends fellow Christians, I will obey. But I usually don't know when others are offended by my actions, and this is a pretty constricting command. Am I to live at the mercy of others' proneness to take offense? I'm not mocking Scripture here; I'm wanting to understand it. Don't you? Is this really what Paul means?

KJV English also uses prepositions in an odd way with the word "offend," and I am at times left scratching my head. Aren't you? At the very least, this is not the way we would say it—or possibly, I am missing some meaning here that the KJV translators intended.

> Jeremiah said unto king Zedekiah, What have I **offended** against thee, or against thy servants, or against this people, that ye have put me in prison? (Jer. 37:18)

We wouldn't say, "What have I offended against thee," in a situation like that; we'd say, "How have I offended you?"—right?

Or take this one, speaking of the way people from Jesus's hometown of Nazareth reacted to him:

> And they were **offended** in him. (Matt. 13:57)

Have you ever heard anyone say they were offended *in* someone else?

Last one:

> Hezekiah king of Judah sent to the king of Assyria to Lachish, saying, I have **offended**; return from me: that which thou puttest on me will I bear. (2 Kings 18:14)

Doesn't that strike your ear in a funny way? We would say, "I have offended *you*," not "I have offended," full stop.

I've been thinking a lot about something a local pastor told me once. I put it in *Authorized*. He said to me,

> I would say [you and I] have approached this subject from different angles. Where we both have come across difficulties of understanding, I have seen it as part of my Bible study . . . and have not considered it as a translation issue.[1]

I said in my book that I admired that spirit. When we come across something difficult in the Bible, this ought to provoke study.

But this pastor's perspective inadvertently omitted something very important: the effects of language change. If the difficulty of some Bible statement is due to what God said, then I need to suffer and pray and work through that difficulty. But if the difficulty comes from the way English has changed over time, then I need to put on a different set of lenses. The difficulty, in this case, is not with "the Bible" but with the effects of language change on one beloved translation of the Bible.

Something is going on with this word "offend." Sometimes in the KJV it doesn't mean what I'll bet most readers assume it means. It is a false friend.

There are around a dozen different Hebrew and Greek words that are translated as "offend" in the KJV. Let's go back to where we began, with Matthew 5:29. The Greek word translated "offend" here had two major senses in Jesus's day. One of them you will recognize, the other you won't.

First, the one you will recognize: "to shock through word or action, give offense to, anger, shock" (BDAG). As we'll see in the next step, and as you already must know, this is what "offend" means in English today. So, there are definitely places in the KJV

1. Private email; name withheld.

where "offend" is *not* a false friend. Here's a place where modern readers will not be misled:

> Then came his disciples, and said unto him, Knowest thou that the Pharisees were **offended**, after they heard this saying? (Matt. 15:12)

This sense doesn't fit in Matthew 5:29, however. How can eyes "offend" people? How can they shock through word or action? They can't—unless Jesus is being exceptionally obscure.

But there's another sense of the relevant Greek word, and it's this:

> to cause to be brought to a downfall, cause to sin (the sin may consist in a breach of the moral law, in unbelief, or in the acceptance of false teachings). (BDAG)

This sense gets used numerous times in the New Testament. "Whoever **causes** one of these little ones who believe in Me **to sin**" (Matt. 18:6 NKJV) is one of them. "If food **makes** my brother **stumble**, I will never again eat meat" (1 Cor. 8:13 NKJV)—that's another. Jesus's statement to the disciples in the garden uses this sense too: "All of you will be **made to stumble** because of Me this night" (Matt. 26:31 NKJV). Doesn't that make better sense to today's reader than "All ye shall **be offended**" (v. 31)?

And that "caused to stumble" sense fits perfectly in Matthew 5:29—"If your right eye **causes** you **to sin**, pluck it out." That is, of course, how every other major English translation takes the phrase.

So, did the KJV translators get it wrong? Why did they say, "If thine eye *offend* thee"?

Because, of course, "offend" in contemporary English doesn't mean "to cause to sin." It means to "cause to feel upset, annoyed, or resentful" (NOAD). My dictionary gives this example sentence: "Viewers said they had been **offended** by bad language" (NOAD). People always tell me they don't get offended easily, and of course, it is a matter of Christian charity at times to not let yourself be offended. On the other hand, it can be good to find things offensive. I'll never forget watching a corny Christian movie and nonetheless really being affected by a particular scene. A time-traveling theology professor from the Victorian period goes to see a modern movie with a church group. Suddenly, he bursts out of the theater doors into the lobby, shouting that someone has just taken the Lord's name in vain! He was offended, deeply offended, to hear this. Does it say something good about us that we are not so offended? I want at times to be offended—to be deeply offended by evil.

But this just can't be what the word "offend" meant in the KJV, in 1611, in Matthew 5:29. I cannot make any sense, not really, out of "If thine eye offend thee"—not if "offend" meant in 1611 what it means today. Eyes can't offend. Unless I am to conclude that the KJV translators made a mistake (and I almost never like to conclude that), there's got to be another explanation.

Wouldn't you know it . . . there are in the OED both transitive and intransitive senses of this word "offend" that fit the Hebrew and Greek perfectly at some of the puzzling places we've just looked at. The senses are very similar:

> to be a stumbling block, or cause spiritual or moral difficulty, to (a person); to shock morally or spiritually; to cause to sin. *Obsolete.*

Both of these senses are obsolete. We have caught a false friend. The KJV translators did not make a mistake. English has simply changed over time. This sense doesn't exist anymore in contemporary English.

Stumbling over "Offend"

Now, let's get clear what I'm *not* saying; I'm *not* saying that every time "offend" occurs in the KJV it means "to cause to sin." Think of "If any man **offend** not in word, the same is a perfect man" (James 3:2). "Offend" there is translating a totally different Greek word than the one we've been discussing, a word meaning "stumble" or "trip." The syntax is a little confusing there for modern readers; it means, "If anybody doesn't trip up in what they say, that person is perfect." There's an OED sense for that usage too:

> to make a false step or stumble morally; to commit a sin, to fail in duty; to do wrong, transgress, infringe a rule.

You simply have to know that "offend" can at times mean "stumble" or "cause to stumble," or you will either puzzle over or actively misunderstand a number of key KJV verses. "If meat maketh my brother to **offend**" (1 Cor. 8:13) now makes a lot more sense than if you think "offending" has to do with saying mean things.

I don't think *all* KJV readers out there are misunderstanding "offend" in Matthew 5:29. My educated guess is that a lot of contemporary English speakers are regularly misunderstanding "offend" in various passages in the KJV because of language change.

Sometimes my YouTube commenters don't believe that I'm telling the truth when I say that I misunderstood a given KJV word. One way to demonstrate that I really did misunderstand Matthew 5:29 as many others do, and I'm not making it up, is to point to online sermons. Obligingly, a viewer of my channel sent me a YouTube video of a preacher who preached a whole sermon about how people shouldn't offend each other in relationships. He quoted Jesus's statement that "it must needs be that offenses come" (Matt. 18:7), and he explained that as meaning "offenses are unavoidable." In other words, we will always offend other people.[2]

He brought up this verse as a sort of proof text, a jumping off point for his theme:

> Yet hath he not root in himself, but dureth for a while: for when tribulation or persecution ariseth because of the word, by and by he is **offended**. (Matt. 13:21)

It seems to me that he was offended by a false friend.

22. Overcharge

> But if any have caused grief, he hath not grieved me, but in part: that I may not **overcharge** you all. (2 Cor. 2:5)

What do you think "overcharge" means in this verse?

____

____

Not all false friends are false friends to all KJV readers, but I hope you've seen by now that I'm not just making stuff up; I'm appealing to more than just my own experience with the KJV. I'm appealing to the dictionary, the only reliable access we have to others' experience.

Does that make sense? Yes, you can poll people to discover how they are understanding (or misunderstanding) a given false

2. I will not provide the link to this sermon because I don't want others to be tempted to mock a preacher who committed the very same error I did for much of my life. I feel certain that a YouTube search will easily find him or someone else who made the same flub.

friend; but I've done it, and it's incredibly time-consuming and difficult. But, in essence, a good dictionary has already "polled" people—by listening carefully to the way they use given words.

Perhaps "overcharge" in 2 Corinthians 2:5 is a word you've always understood just fine in the sense intended by the KJV translators. But, as we'll see yet again, the dictionary suggests that you might not have.

In 2 Corinthians 2, Paul may be talking about the same person he was talking about in 1 Corinthians 5, namely the guy who had married his stepmother. If that common supposition is correct, Paul told the church to cast this guy out, delivering him to Satan for the destruction of his flesh. But by the time he sends 2 Corinthians, he thinks the punishment has been enough:

> Sufficient to such a man is this punishment, which was inflicted of many. So that contrariwise ye ought rather to forgive him, and comfort him, lest perhaps such a one should be swallowed up with overmuch sorrow. (2 Cor. 2:6–7)

Fishing for a False Friend

"Overcharge" is not a dead word, of course. We still have this word, but quite clearly, we don't use it the way the KJV translators did here. We've got a contextual conflict. And it's an obvious one. It's such an obvious one that I think many KJV readers, especially experienced ones, will just sort of pick up from context the gist of what Paul means.

But I'm not sure I did, as a KJV reader in my teen years, and I think I was a pretty good reader at the time. I don't have a specific recollection about how I understood the relevant phrase, "that I may not overcharge you all." I think I just drew a blank.

BDAG says that this word translated "overcharge" means "to be a burden to, weigh down, burden," and it makes a comment specific to this passage:

> Second Corinthians 2:5 seems to have the mng. "in order not to heap up too great a burden of words" = in order not to say too much (Heinrici, Schmiedel, Ltzm., H-DWendland), although there are no ex[amples] of it in this m[eaning]. Other possibilities are *exaggerate, be too severe with.* (BDAG)

BDAG is a little unsure of Paul's precise nuance here. But the Greek word clearly did not mean to Paul what "overcharge" means to us.

NOAD gives two senses for this word:

> 1 charge (someone) too high a price for goods or a service: that makes it easy for wheeler-dealers to **overcharge** customers.

> 2 put too much electric charge into (a battery): large generators can **overcharge** batteries.

Neither sense fits the Greek word in 2 Corinthians 2:5. Paul isn't talking about money, and I'm pretty sure he wasn't predicting the invention of electric cars. We need to turn to the OED. I think the KJV translators had to mean something from within the first sense in the OED, and I think it has to be sense 1a:

> to load, fill, or supply to excess (with something); to overload, overburden; to overstock, overfill.

There's that word "overburden." That's a perfect match with our Greek word.

This sense is very like that second one in NOAD—as long as there's no battery or electrical idea required. The OED does not name this sense as obsolete, as I admit I expected.

I publicly admit that by my method, the OED does *not* prove that this word is a false friend. Some people out there, according to the dictionary, will read this verse and understand "overcharge" to mean "overburden."

But I've got a problem, and I wonder if you have it too. I simply did not know this sense of the word, and even now that I know it, I have a hard time making my brain process "overcharge" in this context to mean "overburden." Maybe I'm just not well-educated enough. Maybe the brain cell in charge of "overcharge" was damaged during one of the seasons I played tackle football. Who knows why I have a hard time reading the word this way?

However, I think most of us are in the same boat. I think the next edition of the OED will mark this sense of the word as obsolete because this sense has died. I think only the financial overcharging and the electrical overcharging remain in our English at this precise moment.[3]

Let's turn back to a part of step 1 I didn't use, because I've got work to do today, and you're not paying me enough to go to all the trouble of checking hundreds of lines in a linguistic corpus. Instead, I'm going to check the contemporary English translations we're using in this book.

A reminder: There's no textual variant here; they're all dealing with the same Greek word, and yet the NKJV goes with "not to be too severe" and the SKJV goes with "not [to] overburden you all."

The NKJV does not use the word "overcharge" even once. Why not? Because most people hear "charge too much money" or "left plugged into the wall too long" in that word. The relevant sense is too rare, approaching obsolete.

3. Indeed, these are the two (and only two) senses in NOAD, and this is one of many examples that have led me to view NOAD as the best dictionary of contemporary American English. It describes the way we actually use words—without holding on too long (as I think MW does) to older senses no one uses anymore.

One Other Use

There is just one other use of "overcharge" in the KJV. It's in the Gospels:

> Take heed to yourselves, lest at any time your hearts be **overcharged** with surfeiting, and drunkenness, and cares of this life, and so that day come upon you unawares. (Luke 21:34)

"Overcharged with surfeiting" is difficult on two levels—the main two levels of difficulty that I discuss all the time: dead words and false friends. We still have the word "surfeit," as in "There was a **surfeit** of choices in the spatula section." But I have only ever heard it as a noun, never a verb.[4] I think "surfeiting," as a verbal idea, is a dead word. And I think "overcharged" is a false friend. Add the two together, and we have a difficult tangle.

When we use our fishing tools, however, this is what we get:

> Take heed to yourselves, lest your hearts be **weighed down with carousing**, drunkenness, and cares of this life, and that Day come on you unexpectedly.

That just happens to be the NKJV. "Carousing" isn't necessarily an easy word, but in my judgment, it is still used more often than "surfeiting." Merely being able to distinguish dead words and false friends will help us understand this statement of Jesus.

Differences of Opinion Among Friends

There is room for good Christians to disagree about specific questions of KJV readability. You could use the fishing methods

4. Though, admittedly, my favorite contemporary dictionary, NOAD, thinks a verbal sense still exists in American English.

I'm teaching and still come to a different conclusion about "overcharge" than I did in this chapter. The dictionaries leave space for disagreement.

But I wonder: What did you write down when I asked you what "overcharge" in that context meant to you? I wonder how many readers wrote down "overburden"? I'm betting very few did—*and I don't blame you.* In fact, I'm one of you.

23. Evil

> I [the LORD] form the light, and create darkness: I make peace, and create **evil**: I the LORD do all these things. (Isa. 45:7)

What do you think "evil" means in this verse?

____

____

THE WORD "EVIL" shows up 624 times in 579 verses in the King James Version.

If you're committed to believing every word of the Bible, as I am, some of the uses of "evil" are problematic if not understood correctly.

Like the verse you carefully read above (after which point you diligently recorded in writing your understanding of the bolded word contained therein):

> I [the LORD] form the light, and create darkness: I make peace, and create **evil**: I the LORD do all these things. (Isa. 45:7)

Or this verse:

> Shall a trumpet be blown in the city, and the people not be afraid? Shall there be **evil** in a city, and the LORD hath not done it? (Amos 3:6)

When modern American Christian readers (such as myself) encounter oddities like this, we often just kind of sidle past them. We figure we must be missing something. And we are. But it's not something theological, necessarily. It's something linguistic. It's language change.

Fishing for a False Friend

I'll limit myself to just the two verses I've already quoted, the ones that say the Lord "creates" evil and "does" evil. Those will be tough enough.

The Hebrew word for the "evil" that God "creates" in Isaiah 45:7 can mean not just "evil" but also the softer "harm" (HALOT). For example, the psalmist says of the Lord in Psalm 54:5, "He shall reward evil unto mine enemies." In context, "evil" here almost certainly doesn't mean "wickedness"—as it often does elsewhere. It means "misfortune" or "harm."

The Hebrew word for the "evil" that God "does" in Amos 3:6 is almost the same word as the one we just looked at (this is tough to explain). It can mean not just "evil" but also "misfortune" or "disaster." For example, Jeremiah observes to the Lord that it is because of Israel's sin that much "evil" has been brought on them by the Lord (32:23).

Does contemporary English have a sense of "evil" that is softer than "moral wickedness"? It surely has the latter sense; NOAD defines "evil" as "profound immorality and wickedness, especially when regarded as a supernatural force." It gives this sample sentence: "The world is stalked by relentless evil."

NOAD does have a softer sense for the noun "evil," a sense that fits our two passages:

> something which is harmful or undesirable: the various social **evils** of our modern world.

The OED, of course, gives the same sense—but it complicates matters. Look at sense 2.6:

> a calamity, disaster, misfortune. *Obsolete.*

The OED names the same sense we saw in all three contemporary dictionaries, but it marks that sense as obsolete.

Welcome to the real world, a world in which language is not math, in which there are gray areas and edge cases—and entirely different countries that use the language differently. By my own methods, it seems that many KJV readers today ought to be able to understand what the KJV translators meant by having the Lord say, "I . . . create evil."

But I didn't. I didn't understand. And at least one OED lexicographer said I shouldn't have to. They, too, felt that this sense was no longer present in our English.

Check Other Translations

Without a formal study testing the way regular readers understand this passage in various translations, you will occasionally hook a false friend that is still breathing while you try to weigh it with your handy fish scale. When it takes in a breath, it will weigh enough that you can keep it; but when it exhales, it goes below the required weight—and maybe you will have to throw it back.

I give this example to help make certain you understand what the KJV translators (and more importantly, the Spirit of

God himself) intended in two potentially confusing passages. I also give this example to teach you another principle I use: If a word used by the KJV technically works, but there are some reasons to believe it might cause confusion because of language change, check the translations. If none of them choose precisely the same word the KJV translators did, it's probably no longer the best word to choose in your sermon or lesson. The NKJV uses "calamity" in Isaiah 45:7, for example, while the SKJV uses "disaster"—not "evil."

My slowly distending English gut tells me that some people will misunderstand these verses in the KJV because of language change. I could be wrong. But if I'm right, *we have verses that some readers will see as blaming God for evil.* When the theological stakes are this high, I'd rather err on the side of calling this a false friend.

24. Curiously

> My substance was not hid from thee, when I was made in secret, and **curiously** wrought in the lowest parts of the earth. (Ps. 139:15)

What do you think "curiously" means in this verse?

____

____

ONE OF MY FAVORITE psalms throughout my whole Christian life has been Psalm 139. I grew up reading it and—simply by numerous rereadings—memorizing it in the King James Version.

> O LORD, thou hast searched me, and known me. (139:1)

I found this both comforting and fearful, in a good way: God knows me, good and bad. But the emphasis of the psalm is surely comfort: God's presence is meant to calm our fears, to bid our sorrows cease. That's why I love this psalm, and why I think I especially loved it during my adolescence when I was trying to figure out my place in the world.

There are also several key words in the psalm that either puzzled me or (as I now know) misled me because language has changed in the last four-hundred-plus years. There are, I would say, four words in Psalm 139 that because of language change don't mean to us what they meant to the Elizabethans. Only one is unmistakably a false friend: It's the word "curiously."

Fishing for a False Friend

I believe I had a little trouble with this word "curiously" as a kid. It seemed to mean "secretly," maybe. Or was I just getting that from the previous phrase? Or perhaps it meant that God was watching the creation of David with deep interest, wishing to learn about his own creation of humankind. In other words, he was "curious" about the formation of the infant David's body. "Curiously" can also mean "strangely" or "unusually." Like "That sentence was curiously worded," or "Curiously, I find pickleball riveting." God, in other words, has his own odd ways of doing things. For example, it was unusual for David to have been made underground. Maybe that's how I took this phrase.

In this book I have tried to train you, fisher, to notice when a KJV word sounds . . . curious. I've tried to urge you, in fact, to *be* curious about the meaning of such words, to follow up on your curiosity and study them with the best tools available. The mere fact that I could sort of make multiple different meanings of "curiously" work in Psalm 139:15 by itself suggests that we ought to consider the possibility that language change is involved.

The Hebrew word translated "curiously" in the KJV at Psalm 139:15 brings a little bit of uncertainty. HALOT says that it means "formed," but it is itself a form of a word that more typically means "woven" or "embroidered." I checked many commentators, and they mostly did what I just did: They suggested that there might be a metaphor here in which David compares God's formation of his body in the womb to the intricate weaving of a tapestry.

"Curiously" clearly can't mean either "formed" or "embroidered." The word has two main meanings in our English:

> in a way that shows eagerness to know or learn something. . . .

> In a strange and unusual way. (NOAD)

I've already shown that these don't make the best sense in Psalm 139:15. They also don't happen to make sense in the other KJV phrase that uses the word "curious" most frequently: "the curious girdle of the ephod," a description of a portion of the special garments worn by priests. Those garments aren't "eager to know or learn something"; neither are they "strange and unusual."

Let's turn, then, to the OED. It includes a sense that fits Psalm 139 and also the phrase, "the curious girdle of the ephod."[5]

> With careful art, skillfully, elaborately, exquisitely, cunningly.

The OED editors mark this as "archaic." The AHD and MW have this sense too (and mark it as archaic), but NOAD doesn't

5. I'm quoting the OED entry for "curiously," but the one for "curious" is essentially identical for the relevant sense.

even contain it. In my judgment, this means most KJV readers today will misunderstand what David meant when he said that he was "curiously wrought in the lowest parts of the earth." It meant he was "skillfully" or "elaborately" or "exquisitely" or "cunningly" made. This was the KJV translators' brilliant way of capturing the meaning of the Hebrew word, which seemed to mean "embroidered."

This false friend will not cause false doctrine. It will just cause static.

When Bezalel was called by the Lord "to devise curious works," he wasn't making strange works. When God instructed the Israelites to make a "curious girdle of the ephod," he didn't intend for them to make a weird or unusual girdle of the ephod.

Stay Curious

Let's remember something: When the NKJV and SKJV use the words "intricately" and "skillfully" instead of the KJV's "curiously" in Psalm 139:15, *they are communicating the same idea as the KJV*. They have to use a different word to do it, however, because "curiously" doesn't have the same set of senses today.

I did *not* fail to get the point of Psalm 139 as a teenager because of this false friend in the KJV (or because of any of the other archaisms in the KJV translation of the psalm). Psalm 139 had a lasting impact on my life despite my misunderstanding of "curiously wrought." But I did miss something that would have been helpful to me.

25. Passenger

> A foolish woman is clamorous: she is simple, and knoweth nothing.
> For she sitteth at the door of her house, on a seat in the high places of the city,
> To call **passengers** who go right on their ways. (Prov. 9:13–15)

What do you think "passengers" means in this verse?

WHAT IF YOU LOOK UP a Bible word and the dictionaries disagree?

I'm not talking about Hebrew or Greek; I'm talking about good old, down-home English. The language in which my fathers lied, the language in which the pilgrims cried, the language I learned at Mountainside . . . Christian Academy in Schroon Lake, New York, between 1988 and 1993.

I'll give an example that a YouTube viewer sent me: the word "passenger."

I used to be a passenger twice a day on the bus from my home to my work forty-five minutes away. I loved the bus. I wrote a whole book on that bus one year, as I've mentioned.[6] I'm still a passenger every other week or so when I carpool with my buddy Jim to our weekly ultimate frisbee game. We've done this for years. Jim and I always have a nice time talking theology or business or ultimate when I'm a passenger in his Silverado, or when he is a passenger in my Yukon.

6. Mark Ward, *Bible 6: Basics for a Biblical Worldview* (BJU Press, 2021).

Back to the KJV: A viewer sent me the passage above, which is from the famous chapter in Proverbs that contrasts Lady Wisdom and Dame Folly.

You know what a passenger is. It's someone who rides in a vehicle but isn't driving it. The foolish, adulterous woman is calling out to men who are riding on donkey carts they've hired—ancient taxis. Right?

Fishing for a False Friend

That's maybe a little funny, though, because why would she be calling to the passengers and not the drivers? I guess the passengers could be of higher status because they have money to hire drivers? I think most people would never notice that this is even possibly odd. I didn't, and I read this chapter many times in the KJV as a young man. Most people, I think, would just assume that ancient people talked a little funny, and they would go on with their enviable, non-nerdy lives.

But not us—oh no, not us! We few, we nerdy few, we shall go once more into the breach, my friends! And normally, at this point in my investigation of some apparent oddity in KJV English, I'd look up which Hebrew word "passenger" is translating in a responsible original-language lexicon. But I have something interesting to show you in English dictionaries first, like I promised. If you follow me, you will gain elite dictionary skills.

That's right, we're skipping step 2 for now. Don't be alarmed. We'll still get our fish.

I promised in the first chapter that I'd explain both here and in appendix 1828 why I use NOAD for step 3 in this book, even though I don't use NOAD alone in my own study. Here are the four top English dictionaries I use all the time—and I do mean all the time:

Merriam-Webster Unabridged (MW)
American Heritage (AHD)
New Oxford American (NOAD; the one that's on every Mac)
Oxford English (OED)

What is the job of these dictionaries? It's to describe. Dictionaries describe a language as it is then spoken by a certain set of speakers. Why? So that those who want to understand that language can do so. They also do it so that those who want to write or speak in that language can be sure to be both understood and—this is important—respected, not snickered at. People who use dictionaries don't want to use words in a way considered erroneous by the standard-bearers of that language: the elites, journalists, writers, teachers, and employers out there.

That's why the word "American" appears in the title of two of these dictionaries and why it kind of implicitly appears in the title of a third with the word "Webster," which is the last name of Noah Webster, America's greatest lexicographer.[7] Three of these dictionaries, then, tell you in their names that they are describing *American* English. They might note certain British usages—such as the way MW notes that "bloody," in British English, is "informal" and "sometimes offensive." But they have to specify "British" for that sense of "bloody." They don't need to mention "American" next to all the other senses or any of the senses in the entire dictionary—any more than my local grocery store, which has a sign for the "international food" aisle, needs to have "American food" in big letters above all the other aisles. No, American is the default in my grocery store as it is in MW. Same with AHD. Same with NOAD.

7. Merriam is the last name of the brothers who bought the rights to Webster's *An American Dictionary* after Webster died—that's why the logo on the website says "since 1828," even though the Merriams didn't come along until fifteen years later. They subsequently revised Webster's work, and now we have Merriam-Webster.

So, English dictionaries typically describe the language of a particular place, like the United States of America as opposed to Great Britain or Kenya or Australia or Singapore, all of which speak English. They also often describe the language of a particular time, usually *now*.

That's where the fourth dictionary on the list, the OED, most significantly differs from the others, as you know by now. It does presume British English as the standard, I'd say, but its true distinguishing mark is that it describes English over all of time (of course, before British colonialism, English was spoken in only one place, an Oregon-sized island off the coast of France).

Most users of dictionaries want to know what a word means *now*, today, among speakers and writers of current English in a particular locale. So, though contemporary dictionaries like MW, AHD, and NOAD all include some archaic senses (and label them as such), it's their job to notice when a certain word or sense hasn't been used in so long that it really probably ought to be left out of the dictionary.

Now, back to "passenger." If you do bother to look up this word-you-already-know[8] in all four of these dictionaries, you will see they disagree about "passenger," and they do it in a way that will help you get a good snapshot of their overall tendencies. I have seen these tendencies repeatedly with other words. If you are nerdy and motivated enough to follow me here, you'll get something valuable, I promise. You'll gain some power over The Dictionary.

Merriam-Webster Dictionary

Let's start with MW. This dictionary lists as its very first sense something that surprised me: "one who passes by: traveler, wayfarer." On the one hand, this makes perfect sense in the Proverbs

8. And who does that? Well, me, I guess.

passage we started with. This would mean that Dame Folly is not crying out to men who are riding in the passenger seat on carts someone else is driving; no, she is calling out to travelers, to wayfarers. This works much better in context than "rider in a vehicle one is not driving." But on the other hand, I have never in my entire life heard anyone use the word "passenger" to mean "traveler" or "wayfarer."

Now, passengers are typically travelers, even if they're just traveling to Walmart with their mom. But I've only ever heard and used the word "passenger" to speak of people who are, again, riding in a vehicle they aren't driving. Just yesterday, I told someone in my family to open the "passenger" door on my truck. I didn't mean the wayfarer door.

Why is this "wayfarer" sense listed first? Doesn't listing a sense first usually mean that the lexicographers who wrote this entry regard this to be the most common sense of the word? Even though I ponied up for an annual subscription to MW online, I had to email them to ask for the front matter (*the things I do for you*). And this is what I found:

> The order of senses is historical: the one known to have been first used in English is entered first.[9]

If you read Proverbs 9:15 in the KJV, and if you think to look up "passenger," and if you happen to choose MW, you'll see the right sense.

But only because, as I'll argue, MW has held on to this sense for too long. At least they listed it first, but that will only help you if you know what being listed first means. I'm confused, honestly, as to why they didn't mark the sense as "archaic."

9. An employee at Merriam-Webster sent me a one-page PDF containing this wording. I have nothing to cite. But I found that this precise language goes back to the 1963 edition of the dictionary.

American Heritage Dictionary

This means I'm relieved when I turn to the AHD and see that, though they also include this sense I've never heard, they explain why I've never heard it by labeling it "archaic." I find myself wondering, however, if even this was necessary. This is a judgment call; I've read a lot of things in my forty-plus trips around the sun—well, starting after about the fifth trip. And I've been listening to people flap their English gums for all that time too. If I've never encountered this sense of the word, maybe it's dead enough to just drop it out of the dictionary. Save the space; save the ink; save a tree; save the small bugs living in the tree who don't speak English anyway and couldn't care less about KJV archaisms.

New Oxford American Dictionary

This indeed is the judgment that was made by the happy, peppy people behind the NOAD. They don't even mention the "traveler" or "wayfarer" sense.

Oxford English Dictionary

It's the OED's job to mention old senses, and they surely do, giving "a person who passes by or through a place; a traveller, esp. a traveller on foot." And they expertly cover both place and time here by adding that this sense was "chiefly Scottish in later use" but is now obsolete.

In the judgment of three out of the four major dictionaries I check all the time—two of which are paid services and another being the most eminent and respected English dictionary in the entire galaxy—the sense of "passenger" used by the KJV translators here is somewhere between archaic and not worth mentioning.

Assessment

The point of this detailed exercise is about to arrive. I'm going to offer what I hope will be useful generalizations about these four major English dictionaries. Because with "passenger," each of these dictionaries has done what I have seen each of them do many, many times.

MW held on to this sense far too long and ranked it far too high. I am certain that I have seen them do this before—several times making a sense that is totally ignored by NOAD their top sense. When my major dictionaries differ, this is characteristic of *Merriam-Webster*.

AHD held on to this sense too long, too, but they have always been more sensitive in their very structure to current usage because they use a "usage panel," a group of specialists they call on to vote on certain disputed uses or senses. John McWhorter told me that the AHD has closed up shop and that his usage panel duties have been shuttered. I was super bummed, because I'd hoped that he could get a redheaded specialist in biblical and theological jargon onto the panel. Alas, my dreams were crushed. The AHD's last edition came out in 2011. Who knows if there will ever be another. The AHD, anyhow, was conservative and kept this sense but did mark it as archaic. When my major dictionaries differ, this is characteristic of *American Heritage*.

NOAD is lean and lithe, like a graceful lexicographer-ballerina. It's a little known not-fact that many ballerinas retire on their thirtieth birthdays and go into lexicography or library science. That's why both lexicographers and librarians characteristically wear their hair in buns, which is also a not-fact for you to not know. Anyway, NOAD did its job: It described English as it now is, no more and no less. When my major dictionaries differ, this is characteristic of NOAD.

Of course, the OED did its job too. There are times when the OED is behind the times because it is such a massive work that some of its entries haven't been updated for many decades, even a century. I'm not kidding. Their website, which I use practically every day, tells you on any given entry when that entry was last updated.

But with "passenger," the OED nailed it. When my major dictionaries differ, this is characteristic of the OED. I trust it. These lexicographers do not just good work but great work, the best work. I smiled writing these lines, because I am so blessed to live in a culture that can produce and sustain a project like the OED. There is no OED for countless languages of the world; the cultures that speak those languages don't have the necessary strength of institutional might or economic base. English speakers have been given so many great gifts. So many.

Of course, the KJV is one of those gifts. And turning back to it—and back to my regular process for such words—let's look up in a responsible original-language lexicon the Hebrew word that was translated "passengers" in Proverbs 9. It just means "those who pass by." That is what the NKJV says. That's also what the Geneva Bible had before the KJV. And *that's what the KJV translators meant.*

We've caught a false friend. It's (admittedly incredibly) minor, but it's definite. Today's readers are unlikely to realize they're misunderstanding, because of four centuries of language change, the choice of the KJV translators. The value of this particular false friend lies not mainly in its intrinsic importance but in the opportunity it affords us to notice the tendencies of major dictionaries.

"The Dictionary"

I've been told my whole life by fellow Bible readers, "Don't be lazy in your Bible study. If you come across a word you don't know, just pull out The Dictionary"—capital T, capital D. But I would never have thought to look up the word "passenger." I thought I already knew it. The way I use the word worked well enough in context in Proverbs 9—and in the one other passage in which it occurs, in Ezekiel 39—that I would never have thought to look this up if a perceptive reader trained in my methods hadn't brought it to my attention. And if you do look up this word, you will discover that there is no "The Dictionary." There are multiple dictionaries, all made by humans with differing purposes and methods, and sometimes with differing ideas about how to most usefully and accurately describe this awesome gift we call English.

26. Constantly

> These things I will that thou affirm **constantly**. (Titus 3:8)

What do you think "constantly" means in this verse?

____

____

CAN KIDS UNDERSTAND the KJV? I did.

Or I thought I did.

Now I know that I did—and I didn't. I understood most of what I read—and I want everyone to hear me say that again: *I believe I understood the great majority of what I read in the KJV when I was a kid between the ages of nine and eighteen.* I read mostly familiar passages, of course: Genesis, Exodus, the Gospels, Paul's letters, James, Psalms, Proverbs. I generally understood the KJV.

But some of it I did not understand. I read and even memorized many words in the KJV, and many sentences, that I later realized I was misunderstanding. Some of those misunderstandings were due to inexperience and immaturity, but not a few of them were due to subtle changes in English over four-plus centuries. I wasn't understanding what I read, even though I thought I was.

I'm going to give an example, and for this example, I polled five real, live, scientifically verifiable kids—kids who have all grown up in church—to see if they would make one of the same mistakes I did. I used the kids I happened to have on hand while visiting my sister—my three (ages thirteen, eleven, and eight) and her two (ages twelve and five). I did not coach the kids—that is, I told them to simply answer me honestly, whatever I asked. No kid heard the answers given by the other kids.

I said, "I'm going to ask you two questions about the meaning of some words in the KJV. Give me your honest answer. So Peter, one of Jesus's disciples, was stuck in prison, but an angel let him out and he walked over to a home where he knew Christians would be." Then I read them these verses:

> And as Peter knocked at the door of the gate, a damsel came to hearken, named Rhoda. And when she knew Peter's voice, she opened not the gate for gladness, but ran in, and told how Peter stood before the gate. And they said unto her, Thou art mad. But she **constantly** affirmed that it was even so. (Acts 12:13–15)

I asked them, "What does the word 'constantly' mean?" Here were the answers I received, verbatim:

A. (13): Uh, repeatedly, like, and you won't stop.
E. (12): Constantly is like, or is like, it is sort of like doing it over and over and over again.
M. (11): Uh, a bunch over and over again.
E. (8): It means, it means stuff like keeps happening. Like, uh, "I'm constantly hitting a ball at your face."
E. (5): Well, I don't know, weally.

I continued: "Now the second and last question. I will read to you some instructions that the apostle Paul gave to the younger pastor Titus. He tells him about the way Jesus saves us from sin, and the way that we will inherit eternal life, and then he says this: 'These things I will that thou affirm **constantly**' (Titus 3:8). What does it mean to affirm something 'constantly'?"

They answered:

A. (13): Um, just over and over again. You know, same as last time.

E. (12): It's like saying, "Yeah, yeah, this is so, this is so, this is so"—over and over again.

E. (8): It means you are like, um, saying that this happened. Like, "I saw a dragon in the sky," and you won't stop saying it. But people don't believe you.

(The other two children did not know.)

We now have a tiny usage sample from a young panel, a panel whose reading skills are all above average, by the way (except for the littlest member, who was not able to read at the time). For what it's worth, these kids understood this word "constantly" in the KJV exactly as I did until very shortly before I asked them about it.[10]

The word "constantly" appears three times in the KJV; I will focus in this chapter on only the two that I asked the kids about: Rhoda "**constantly** affirmed" that Peter was at the gate in Acts 12, and Paul wants Titus to "affirm **constantly**" the truths of the gospel.

Fishing for a False Friend

You'd have to be a pretty subtle reader to notice this, but Rhoda didn't have much time to affirm something over and over. Someone who does something "constantly" usually does that thing

10. YouTube commenter Wesley Tyler pointed this one out to me.

over and over during a period of time—maybe hours, weeks, or a lifetime.

The way "constantly" is used in Acts 12 does not rule out the possibility of our modern-day meaning. And I certainly never noticed that it sounded odd during my multiple times reading the story in the KJV as a child. Apparently, my children and my niece and nephew didn't either.

These two passages—Acts 12:15 and Titus 3:8—use different Greek words, though the KJV translates them the same way into English (which is not a problem, by the way—the KJV translators did *not* make a mistake in either place). In Acts 12:15, the relevant Greek word means "to be emphatic or resolute about something." You can translate it "to insist, maintain firmly." This is how the modern translations render it. Here's the NKJV:

> But they said to her, "You are beside yourself!" Yet she **kept insisting** that it was so. So they said, "It is his angel."

In Titus 3:8, the relevant Greek word means something very similar: to "speak confidently, insist."

So, why did the KJV translators choose the word "constantly"—"constantly affirm"? "Constantly" would seem to be a time reference (to say something over and over, as the kids and I all thought) instead of as a reference to the speaker's spirit (to say something insistently or confidently). This is a minor difference, but it's a difference. Did Rhoda say the same thing over and over, or did she insist confidently? More importantly, are preachers supposed to repeat certain truths over and over again, or to insist on those truths confidently?

How do contemporary dictionaries define this word, "constantly"?

NOAD takes this as I did my whole life and says that "constantly" means "continuously over a period of time; always." It gives these sample sentences: "The world is **constantly** changing," and "He was **constantly** on her mind." This sense does not fit the Greek word in either passage we've been looking at.

The OED, of course, nails it to the wall and throws dozens of darts mercilessly at its heart. It presents this sense:

> with assurance or certitude; confidently, firmly, assuredly.

It also names this sense as obsolete. We have another false friend.

Get this: The OED even lists Acts 12:15 from the 1611 KJV as one of its example uses! And alongside that verse, it also gives an example from Shakespeare's *Measure for Measure*:

> I doe constantly beleeue you.

I think modern audiences will find this sounds funny but will not quite know what is being said. Even though I think a lot of educated people know that "constant" used to mean "faithful," I judge that few will realize that "constantly" meant "faithfully" or "confidently" or "firmly."

That is what Rhoda was doing: She was confidently, firmly, and assuredly insisting that Peter was at the gate.

That is also what Paul was calling on Titus to do: to confidently, firmly, and assuredly insist on the truth of the gracious justification given to us, not for works of righteousness we have done but solely through the mercy of God and the sacrifice of Christ.

Contemporary False Friends?

I am constantly asked by YouTube commenters why I don't mention false friends in contemporary English versions. It's because, by and large, they don't exist. By definition, false friends are the result of language change, and contemporary translations such as the NKJV and SKJV use contemporary English.

But here in Titus 3:8, those two modern versions do retain this false friend. Ironically, then, whereas I do not believe the KJV translators committed an error by using the word "constantly" there, I think the NKJV and SKJV did err when they chose to retain it. English has changed since 1611, and they failed to recognize this.

I am also constantly told that I should be able to learn the meaning of false friends from context with no help from other sources. There's some truth here. In fact, one of my little survey helpers did just this. E. got the gist from the story, and she talked about how Rhoda spoke to the early Christians while Peter waited outside, adding, "Which might normally push somebody, but then it's like, but then it's like, but then she's insisting, so it's kind of, you know . . ."

That idea of "insisting" is practically demanded by the context. I don't think my misunderstanding of this passage was significant, frankly, because we're not talking about doctrine. We're talking about a minor point in a neat story, a point that is clear enough despite my small misunderstanding. Even my twelve-year-old niece got this.

But Titus 3:8 is a bit different—at least for me, anyway, because I am a Christian preacher. I am very, very sensitive to the question of what I should preach and then leave in people's hands and what truths I should insist on. I gave a talk on dating to our church teens recently, and I made a very clear line between cultural practices I think are wise (like waiting to date until you're ready to be married—something the Bible does not demand) and truths I insist on (like the necessity for sexual chastity, which the Bible does demand). The distinction is the former are things I maintain as truth but will not bring up constantly to them.

So, does Paul tell Titus to affirm certain things over and over or to insist on those things? There is a difference. There's a nuance here that I'd like to get as a preacher. Titus 3:8 is one of countless KJV phrases that landed in my memory despite, I assume, not being an Awana memory verse. And because of language change, I misunderstood it. It didn't even occur to me that I might be wrong. *It is incredibly difficult to make yourself remember to question the first meaning that comes to your mind regarding a word you use constantly.*

I referenced some good commentaries I have (in Logos, of course). I checked several modern commentators and one Reformation-era commentator. They pointed back to everything in Titus 3 as "the things" that Titus is supposed to insist on. That would include:

Being submissive to rulers and authorities.

Being obedient.

Being ready for every good work.

Speaking evil of no one.

Avoiding quarreling.

Being gentle.

Showing perfect courtesy toward all people.

Knowing that in our own pre-Christian lives we were foolish and disobedient, slaves to sin and hatred.

Knowing the precious gospel itself—the by-faith-alone gospel that Paul so beautifully describes.

These are the things that Paul tells Titus to insist on, to confidently affirm, to focus on. These are all nonnegotiable in the Christian life. In order to insist on these things, they are going to have to be repeated constantly. That's true. But that's not what Paul said. He told Titus to insist.

I know I sometimes see fine distinctions in meaning between Elizabethan English and contemporary English, and I know that this subtlety is frustrating to some non-nerds out there. But I'm reminded of one more thing stated by twelve-year-old E.:

> Which yet again is kind of annoying. But still . . . it kind of shows that somebody probably either is mad, as in like [she twirls her finger in the air near her head to indicate that someone is crazy], or that they know what they're seeing.

For me, I'm pretty sure it's the latter.

27. Occupy

> And he called his ten servants, and delivered them ten pounds, and said unto them, **Occupy** till I come. (Luke 19:13)

What do you think "occupy" means in this verse?

THE OCCUPY WALL STREET movement was many, many twenty-four-hour news cycles ago. If any of the participants were Christians, Luke 19:13 in the KJV may have proved a tempting proof text for their protest signs: "Occupy till I come."

If there are any young children out there whose parents feel desperate for some alone time, such parents might also be tempted to reinforce their instructions with a Bible quotation: "Occupy yourself till I come back."

But what does that phrase mean? Have you ever wondered?

Fishing for a False Friend

The word "occupy" doesn't occur very often in the KJV. It sounds a little funny to my ear in its first occurrence:

> All the gold that was **occupied** for the work in all the work of the holy place, even the gold of the offering, was twenty and nine talents. (Exod. 38:24)

Gold isn't something you can "occupy" in contemporary English. This is one of those impossible collocations we met in chapter 2—words that don't go together. Like "He was driving a curtain," or "She bought ten pieces of forever." You can't drive curtains; you can't buy forever—let alone in pieces. Just because a sentence is grammatical doesn't mean it's possible. Colorless green ideas sleep furiously, that's what I always say.

The next use of the word "occupy" in the KJV comes from the lips of Samson, who tells Delilah this get-off-my-back lie:

> If they bind me fast with new ropes that never were **occupied**, then shall I be weak, and be as another man. (Judg. 16:11)

This is a strange choice of words but not an impossible one. Perhaps a clue; perhaps not.

It's in Ezekiel 27 that we get six uses of "occupy" that make the most nonsense. Read through these and see what you can get out of "occupy." I warn you; this will be demanding.

> All the ships of the sea with their mariners were in thee to **occupy** thy merchandise. . . .
>
> Syria was thy merchant by reason of the multitude of the wares of thy making: they **occupied** in thy fairs with emeralds, purple, and broidered work, and fine linen, and coral, and agate. . . .
>
> Dan also and Javan going to and fro **occupied** in thy fairs: bright iron, cassia, and calamus, were in thy market. . . .

> Arabia, and all the princes of Kedar, they **occupied** with thee in lambs, and rams, and goats: in these were they thy merchants.
>
> The merchants of Sheba and Raamah, they were thy merchants: they **occupied** in thy fairs with chief of all spices, and with all precious stones, and gold. . . .
>
> Thy riches, and thy fairs, thy merchandise, thy mariners, and thy pilots, thy calkers, and the **occupiers** of thy merchandise, and all thy men of war, that are in thee, and in all thy company which is in the midst of thee, shall fall into the midst of the seas in the day of thy ruin. (vv. 9, 16, 19, 21–22, 27)

Here's what I'm getting at: In this passage, at least, occupying has something to do with merchants taking up space in stalls at the market. Maybe? I'm afraid that when I did make attempts at the prophets in the KJV in my late teens, I was probably just assuming I wouldn't fully understand, so I don't ever remember noticing that "occupy" was an odd word to use here.

And how all this helps me with Jesus's statement "Occupy till I come" I wouldn't know—except I peeked ahead to the end of this chapter. So, I do know. And soon I'll tell you.

There are three totally different Hebrew words the KJV translates as "occupy" in Ezekiel 27. One means "conduct trade, barter" (HALOT); another is somewhat obscure but seems to mean "to give for" (HALOT); the last means "trader, dealer, wholesaler, merchant" (HALOT).

As for the Greek word translated "occupy" in the phrase "Occupy till I come," this word, too, means "do business" or "trade" (BDAG). Indeed, the NKJV uses "Do business till I come," and the SKJV uses "Engage in business until I come."

The English word "occupy" has three main senses today, according to NOAD:

1. You can occupy a residence or a space of some kind: "The apartment she occupies in Manhattan"; "Two long

windows occupied almost the whole wall"; "On the corporate ladder, they occupy the lowest rungs."

2. You can occupy yourself with particular thoughts or activities: "Her mind was occupied with alarming questions"; "Sarah occupied herself taking the coffee cups over to the sink."
3. You can occupy an area of land by military or other violent action: "The region was occupied by Britain during World War I."

I don't see anything about trading or bartering. So, for my whole life, until this book, I assumed that Jesus, when he said, "Occupy till I come," was using that second sense. A certain nobleman goes into a far country to get a kingdom; his plan is to come back, so he calls ten of his servants and gives them money, saying, "Hang in there till I come back, guys." Or "Occupy yourselves with something; don't get into trouble."[11]

In other words, I think most KJV readers today hear from Jesus the message a mother gives to a nearby seven-year-old while she makes a phone call: "Can you please just occupy yourself?" My brain just added the word "yourself" when I couldn't make sense of "Occupy till I come." Brains do this, I have observed. They insist on making some kind of sense of things if they possibly can.

But this sense of "occupy" does not fit the Greek or Hebrew. *Did we finally catch the KJV translators in an error?*

No. There is an older, obsolete sense of this word "occupy" in the OED that fits the Greek and Hebrew words perfectly:

11. The exceptional reader (see "nerd" or "pedant") may have noticed that in "Occupy till I come," "occupy" is intransitive, and contemporary English doesn't have an intransitive use of "occupy." NOAD specifies that all its senses are "with object." I think most KJV readers today supply a silent "yourself" in Luke 19:13: "Occupy *yourself* till I come." I believe I did this.

> intransitive. To be busy or employed (in some capacity); to exercise one's craft or function; to practise; to do business, to work. *Obsolete.*

No Loafing

Doesn't this make instant sense of what Jesus has the master saying in that parable? The pastor friend who sent me this example said, "You'll miss the whole point of the parable if you think that the nobleman simply told the servants to 'hang around' until he came back."

In other words, Jesus pictures himself as a nobleman who goes away to receive a kingdom, and he expects his citizens to invest wisely the money he has left them. Indeed, when he returns, he calls in the servants to whom he had given money, and he asks them "how much every man had gained by trading" (Luke 19:15).

"Occupy till I come" meant to speakers of Elizabethan English just what the NKJV and SKJV mean to speakers of contemporary English: "Do business till I come back"; "Engage in trade till I return." As always in this book, the KJV translators did no wrong. But neither did I when I misunderstood this phrase for decades without realizing it.

28. World

> And whosoever speaketh a word against the Son of man, it shall be forgiven him: but whosoever speaketh against the Holy Ghost, it shall not be forgiven him, neither in this **world**, neither in the **world** to come. (Matt. 12:32)

What do you think "world" means in this verse?

AS I WRITE THESE WORDS—in a hotel in the Chicago area, as it happens—I am forty-three years old. I have been a full-time Bible nerd for around two decades. I have taught the Bible at countless evangelistic events and Sunday school classes, and in sermons, articles, blog posts, and videos. I went to seminary for more years than you can shake a shoe at, and I took about ten semesters of Greek. Most importantly, I have been in church since literally before I was born. I picked up at some point that the word "world" in the New Testament sometimes *actually* means something like "age," a period of time. I think tons of Christians know this.

It never occurred to me at any time during all of the experiences I've described to consider the possibility that language change might be involved until a good friend and brother pointed it out to me quite recently.

It would take a pretty skilled reader with a great memory to notice that "world" might, in some places, be a false friend. *Maybe*, if someone did a word study on "world" and happened to read KJV uses of the word alongside the NKJV and SKJV, they might notice that the word the KJV itself usually translates as "world" is twice translated "age" in the KJV New Testament (Eph. 2:7; Col. 1:26).

But if you regularly check translations such as the NKJV and SKJV next to your KJV, you'll see that there are multiple places where the KJV uses "world" but the new translations use "age."

If you've been trained up to be a fisher of false friends, maybe it will occur to you to wonder—as it did not to me, despite careful study of the Bible's teaching on the "world"—whether indeed language change is up to one or more of its old tricks. Maybe it's grabbing the bait off the hook and swimming to a place where fishers can't catch it.

Fishing for a False Friend

The Greek word we're interested in here has one major aspect and one less than major aspect: It can refer to time and (less often) it can refer to space.

It has several time-related senses. The most important is "a long period of time, without reference to beginning or end" (BDAG). Here are a few places in the New Testament where BDAG says that's what the word is doing. I'll quote these verses with that definition inserted in place of our word:

> As he saith also in another place, Thou art a priest for [a long period of time, without reference to beginning or end] after the order of Melchisedec. (Heb. 5:6)

That makes sense, right? Jesus is a priest forever—no beginning or end. One more example. Here's Mary, at the very end of her beautiful and theologically rich Magnificat, her song of praise:

> He hath holpen his servant Israel, in remembrance of his mercy; As he spake to our fathers, To Abraham, and to his seed for [a long period of time, without reference to beginning or end]. (Luke 1:54–55)

These are both clearly time references.

The next sense of the word is also a time reference: "a segment of time as a particular unit of history, age" (BDAG).

> Let no man deceive himself. If any man among you seemeth to be wise in this [segment of time as a particular unit of history, age], let him become a fool, that he may be wise. (1 Cor. 3:18)

And one more for good measure:

> Who gave himself for our sins, that he might deliver us from this present evil [segment of time as a particular unit of history, age]. (Gal. 1:4)

The third sense this word can carry, depending on the context, is not a reference to time but to space: "the world as a spatial concept" (BDAG). Whereas BDAG listed a couple dozen passages in which the time senses were used, it lists only a few in which this spatial one appears. Here are the two clearest examples:

> Hath in these last days spoken unto us by his Son, whom he hath appointed heir of all things, by whom also he made [the world as a spatial concept]. (Heb. 1:2)

> Through faith we understand that [the world as a spatial concept] [was] framed by the word of God, so that things which are seen were not made of things which do appear. (11:3)

In the judgment of the lexicographers at BDAG, the Greek word we're focusing on—the one in Matthew 12:32, which I asked you about at the beginning of the chapter—is much more likely to be temporal than it is to be spatial. But it *can* be spatial.

Is "world" in contemporary English used the same way? No, it's the opposite: It's a word that *can* have a time reference but usually has a spatial one. I'm warning you, this gets complex. My favorite contemporary American English dictionary gives multiple senses for "world," and it gives *many* example sentences. Almost all of them have to do with space rather than time.

Here's the main spatial sense for "world" in our English:

> the earth, together with all of its countries, peoples, and natural features: *he was doing his bit to save the world.* (NOAD)

Here's one of the time-related uses:

> a particular period of history: *the ancient world.* (NOAD)

NOAD gives three senses (or categories of senses?) for "world." AHD gives twelve. MW gives twenty-one. I told you this was complex! With all three dictionaries, the overall picture is the same, however: "World" in our English is much more likely to be spatial than it is to be temporal—but it *can* be temporal.

We have something of a mismatch—or maybe just a mish-mash, as things are so complex—between the English and the Greek.

Will the OED help us? I think so. I hope so.

I know so.

The OED is going to give us an obsolete sense of "world" that fits the Greek word perfectly and fits the contexts in which the KJV uses the word. Here it is:

> an age or extended period of time in human (or earthly) existence or history; (in plural) ages. . . . *Obsolete.*

The expert lexicographers at the OED see language change here. And they also see something else that is hard for us to see, and it's their job to see. They see English speakers of the past using the word "world" in ways that we just wouldn't today. Here's the key example, from 1600—exactly the time of the King James Bible. This comes from famous Church of England priest Richard Hooker. Ask yourself: Would anyone use "world" this way today?

> Adam and all the fathers before Christ, till Christ's coming, were for so many **worlds** together detained.

Quite obviously, "worlds" here has to have a time reference. And we simply wouldn't use the word this way. I believe we have a false friend in some places where the KJV uses "world." I believe that when the KJV translators translated Matthew 12:32, they chose a word that for them had primarily a time reference but for us has a spatial one.

> And whosoever speaketh a word against the Son of man, it shall be forgiven him: but whosoever speaketh against the Holy Ghost, it shall not be forgiven him, neither in this **world**, neither in the **world** to come.

It's hard to pin down how much a given misunderstanding matters. Could readers today take this to mean that we're getting a wholly new planet (spatial reference) instead of a new age (time reference)? I think so. I don't want to freak out too much about minor misunderstandings; I think that reading the whole Bible carefully and receiving good teaching from a faithful, doctrinally sound pastor will keep people from some erroneous theology they might otherwise believe.

But still, we need to get things right when we can, even on the littler details—the mint, anise, and cumin of Bible interpretation. We need to reel in the false friends before they get rabies (can fish get rabies?) and infect other fish in the pond.

A Complex World

"World" is probably the most complex and difficult false friend in this book. The fact is, "world" still is a legitimate translation of the Greek word we've been focused on—in certain passages. I agree with BDAG in seeing two of those in Hebrews (quoted earlier). Clearly, context in those places demands a spatial reference. Those passages are saying that God created "the worlds," not "the ages."

I almost skipped this word for this book because I felt it was so difficult to nuance, but I didn't because of one key thing: that OED citation. As soon as I read it, I knew immediately that I was not hearing my English. It made me want to explore how often I had misunderstood the KJV's use of the word "world" in the New Testament.

Armed with the knowledge you now have, I encourage you to take these steps and do some more study:

Go to Marble.Bible, select the Greek New Testament, and navigate to Matthew 12:32, the verse we've been focused on most in this chapter. (You can also easily use Logos, Bible.org, or Bible Hub for this step.)

Click on the word "age" in that verse.

Click "Show Passages" at the bottom of the definition pane that opens to the right to show all the passages where the Greek word we've been focusing on appears.

Read through all those passages in the KJV, find the words "world" or "age," and try to decide whether the context indicates that the references are primarily temporal or spatial.

Soon, I think you'll have a few more fish in your basket to bring home for your hungry children.

Amelioration

When a word "ameliorates," it gets better. Some words move from being mean or bad to being positive. A classic example is the Latin word *nescius,* which (many people know) used to mean "ignorant" (see *Oxford Latin Dictionary*) but became our word "nice." Imagine entering a time machine and going back to the days of Paul, hearing a Latin speaker call someone *nescius,* and telling him, "Did you know that in the future, that word will come to be positive?" This will be difficult for the Latin speaker to compute: When could it ever be positive to call someone ignorant? But it will be true.

29. Mansion

In my Father's house are many **mansions**: if it were not so, I would have told you. I go to prepare a place for you. (John 14:2)

What do you think "mansions" means in this verse?

THE WORD "MANSION" appears just once in the King James. My own pastor preached fairly recently on the passage in which it appears, and the sermon was really wonderful. It was careful with the biblical text, and it put on display what Christ is doing for his people's future. This chapter will provide insight into that word "mansion" in the KJV and will borrow a bit from my pastor to provide insight into what it means for Jesus to tell his disciples—and, by extension, us—that he goes to prepare a place for us.

Were you fascinated as a child by this word, as I was? On the one hand, I wanted a heavenly mansion all my own—with a bunk bed in a loft room that featured a slide into a ball pit on the floor below, as well as a fireman's pole. On the other hand, my young mind was confused and intrigued by "mansions" being "in" the Father's house. Tell me you thought this too.

We weren't alone, I think. There's an old gospel song that contrasts the mansions we expect in heaven with the humbler dwellings in which we must now reside on earth. The singer croons that he's satisfied with just a "cottage below." In other words, a 1956 brick-front rambler is really OK for now. But in heaven, he expects something better: "I've got a mansion just over the hilltop."

A mansion, in this telling, is obviously a big, opulent, multi-bedroom home. This is what Ira Stanphill meant when he wrote this 1949 song "Mansion over the Hilltop," a song sung by many gospel groups and even by Elvis himself. There really is only one realistic possibility here: Ira got this song from the word choice in the KJV.

Fishing for a False Friend

Some other translations do have "mansion" here. I was a bit surprised to see that the NKJV sticks with "mansions," which goes all the way back to Tyndale. (It does have a footnote, but we'll get to that.)

I was surprised because there's an obvious contextual conflict: What in the world does it mean for the Father's "house" to have many "mansions"? Mansions *are* houses, right? How can a house have a mansion in it? This is what fascinated me as a kid. Indeed, I think this may just increase the mystique for people. But I'm convinced that this is a false friend.

So, step 2, let's look up the Greek word translated "mansions" in a responsible original-language lexicon. Remember, this is the really important thing: The ultimate standard here, and in every passage, is what the Spirit inspired in Greek, not what translators have said in English. Serious translators almost always get things right; they really do. As I was reading along in my Greek New Testament during my pastor's sermon, I just kept thinking about how simple and straightforward the translation of John 14 is, all over the place. Jesus's words are very clear. His meaning sometimes takes a little more effort to uncover, but the words themselves are not tricky to translate.

The Greek word here is no exception. BDAG gives a very simple definition: "a place in which one stays, *dwelling(-place), room, abode*." In a context like this one, the word means "room." And that makes a lot more sense, right? "In my Father's house, there are many **rooms**." Context indicates that even if the word can mean "dwelling place," as in maybe a whole house, it most certainly doesn't specify a large, opulent house.

Here I think it's unlikely that Jesus is speaking of a whole separate house, because unless Jesus is using "my Father's house" as a stand-in for all of heaven, he just has to mean "rooms." In Jesus's day, large houses could contain multiple separate dwelling places, and those dwelling places might contain several rooms each—sort of like a duplex or triplex today. But he wasn't talking about what we mean by "mansions."

Basically, the Greek word in John 14:2 means "rooms."

(The footnote in the NKJV at this word says "dwellings." I see this as a hedging of bets: Maybe the word does refer to something more than a room. But a "dwelling place" can be a separate dwelling or an apartment in a larger building. This is a defensible translation choice.)

"Rooms" is clearly not what the English word "mansion" means. Look it up in NOAD and you'll get "a large, impressive house." In my entire life—a life in which I have gone around intensely English-ing all over the world—I have never heard anyone use "mansion" to mean "a room inside a big house."[1]

So, step 4: What does the venerable and august OED say? Will it explain to us why in the world the KJV translators chose "mansion" instead of "room" here? Did the KJV translators commit an error? Was the great-great-great-great-grandpappy of a prosperity gospel preacher one of the KJV translators? Did he try to upgrade his heavenly inheritance by changing the humble "room" to the glorious "mansion," as if by mistranslating this word he could force God to stick to a promise he never intended to make?

No. The OED is very clear here. It addresses this very passage of Scripture, John 14:2. Let's stop off first in the etymology section—this is interesting. The OED shows that "mansion" comes from the Latin *manere*, meaning "to remain." In fact, "remain" itself comes from *manere*. "Remnant" likewise comes from this root. The "m" followed by a vowel and then an "n" can suggest this root.

So, though "any large or stately residence" is currently the top sense for this word, there is sense 5a here in the OED for "mansion":

1. I did have a YouTube commenter tell me, "We still use the word 'mansion' here in the UK for a separate dwelling in a large, stately home. There are property listings on estate agents which include 'mansions' to mean such. (Oops, I mean 'realtor' when I say 'estate agent'!)" I asked: "Really?! Do British Christians understand 'mansion' accurately in the KJV, in your experience?" He replied, "Strangely no. . . . Reading 'mansion' in Scripture we would automatically lean to the tradition, probably inspired by hymns and KJV teachers, that it means a single large, stately home."

> each of a number of separate dwelling places or apartments in a large house.

Aha! That's exactly what the Greek word means! We have caught ourselves a false friend. Because, of course, the OED goes on to say that this sense of "mansion" is

> now usually archaic [and used] as a translation of, or in allusion to, John 14:2.

The OED also comments that Tyndale may have used this sense because he was influenced by the Vulgate, the Latin translation of the Bible that was the King James of its day—the venerable and trusted translation that every educated person was familiar with. The Vulgate has *mansiones*.

But in the KJV translators' day, "mansion" could still be used to describe individual rooms or dwelling places in a larger structure. It is to demonstrate this that the OED editors always include citations. Listen to the way one English writer used the word in 1533:

> They came to a low cottage . . . having in it two **mansions**, in one of the which were women and children and in the other only men.

Low cottages today can't have mansions in them, unless they're toy mansions. Say this today, and it doesn't make sense. And listen to this use of "mansion" in the OED from eighty-eight years after the KJV was published:

> Grecian Houses were usually divided into two Parts, in which the Men and women had distinct **Mansions** assigned.

Same thing. You couldn't say this today. You'd say "rooms," or maybe, possibly, "dwelling places."

I'm super sorry, but Jesus was not promising us access to the most expensive listings on Zillow. Jesus did not promise us "mansions."

What Jesus Is Preparing

But what a bummer of a way to end a chapter. I can't stop here. I have to share with you what my pastor shared with me. My wife turned to me during the sermon and said, "I've never heard this before—so cool!"

It makes sense. I looked it up in some commentaries too. As he often does, D. A. Carson puts it insightfully and beautifully, and I'll just quote him:

> It is not that [Jesus] arrives on the scene [in heaven] and then begins to prepare the place; rather, in the context of Johannine theology, it is the going itself, via the cross and resurrection, that prepares the place for Jesus' disciples.[2]

Did you catch that? I always wondered what it meant for Jesus to go make rooms ready for us in his Father's house. Was he being a carpenter again, like he was under his earthly father, Joseph? Carson is saying that this is a word picture meant to tell us that Jesus was preparing a way for us to go remain, to go dwell with God. He continues:

> And if he takes such trouble, all to prepare a place for his own, it is inconceivable that the rest should not follow: *I will come back and take you to be with me that you also may be where I am.*[3]

---

2. D. A. Carson, *The Gospel According to John*, The Pillar New Testament Commentary (Eerdmans, 1991), 489.

3. Carson, *John*, 489.

This is better than a mansion, whether silver- or gold-lined. This is dwelling with Jesus for all eternity. The dwelling place of humanity will be with God. And someday, when God makes a new heaven and a new earth, the dwelling place of God will be with people. In that bright land the ransomed *will* shine, because Christ will be our light. That is a truth to take home to your McMansion.

J. C. Ryle has been explaining to English readers since the nineteenth century that "the word rendered 'mansions' means literally 'abiding-places.'"[4] And still people are confused—through no fault of the KJV translators nor today's readers, who understandably have difficulties keeping up with all the changes in English in the last four-hundred-plus years.

Thankfully, this book is here to help.

4. J. C. Ryle, *Expository Thoughts on John*, vol. 3 (Robert Carter & Brothers, 1880), 55.

Pejoration

SOME WORDS MOVE from mild to offensive, or from positive to crass, over time. This is especially true of things that are inherently private or necessarily icky or filthy. Words for sex, for relieving oneself, for the place where one relieves oneself, and for society's "undesirables" are all ripe for pejoration.

30. Ass

> And it came to pass, as she [Achsah] came unto him, that she moved him to ask of her father a field: and she lighted off her **ass**; and Caleb said unto her, What wouldest thou? (Josh. 15:18)

What do you think "ass" means in this verse?

DAN ALLENDER GREW UP as a complete heathen not far from the picture-perfect evangelical family the Longmans. Young Tremper Longman III, now a well-known evangelical

Old Testament scholar, became best friends with his heathen neighbor Dan. The whole story is really touching; it begins with Tremper showing Christian kindness to an angry young rebel (namely Dan). And though Dan did not follow Tremper in his faith, and though Dan literally never darkened the door of a church, he actually followed Tremper to a religious college, just so they wouldn't have to break up their mutual collection of LPs.

This was the 1970s. Tremper was on his way to becoming a biblical scholar. Dan, on the other hand, was on his way to becoming a deadbeat. And then, as he tells it,

> The point came in the context of the cartel that I worked with putting out a contract on a DEA agent. And all of a sudden I went from being a middle-class drug dealer to being in the big time. I knew that either I was going to jail or I was going to die.[1]

Dan reached out for help—to Tremper, of course. And for the first time in his life, he came to church.

Has this happened to you? A non-Christian friend visits church with you, and suddenly you are hypervigilant; you see and hear everything through their ears. Dan was "the one that believeth not, or one unlearned" that Paul talks about in 1 Corinthians 14. And what did poor Dan, the unlearned, hear in his very first time in a pew?

> The pastor started talking about Balaam's ass. And I'm thinking, "Oh my goodness. What kind of religion have I gotten myself into that Balaam's ass is talking to him?" And about halfway in the sermon he changed to Balaam's donkey. Oh, it was such a relief. It was at this point I realized that all we're dealing with is the possibility that God could use *animals* and not *body parts*.[2]

1. Dick Staub and Dan Allender, "How Dan Allender Broke on Through (to the Other Side)," *Christianity Today*, June 1, 2003, www.christianitytoday.com/2003/06/how-dan-allender-broke-on-through-to-other-side/.

2. Staub and Allender, "How Dan Allender Broke on Through."

I am rather fastidious about allowing bad words to escape my own lips, and I have insisted that my children, too, not use vulgar language. I may even have gone a little too far when my kids were very small. I didn't want them saying the word "butt" because I found it coarse (still do). But when one's children are in diapers, some nomenclature is needed for successful reference to their posteriors. So, we used "bum." Only, the kids—toddlers at the time—started using "bum" the way they would have used the word "butt" if I let them. And they used it all the time. So, I banned it. I tried to explain that it wasn't a bad word, but it wasn't a good word either. Kids think in black-and-white; they had a hard time with this. All they could understand was that Daddy outlawed the word "bum," and if Daddy said no to "bum," it must be bad.

One day, Mommy was out shopping around Christmastime with my little verbally precocious daughter, who had just turned two. Suddenly, a look of profound horror came upon her tiny face. She'd heard the music in the shop, and it was playing the Chordettes' 1954 hit, "Mr. Sandman," the song that begins, "Bum bum bum bum bum bum bum bum bum bum." She said with shock, "Mom! They're saying, 'bum bum'!" To her little ears, the song was a series of bad words sung in cheery harmonies.

At some point after this, I gave up on this word. I have teenagers now, and they can say "bum" if they want.

Have I communicated sufficiently, however, that I don't really find it fun to talk about "ass" (and "bastard," the next entry)? But I just die every time I think of the Dan Allender story; it is nothing short of hilarious. And we need to talk about this, because Dan's experience cannot be unique. I discuss this word in order to offer what I pray is wisdom for how to diagnose the problem "ass" creates. (As for how to deal with it, see the conclusion.)

Fishing for a False Friend

Do you really need me to go through the whole process with "ass"? Let's make it quick.

Dan Allender noticed this false friend for us—hilariously.

The Hebrew and Greek words the KJV translates as "ass" most often mean, of course, "donkey."

"Ass" still shows up in NOAD (and MW and AHD) with the meaning "an animal of the horse family, which is typically smaller than a horse and has longer ears and a braying call." The sense is not labeled as archaic. (I checked with my youngest, now nine, and he said he knew that "ass" means "donkey." He said he knew from the Bible and from songs.)

"Ass" in the horse-like animal sense shows up in the OED, of course, and that sense, too, is not marked as obsolete.

So, what's the problem? "Ass" still means "donkey," right?

Well, perhaps step 5 is in order.

I looked up the word "ass" in the NOW Corpus, and after looking at hundreds of uses—which was not exactly fun for this rather uptight writer—I found only one that referred to a donkey. It was a reference to an ancient Latin novel sometimes called *The Golden Ass*. But no one else I could find used "ass" to refer to the braying animal.

Do you want to know what I saw instead? I saw people being kicked in the bum. I saw some kick-bum recipes. I saw people who were a pain in the bum (such a person might be referred to as a dumb-bum; I saw this). I saw others who were working their bums off. And, of course, I saw plenty of direct references to actual human bums.

Who knew Bible teaching would lead to this?

I can't use a euphemism anymore, because you just have to see these two phrases I also saw at the corpus. If you have your ear tuned to English *as it is actually spoken by real people*, you may have noticed phrases like these:

"fly-ass burrito"
"fake-ass people"

There is a common, though definitely slangy, use of the word "ass" as a piece of grammar. It's what might be called an "infix." Not a *prefix* or *suffix*, but a piece of language that is inserted *within* something, such as a word (or phrase): an infix. Neither NOAD nor MW nor AHD references this usage. So, I checked *Urban Dictionary*, which I find to be pretty spotty and unprofessional (and crass to the point of defiling) but occasionally useful for slang. A lazy lexicographer there noticed this usage but explained it this way: "word inserted between an adjective and a noun for seemingly no reason at all."[3]

I knew this was wrong; people across a language group don't say random stuff repeatedly for no reason. So, I turned to the OED, and sure enough, they had carefully recorded this use.

> As the second element in compounds, forming adjectives with the sense "having or displaying the quality designated by the first element to an extreme or undesirable degree," as broad-ass, snobby-ass, cheap-ass, lame-ass, sorry-ass, stupid-ass, long-ass, etc.

Now, before you shake your head and make some comment about kids today: The OED editors found uses of this infix as far back as 1930.

A linguist wrote a great little piece about this use of "ass" in a journal: He called "ass" in this sense "an intensifer," and he carefully recorded the grammatical rules that attach to it.[4] It's not

3. *Urban Dictionary*, "ass," posted by prudence-mcgee, July 16, 2010, www.urbandictionary.com/define.php?term=ass.

4. For example, he noticed that you can say, "It's a cold-ass night," but not "The night is cold-ass." There are grammatical rules surrounding this slang "word." See Daniel Siddiqi, "The English Intensifier *Ass*," *Snippets* 23 (May 2011): 16–17.

something I would say, but a "fly-ass burrito" is an impressively good burrito, and "fake-ass people" are very fake people, not people with prosthetic bums.

What People Will Say

Why do I mention all this? In order to aid diagnosis, to name *why* "ass" was amusing to Dan Allender . . . and to the fifth-grade girls who (another true story) giggled and wondered why in the world anyone would covet someone else's ass (Exod. 20:17).

When Dan and the fifth-grade girls come into your church, they know the English they know, and they have good reasons for knowing that English. "Ass" means "donkey" far, far less often than it means . . . other things. My educated guess is that "ass" in the donkey sense is used only in historical contexts and in scientific, zoological ones. If someone doesn't happen to enter those contexts, that someone is likely to misunderstand this verse: "And she lighted off her ass" (Josh. 15:18).

I know what people will say: "Dan Allender should have known that the word 'ass' means 'donkey'! Every educated person knows this!" Even more thoughtful and observant people might note that the story of Balaam's ass in Numbers 22 is rather ridiculous if one takes "ass" to mean "bum." Balaam saddles his bum (v. 21); he rides upon his bum (v. 22, though I guess that kind of makes sense); his bum sees the angel of the Lord (v. 23); his bum turns aside out of the way and goes into a field (v. 23); Balaam smites his bum repeatedly (vv. 23, 27); his bum falls down (v. 27); and his bum talks (v. 30). Wouldn't most people recognize that something simply must be wrong in their understanding after hearing all these incredible oddities?

Yes. There's some truth in this criticism. Church is primarily for Christians, and we can't make literally everything we do there intelligible to literally every first-time visitor. Plus, I can attest people can manage to misunderstand even when you do preach a totally clear-bum sermon.

But just read about "Dan" in 1 Corinthians 14:

> Therefore if the whole church comes together in one place, and all speak with tongues, and there come in those who are uninformed or unbelievers, will they not say that you are out of your mind? But if all prophesy, and an unbeliever or an uninformed person comes in, he is convinced by all, he is convicted by all. And thus the secrets of his heart are revealed; and so, falling down on his face, he will worship God and report that God is truly among you. (vv. 23–25 NKJV)

One reason we use intelligible speech in church—the most important reason—is that the body needs to be edified. But another reason is that an unbeliever might visit that day with his Christian boyhood buddy.

If you blame the Dans in the world for misunderstanding, at least do them the honor of understanding why they misunderstood. "Ass" for "donkey" is not higher English; it's older English. The fact that it still exists on the edges of our language—like "beeves" is still used on cattle ranches—does not change this fact.

I'm not telling you what to do here, but I do think you have to consider the Dans.

A Donkey to Be Named Later

Consider this: The word "donkey" did not exist in 1611 when the KJV translators sat down to do their work. It didn't enter English until the late 1700s. "Ass" was simply the common word for that animal when the KJV was published; it clearly isn't now.[5] Very likely because people don't appreciate being forced

5. Fun fact: "Ass" meaning "donkey" and "ass" meaning "bum" have different etymological histories. The former comes from the Latin word for donkey,

to use giggle-inviting double entendres every time they refer to common objects. (Like the time a pastor's wife apologized to me for calling her dog a "bitch," explaining quickly that that's just what you call them when you're a breeder.)

"Ass" in the KJV is a mild false friend everywhere it might call up the wrong idea for a moment before you remember, *Oh yeah, they mean "donkey."* And for some people—nobody but God knows how many—it's a more major false friend because it won't just bring up the wrong picture. It will bring up an offensively wrong picture because it's a current "bad word."[6]

---

asinus; the latter comes from the Old English (Germanic) form *ærs* (later "arse," still used in British English), meaning "bum." And you're going to get one more humorous "ass" story, since you persevered so long in the footnotes. I was in a choir all four years during college, and our beloved director was a rather fastidious and proper man. He dressed neatly; he lived neatly. I owe him a great deal, because I used knowledge he provided when I became a choir director on several occasions. One day our choir was practicing for a Christmas concert in which we'd have to sing from memory, and he was trying to remind us of the words of our song by making hand motions. We sang of the baby Jesus, and he made a cradling motion to help us. We sang of the star above the place where he lay, and he reached his hands up and made them "twinkle" (how does one describe this?) to indicate stars. We sang of the ox and the ass who adored him, and when we came to ass, you can guess where he pointed. His face went red, we all dissolved into laughter, and I'll bet you every single other member of that choir remembers this event to this day. He explained, rather awkwardly, that he was trying to refer to the donkey's tail.

6. One more note: The great Noah Webster himself, in the early 1830s, noticed the problem we're seeing in this chapter. By his day, the KJV had come to contain "some quaint and vulgar phrases which are not relished by those who love a pure style, and which are not in accordance with the general tenor of the language." Webster continues,

> To these may be added many words and phrases, very offensive to delicacy and even to decency. In the opinion of all persons with whom I have conversed on this subject, such words and phrases ought not to be retained in the version. Language which cannot be uttered in company without a violation of decorum, or the rules of good breeding, exposes the scriptures to the scoffs of unbelievers, impairs their authority, and multiplies or confirms the enemies of our holy religion. (Noah Webster, *The Holy Bible, Containing the Old and New Testaments, in the Common Version* [Durrie & Peck, 1833], preface)

31. Bastard

> And a **bastard** shall dwell in Ashdod, and I will cut off the pride of the Philistines. (Zech. 9:6)

What do you think "bastard" means in this verse?

EVERYBODY WHO GREW UP on the King James Version, as I did, knows about those naughty words that cause the teens in Sunday school to titter during Bible-reading time. I am, as I said in the previous chapter, particularly persnickety about the use of bad words in my personal life. Words that take the Lord's name in vain especially I never utter—but also words that profane the marriage bed, or words that otherwise bring the properly private into public, or words that are just plain offensive. So, it feels rather awkward for me to even mention some of the "bad words" in the KJV that appear in this portion of this book.

My discomfort raises what I take to be an important and central question: Did the original readers of the 1611 KJV experience this same discomfort? Did the KJV translators choose some words that they full well knew were widely offensive? Or were these KJV "bad words" neutral back in 1611, only later picking up nasty connotations?

Let's explore.

Fishing for a False Friend

"Bastard" is a word that appears in the KJV three times. For example,

> A **bastard** shall not enter into the congregation of the LORD; even to his tenth generation. (Deut. 23:2)

You probably noticed this false friend if, as you read along, you started backward and did a double take—"No **bastards** are allowed in the congregation of the Lord up to ten generations." What? If you read contemporary translations, you might notice that "bastard" is absent. Modern translations have dropped this word completely. No major modern evangelical English Bible translation uses this word today. The NKJV and SKJV, for example, tend to opt for "illegitimate children" and "person of illegitimate birth" instead. Why?

I'll only cover the New Testament use of this word, for time's sake, though the Old Testament word is similar. Here's the relevant verse, one I memorized in the KJV as a child or teen:

> But if ye be without chastisement, whereof all are partakers, then are ye **bastards**, and not sons. (Heb. 12:8)

The Greek New Testament word translated "bastard" in the KJV here means "illegitimate children," someone born "out of wedlock or of servile origin and therefore without legal status or rights" (BDAG). Older Greek dictionaries do offer the translation "bastard," but by the time BDAG rolls around in the early 2000s, that word is absent.

That's because it's obvious to anyone who's spoken English for any length of time that "bastard" now doesn't often get used to mean "illegitimate child," and even when it does, there is still a strong whiff of nastiness in the word. Much more commonly, the word is just a mean name. It means, according to NOAD, "an unpleasant or despicable person." NOAD gives the example sentence, "He lied to me, the **bastard**!"

When I checked an online corpus, uses of "nosy bastard" and "cheap bastard" and "lying bastard" far outnumbered uses of "bastard son."

Notice something else: In the nasty uses of the word, "bastard" is a substantive, a noun, a thing: "poor bastard." But in the only instances I could find where "bastard" was used to refer to illegitimate children (always sons), it was an adjective: "bastard sons." When, in our English, people refer simply to "a bastard," as a noun, it appears that they intend the *mean* version of that word.

So, did the original readers of the KJV hear this when they read Hebrews 12:8 in the KJV?

> But if ye be without chastisement, whereof all are partakers, then are ye **unpleasant or despicable persons**, and not sons. (Heb. 12:8)

The OED will help us in a moment, but let's do some more exploring first.

"Bastard" is the word the 1568 Bishops' Bible had, and that is the Bible the KJV translators were asked to revise. It's the word Tyndale had before the Bishops' Bible.[7] Was it a mean name in the 1500s?

The truth is, it's a bit difficult to discern, from this distance, what kind of emotional weight this word carried in the sixteenth and early seventeenth centuries. It isn't just language that changes over time; it's culture. Illegitimate children used to face difficulties in Western culture that they just don't face anymore. So, in that sense, "bastard" in 1611 referred to something worse than "illegitimate child" refers to today. Western society has come to believe, in part because of stories of poor illegitimate children like Oliver Twist in Dickens's famous novel, that it's wrong to

7. Wycliffe, following the Vulgate, which he translated, has "adulterers" (*auowtreris*). This seems to be an instance of the English translator transliterating the Latin rather than translating it.

punish children for who their father is or isn't. But even if the cultural *thing* was once bad, it's still possible that *the word itself* used to be more neutral.

And that is exactly what the authoritative and exhaustive OED says, namely that "bastard" was

> originally a neutral designation, and used as such in legal contexts as late as the 20th cent. (see, e.g., quot. 1933), but now tempered by the largely pejorative overtones of the word in modern use.

It is now, they say,

> used as a term of abuse or contempt for a person (esp. a man or boy), now esp. for someone who is callous or wilfully cruel, or who acts ruthlessly out of self-interest.

The OED prides itself in finding the very first recorded instances of a particular word or sense. And under this pejorative sense of the word "bastard," their first use comes from 1675 of a man who was "cursing his Doctor for [being] a Quacking Bastard." So, according to the best source I know, the KJV translators *did not* use a word that was dirty or mean or pejorative in their day when they chose "bastards." The word was neutral in 1611. It just meant "illegitimate children."

Two Acid Tests

But how about today? Let's give "bastard" two acid tests. First, would your pastor ever use the word "bastard" in a sermon outside of reading or referring to the KJV? Second, ask your teen Sunday school class to read Hebrews 12:8 in the KJV and see if they snicker and look at one another.

This word is a false friend in the KJV, and it's not so much because modern readers will misunderstand the literal meaning (although I predict that a certain percentage will indeed be confused, thinking that the writer of Hebrews was being awfully harsh). This word is a false friend because your teens will snicker at the word and teens in 1611 would not have. It would have sounded like the neutral designation it was, not like the bad word it has become today.

Is this a big deal? I don't really think it is. But if you've ever used the KJV in urban or youth ministry, as I have done, you can't tell me you didn't secretly wish for this one word to be updated! And though this isn't a big deal, it's just a little bit more static in the audio Bible, a few more little cracks in the sidewalk in front of your house that you don't notice till your friend stumbles over them.

32. Lewd

> But the Jews which believed not, moved with envy, took unto them certain **lewd** fellows of the baser sort, and gathered a company, and set all the city on an uproar, and assaulted the house of Jason, and sought to bring them out to the people. (Acts 17:5)

What do you think "lewd" means in this verse?

____

____

Some KJV phrases really stick in the mind because of their beauty: "The Lord is my shepherd; I shall not want" (Ps. 23:1). Some stick in the mind because they just strike our modern ears as quaint, even funny. Like "superfluity of naughtiness" (James 1:21)—and one other phrase my wife and I sometimes use just because it makes us laugh. My wife will say, "Hey, honey! Could you look to see who's at my flower cart right now?" And I will respond, "Oh, certain lewd fellows of the baser sort." This phrase comes, of course, from Acts 17, when Paul and Silas were in Thessalonica.

And what does it mean? What is a lewd fellow of a baser sort? This potential false friend was sent to me by a true friend who has sent me multiple false friend submissions, most of them (in my humble opinion) successful.[8] It never occurred to me to look this one up. I thought I knew what "lewd" meant. And I do. In my English. But 1611 English was different from ours, if you haven't noticed by now!

Let's go through our steps.

Fishing for a False Friend

The Greek word here is just the bog-standard word for "evil." This is the only place in the KJV New Testament in which this word is translated with the word "lewd." Elsewhere the KJV translators almost always used "evil" or "wicked."

For example, "A **wicked** and adulterous generation seeketh after a sign," Jesus says in Matthew 16:4. The word "wicked" is translating the Greek word we're examining. Or "Resist not **evil**," Jesus says in Matthew 5:39. Here again, the word "evil" is translating the Greek word we're examining.

The most responsible Greek-English lexicon defines the word this way:

> being morally or socially worthless, wicked, evil, bad, base, worthless, vicious, degenerate. (BDAG)

8. This is Caleb Richardson, a true colaborer in the work I've done on the KJV. Thank you, Caleb.

But that's not what the word "lewd" means in our English. Here's NOAD:

> crude and offensive in a sexual way: she began to gyrate to the music and sing a lewd song.

Literally while writing this chapter, I stumbled across this sentence in a Christian review of a book series my daughter was asking me about. It was listing the sexual references in the book, and it said,

> Celaena tells Chaol of a slave girl being raped and killed in prison. The only reason Celaena wasn't sexually assaulted as well is because the guards were afraid of her. Competitors make **lewd** remarks to Celaena.[9]

"Wickedness" and "evil" are a general category. There are many subcategories or kinds of evil. And lewdness names one of them: sexual sin. The NOAD absolutely nails it, in my opinion. This is the way I have heard the word used my entire life. Something that is "lewd" is not just sexually unchaste. It's sexually unchaste in a crude, offensive way.

"Lewdness" is a sexual word. The Greek word being translated in Acts 17:5 is not a sexual word; it's more general. So, why did the KJV translators choose the word "lewd" in this one place to translate this word?

As it often does, the OED has the answer. The OED, of course, records the current sense of the word—a sense that does go back a long time.

> Lascivious, lecherous; (also) involving or relating to sexual activity. Later usually: sexually explicit, offensive, or crudely suggestive; obscene, indecent.

9. "Book Review: Throne of Glass—'Throne of Glass' Series," Plugged In, accessed January 29, 2026, www.pluggedin.com/book-reviews/throne-of-glass/.

The OED comments that this is “the only surviving sense.” The other five senses it lists have all dropped out of the language. No one says “lewd” and means those other things anymore. Let’s see if any of them fit Acts 17:5 and the phrase “lewd fellows of a baser sort.”

First obsolete sense: “of a person: not in holy orders, not clerical; lay” (OED). Well, that doesn’t fit. There’s no way the Jews of Thessalonica collected laypeople of a baser sort. That’s not it. Also, the OED suggests that the “layperson” sense wasn’t in use anymore at the time the KJV was being translated.

Second obsolete sense: “esp. of a person: lacking in education, unlettered” (OED). I suppose that could fit the context, but it doesn’t fit the Greek word. It’s not evil to be unlettered.

Another obsolete sense: “of a person, action, assertion, belief, etc.: lacking in judgement or wisdom; stupid, foolish; unskillful, bungling” (OED). No, that’s not who you call when you want someone run out of town. They’ll mess it all up.

Another obsolete sense: “common, ordinary; of low social status” (OED). That fits the context, but it doesn’t fit the Greek word. It’s not evil to be of low social status.

This is what we have left, the last obsolete sense I’ll mention: “of a person, action, etc.: bad, wicked, unprincipled; good-for-nothing, worthless” (OED).

That’s just got to be it. It fits the context. It fits the Greek word. But it’s an obsolete sense because there’s nothing about sexual crudeness entailed.

Let’s be clear: In 1611, depending on the context, English speakers could use the word “lewd” to mean quite a number of different things. One of the things the word could be used to mean at that time, in that version of English, was just what the context in Acts 17:5 called for.

But today, in our English, the word “lewd” has only one sense—a sexual sense. When we hear “lewd fellows of the baser sort,” we necessarily hear a component of meaning that wasn’t in the Greek and wasn't in the minds of the KJV translators. We misunderstand, and we do so without realizing it.

I know I did, until a friend sent it to me. Within moments, I started writing this entry.

Postscript

There are other uses of "lewdness," in the Old Testament especially, that I didn't discuss. I think many or most of them probably do contain that sexual component of meaning.

Here's one, from the blistering condemnation of Israel in Ezekiel:

> Thou calledst to remembrance the **lewdness** of thy youth, in bruising thy teats by the Egyptians for the paps of thy youth. (23:21)

The NKJV still uses the word "lewdness" here, because that sexual component of meaning absolutely belongs:

> Thus you called to remembrance the **lewdness** of your youth,
> When the Egyptians pressed your bosom
> Because of your youthful breasts.

Hosea 2:10 is similar. Both the KJV and the NKJV have the Lord saying the same thing, with the same word: "Now I will uncover her lewdness in the sight of her lovers." (Well, the KJV uses "discover," which is another false friend—but that's for another day.)

I think there's probably one other place in the KJV where the word "lewd" is a false friend. It's in Acts again.

> When Paul was now about to open his mouth, Gallio said unto the Jews, If it were a matter of wrong or wicked **lewdness**, O ye Jews, reason would that I should bear with you. (Acts 18:14)

The Greek word being translated there also has no note of sexual sin. It's just a word meaning "serious crime." And that's how the NKJV translates it.

If you read the KJV exclusively, and if you don't have the tackle box I offer throughout this book, you will misunderstand—just a little—the intent of the Spirit in two passages in Acts.

But here's the thing: I have all the conceptual tools I'm offering you. I have Bible study tools out the kazoo. And I still missed it. Because it is so, so hard to make yourself remember to doubt your intuitive understanding of words you know. Sometimes people praise me and sometimes people condemn me for using difficult words in my writing. I don't mind saying that I have one of the top five largest vocabularies in my household. I knew the word "lewd." But I only knew what it meant in my English, not someone else's.

33. Peculiar

> For thou art an holy people unto the LORD thy God, and the LORD hath chosen thee to be a **peculiar** people unto himself, above all the nations that are upon the earth. (Deut. 14:2)

What do you think "peculiar" means in this verse?

____

____

TITUS 2:14 IN THE KJV says that Jesus "gave himself for us, that he might redeem us from all iniquity, and purify unto himself a **peculiar** people."

If you go to enough homeschool conventions, you will see these people. The only time they've ever been even close to cool is when Nike came out with a short-lived line of women's athletic culottes in 1986. Their children are all named after the fruit of the Spirit, and they need all the fruit: The baby's name is "Self-Control." Everything they eat is made with home-ground whole wheat. They are birthers and flat-earthers, and their favorite candy is Werther's. They are a peculiar people.

OK, OK, that was a bit more acid than I intended. I think large families can be, and often are, a glory. There's also nothing wrong with Bible names, and my family homeschooled for seven years and is just about to do it again. Fact is, my family is a bit odd, compared to prevailing cultural norms. And I sure hope that in many other ways we seem odd to our non-Christian neighbors. If I'm poking a little fun at people who've been kind to me, perhaps it's because I resemble them so much—and sassy Christian school brats like I was could definitely be due for our own roasting.

Fishing for a False Friend

The point of this way-too-biting humor is to play with the apparent meaning of the KJV wording of Titus 2:14. It sure seems like the Bible is telling us to be weird, right? "Peculiar people" are socially or culturally out of step. Peculiar people make funny faces and awkward motions. Is Paul calling Christian people weird, strange, or odd?

This word "peculiar" gets used in other places in the KJV that also seem peculiar to contemporary English ears. There are two places in Deuteronomy that say effectively the same thing as Titus 2. In fact, it's very interesting that Paul applies to Christians basically the language that God applied to Israel:

> Thou art an holy people unto the Lord thy God, and the Lord hath chosen thee to be a **peculiar** people unto himself, above all the nations that are upon the earth. (Deut. 14:2)

> And the Lord hath avouched thee this day to be his **peculiar** people, as he hath promised thee, and that thou shouldest keep all his commandments. (Deut. 26:18)

There's some important truth here, a very significant biblical theme we'll get back to at the end of the chapter, and language change in English over time is obscuring this theme here for some Bible readers. "Peculiar" is indeed a false friend.

When we turn to the lexicons, we find that the Greek word translated "peculiar" in Titus just means "a special or a distinctive possession of someone," according to Louw-Nida (LN).[10] The Hebrew word translated "peculiar," in the two Deuteronomy passages I just read, means the same thing: someone's "personal property" (HALOT).

So, why does the KJV say "peculiar"? This word today, in our English, means "strange or odd, unusual" (NOAD). But you knew that. When contemporary English speakers use "peculiar" to describe people, they pretty much never mean something positive. You've never in your life heard the word "peculiar" used the way the KJV uses it here—outside of the KJV, of course.

So, is the KJV wrong? Or was it wrong way back in 1611 when it was translated? No. Language has simply changed over time in ways that make "peculiar people" into a subtle misdirection.

How do I know this? Because the OED defines the word "peculiar" this way:

> of property, possessions, etc.: that belongs or relates to one person, place, or group, as distinct from others; that is a person's private property. Usually modified by a possessive.

10. Johannes P. Louw and Eugene Albert Nida, *Greek-English Lexicon of the New Testament: Based on Semantic Domains* (United Bible Societies, 1996), 558.

This is exactly what the relevant Greek and Hebrew words mean, and that means it just has to be the sense of "peculiar" that the KJV translators intended to use here. And yet, the OED marks this sense as obsolete. This sense of the word doesn't exist in our English. However, we still have the word—and our current senses of it sort of work in the phrases referring to "peculiar people"—so they're misleading. Do you see?

The Peculiar Development of English

I now want to address an idea I see pop up frequently enough. It's the idea that a current sense of the word "peculiar" ought to make it super easy to discern what the KJV is saying when it refers to "a peculiar people." The objection goes, "Why can't people just look up KJV words—do a little Bible study?"

Part of this is true: We do have a use of "peculiar" that is very close to what this word meant in 1611 English; it's "belonging exclusively to." NOAD's example sentence for this sense is "The air hung with an antiseptic aroma **peculiar** to hospitals."

"Peculiar to hospitals" means it is proper to hospitals, possessed by hospitals, uniquely associated with hospitals, belonging exclusively to hospitals. Should Christian people stop being lazy and dumb and start realizing that this is what "peculiar" means in the phrase "a peculiar people"?

No. Consider this: Our language, for reasons I don't know, requires that if we use that sense of "peculiar," we put the word "to" after it. The dictionary says this, and you know this. It's a tiny bit like Spanish, where if you want to say, "I saw the building," you say, "Yo ví el edificio," which is, word for word, what we say in English: *I saw the building*. But if you see a person, like Julio, you have to say, "Yo ví a Julio." That is, literally, something like "I saw *at* Julio," or "I saw *to* Julio." Why, Spanish, why do we have to say it like this? I don't know, but we've gotta.

Same with "peculiar." If we want to use it today in the sense most similar to the way it's used in the KJV, we have to use this construction: a noun peculiar *to* another noun.

"A tradition **peculiar to** that family."

"A custom **peculiar to** that culture."

"A style of pottery **peculiar to** that region."

You can't say, "That tradition is peculiar," or "What a peculiar custom!" and expect English speakers to understand that what you *really* mean is not that it's odd but that it belongs to someone in particular.

So, needless to say—except it's not needless, so I'm saying it—"a peculiar people" does not and cannot mean, in our English, "a people peculiar to the Lord." *Even that*, if the KJV said it like that, would probably compute as "a group of people whom the Lord finds peculiar."

Now, I try to be honest and fair in my work, and I think there *are* places in the KJV where pretty good readers will basically ferret out the meaning of the word "peculiar." Indeed, like a ferret, they will go down into the pond of Elizabethan English and come back out with accurate understandings, like fish, dangling helplessly from their mouths.

Listen to this verse:

> If ye will obey my voice indeed, and keep my covenant, then ye shall be a **peculiar** treasure unto me above all people: for all the earth is mine. (Exod. 19:5)

In this context, there are contextual redundancies—other ideas in the sentence—that define what "peculiar" means. Their peculiarity doesn't involve mismatched socks or weird handshakes or those funny glasses that go dark in the sunshine; it involves being a treasure "above all people" in an earth God owns in its entirety. That phrase will help an attentive reader guess at the older meaning of the word "peculiar" and gain a better understanding of this glorious expression of God's love!

A psalmist says something very similar:

> For the LORD hath chosen Jacob unto himself, and Israel for his **peculiar** treasure. (Ps. 135:4)

I think a lot of contemporary readers will get this, after, I suppose, a little experience with the KJV.

But then they will have to admit that the use of "peculiar" in Ecclesiastes 2:8 may or may not be understood by contemporary speakers, considering, again, that the OED says the sense of "peculiar" that the KJV translators intended is no longer present in our English.

> I gathered me also silver and gold, and the **peculiar** treasure of kings and of the provinces: I gat me men singers and women singers, and the delights of the sons of men, as musical instruments, and that of all sorts. (Eccles. 2:8)

To me, that kinda sounds like Solomon tried out weird curios found in the cabinets of other kings. Like he went to an ancient Ripley's Believe It or Not when it was traveling through Damascus.

Now, given the likelihood of people today misunderstanding the various uses of this word in the KJV, would you mind reading the NKJV for a few moments?

> Now therefore, if you will indeed obey My voice and keep My covenant, then you shall be a **special treasure** to Me above all people; for all the earth is Mine. (Exod. 19:5 NKJV)

> For the LORD has chosen Jacob for Himself, Israel for His **special treasure**. (Ps. 135:4 NKJV)

> Who gave Himself for us, that He might redeem us from every lawless deed and purify for Himself **His own special people**, zealous for good works. (Titus 2:14 NKJV)

I've heard many lovers of the KJV, including teenage me, insist that we shouldn't dumb down the Bible for lazy people. But does "special treasure" really sound like dummy English? If this is dummy English, I am a proud and convinced dummy. That, to me, is beautiful language describing an even more beautiful truth. I wouldn't want anyone to miss it.

34. Outlandish

> Did not Solomon king of Israel sin by these things? Yet among many nations was there no king like him, who was beloved of his God, and God made him king over all Israel: nevertheless even him did **outlandish** women cause to sin. (Neh. 13:26)

What do you think "outlandish" means in this verse?

IF YOU HEAR THE WORD "outlandish" today, you might find it used the way it is in these examples from the dictionary:

> Sherri was wearing **outlandish**, brightly colored clothes.

> Jim was known for espousing the most **outlandish** ideas. (NOAD)

The word "outlandish" appears just once in the KJV, in the verse quoted above. It comes at the end of the last narrative, chronologically, in the Old Testament. This is part of an understandable tirade given by Nehemiah against Jewish men who returned from Babylonian exile only to repeat the sins that got their forebears exiled in the first place. Nehemiah literally tore their hair out.

If our understanding of "outlandish" comes from uses like the ones above, where it is used to describe clothes and ideas, what might we think *outlandish women* are?

Fishing for a False Friend

I've seen these outlandish women—they flounce around in crazy clothes, they do weird things. Search the web for "outlandish women" (be careful, of course), and you may find what I did, an article entitled "17 Outlandish Women You Never Knew Existed."[11]

The first outlandish woman in this article is Aneta Florczyk, whom the website said was "four-time winner of the world's strongest woman" and so incredibly strong "that she can hold fully grown men above her head and has become the most successful woman power-lifter in history."[12]

The next was a lady who let her hair grow for eight years, and now it's nineteen feet long. The next was a lady who works very hard to make herself look just like Barbie. Another was a lady whose body was almost completely covered in tattoos. Another was a contortionist who could bend all the way backward and poke her face through her legs from behind. Another has a

11. Minor FYI: I don't recommend you search for this piece; the pictures turned nasty and I closed the tab. But for the purposes of science, I provide here the source: Neeraj, "17 Outlandish Women You Never Knew Existed," Funistan, December 23, 2017, www.funistan.com/viewtopic.php?f=48&t=8851, accessed April 4, 2024.

12. Neeraj, "17 Outlandish Women."

super, super long neck because she's from a tribe in Myanmar that stretches women's necks with golden rings.

Outlandish Women

Now, why would these outlandish women cause Solomon to sin? That's the question. What would make a woman outlandish in ancient Israel? My imagination has been sparked! I'm guessing there was Hazzelelponina of the Negev, who could ride two donkeys at once while standing up, one foot on each donkey's back. There were Abital and Achsah of the tribe of Asher, twins, who could do a dance routine in which their movements were uncannily in sync, like ancient but perfect robots. There was also Mahala, who was incredibly tall and could sing in a strange language no one knew, and rumor had it that her mother was one of the Nephilim.

Outlandish women. *And they got him.* They got Solomon! He loved the circus, I guess, and this made him neglect his kingly duties. They made even wise Solomon sin.

OK, I've got to stop this now. I can't keep pretending I don't know what "outlandish women" in Nehemiah 13 means.

But do you know?

The Hebrew word translated "outlandish" here just means "foreign." Maybe you can already see where this is headed. But let's trace our usual steps anyway.

Next step: Contemporary dictionaries say that "outlandish" now means "looking or sounding bizarre or unfamiliar" (NOAD). That's the sense I've been assuming in this chapter.

But the OED, of course, tells us that in 1611, the word "outlandish" could mean something different:

> of or belonging to a foreign country; foreign, alien; not native or indigenous.

This is quite obviously what the word meant to the KJV translators when they used it in Nehemiah 13. The "outlandish women" who caused Solomon to sin were from outside the land—they were foreigners. He heaped to himself foreign wives in open disobedience to God's laws, and they turned his heart.

Now, the OED does not call this sense obsolete but *archaic*. The same goes for other major dictionaries I use and trust. But I feel certain I have never heard anyone use the word "outlandish" to mean "from a foreign country." I don't think this sense should be labeled archaic; I think it should be labeled obsolete. It's not that I care to make my point in this chapter stronger. I think my point is strong enough. I just love language, and I want to have a fallback in English lexicography if my employment as a Bible nerd ever falls through.

So, I'm going to take that rare bonus step in my false friends process. I'm going to check a linguistic corpus.

I looked through the NOW Corpus to see how the word "outlandish" is used today. I found outlandish claims, outlandish rumors, outlandish antics, outlandish ideas, outlandish approaches. I also found outlandish things, statements, premises, plot points in a TV show, judicial decisions, sensibilities, outfits, allegations, conspiracy theories, hijinks, and hairstyles.

I looked through hundreds of recent uses of this word in written English from all over the world, and I couldn't find a single instance in which "outlandish" was used to mean "from a foreign country."

Archaic Versus Obsolete Usage

Do you understand what this means? We're so used to thinking of a language as something defined by the dictionary (and I find I have to repeat this over and over); it's not. The dictionary is supposed to reflect the way we actually use the language. It's OK if a dictionary, such as the OED, takes a broader view of the language, if it faithfully catalogs older uses. But there is a difference between archaic and obsolete. "Archaic" means you may still possibly encounter a given sense of a word on the edges of the language, or in literature that lots of people still read, say, from the last century. That may be so; I might find that the word "outlandish" was last used to mean "from a foreign country" in 1976.

But people learn their native languages implicitly through hearing them and, later and less so, through reading them. They do not primarily learn their mother tongues from dictionaries or even vocab lists in school. So, if no one uses "outlandish" to mean "from a foreign country," they cannot be expected to understand that sense in the KJV.

Solomon's story is well-known enough, and the etymological parts of "outlandish" are clear enough, that I'll bet a lot of readers are picking up this false friend from context in Nehemiah 13. I'll also bet a lot aren't, even pretty good readers—*especially* good readers—who know the way the word "outlandish" is used today. Only a large study would confirm my prediction here, and I'd love to do such a study with a major polling organization. We shall see.

Syntactical Change

I AM A BIBLICAL PHILOLOGIST; I love words. Grammar doesn't excite me quite so much. Whereas I have worked hard to master the tools that help me understand word meaning in Elizabethan English, contemporary English, Old Testament Hebrew, and New Testament Greek, I'm not so skilled at describing grammatical or syntactical features in all these languages—in other words, those elements of language that have to do with word order. My weakest syntactical link is Elizabethan English. I don't have the labels handy for describing its grammar versus ours. But I can definitely recognize when they differ. In this section, meet two examples where this syntactical change occurs.

35. Drink Ye All of It

> And he took the cup, and gave thanks, and gave it to them, saying, **Drink ye all of it**. (Matt. 26:27)

What do you think "drink ye all of it" means in this verse?

I THINK I CAN CATCH FISH. But some guys can catch sea monsters.

In other words, I have worked very hard to be a word nerd, a connoisseur and purveyor of sesquipedalian delights, but I find grammar and syntax to be much more challenging. The simple fact is that you can look up "sesquipedalian" in the dictionary if you don't know it (it means "characterized by long words; long-winded" [NOAD]); but what if you don't know whether "drink ye all of it" means "All of you, drink it," or "You must drink it all, down to the dregs"? What word would you look up? Which of the words in the KJV phrase do you not already know?

Drink? Ye? All? Of? It?

One of these is indeed a false friend—and the syntax is making it so hard to spot that I'm willing to call the syntax itself a false friend, at least of a sort (it won't go on my official list). In this chapter, I'll try to untangle this knot. In the process, we'll catch a sea monster that has a fish—a very large fish—in its mouth.

Fishing for a False Friend

Let's untangle "drink ye all of it" syntactically. We can do that by first defining the words.

"Drink" is an imperative here, a command—though not a stern one. It's more like an invitation.

"Ye" is a *plural* second person pronoun: The imperative is given to all of the disciples who are present with Jesus at the Last Supper.

"All" is the total amount of whatever the "of" points to—or is it? We'll come back to this in a second.

"Of" is a preposition with a lot of uses. Let's try a few of them here:

"Indicating an association between two entities, typically one of belonging: *the son of a friend* | *the coast of Italy*" (NOAD). So "all of it" would mean that "all" belongs to the "it"? No, that doesn't work.

"Indicating the material or substance constituting something: *the house was built of bricks* | *walls of stone*" (NOAD). So "all of it" would mean that the "all" is made of the "it"? No, that doesn't work.

The only sense that really works, in my judgment, is the one I always assumed was meant: "expressing the relationship between a part and a whole: *the sleeve of his coat* | *in the back of the car* | *the days of the week* | *a series of programs* | *a piece of cake* | *a lot of money*" (NOAD). In this case, then, "all of it," when referring to a drink, means "every part of the drink."

"It" in this context, of course, just has to refer to the cup Jesus has picked up, the one that contained a representation of his blood.

You can count on it: If anyone says, "I want you to drink *all of it*" in my home, it's either Mom or Dad, and the person to whom we are speaking is one particular child who doesn't like taking medicine. This child is, as of this writing, not a fan of certain cough medicines. This child is also sometimes what child psychologists call "a stinker." This child will consume a tiny bit of the medicine and then put it down in disgust. "You have to drink *all of it*," we parents say.

That's what I always assumed Jesus was saying to the disciples at the Last Supper when I was growing up: "Drink it down to the last drop!"

But what if we try to rearrange the words in the sentence to match current English syntax? I think we run right into a problem, because this exercise helps me realize that there are at least two possibilities: (a) "You must drink all of it," and (b) "You must all drink it." In other words, does the "all" go with the "drink" or the "it"? Does it refer to all of the contents of the cup or all of the disciples who are present?

Are the two major options making sense to you? And is language change playing a role here?

Well, yes, or "drink ye all of it" wouldn't be in this book. But what exactly do we look up?

The Greek word for "drink" just means "drink." The Greek word for "all" just means "all." It's the word "of" that we need to look up, at least as a first step. Odd uses of the word "of" in the KJV can't always be looked up in the Hebrew or Greek, because there usually isn't a one-word equivalent in the original languages. "Of" is used to express a grammatical relationship rather than to translate a word. Sorry.

> What if some did not believe? shall their unbelief make the faith **of** God without effect? (Rom. 3:3)

Doesn't that "of" sound a little funny? There is nothing to look up. We have to be able to read Greek to see what's going on (or ask a knowledgeable pastor, or check a commentary, or just look at the NKJV: "Will their unbelief make the faithfulness of God without effect?").

But this one time (with "drink ye all **of** it"), there is a single Greek word that "of" is translating! Here's what it means in a context like this one:

> marker denoting separation, from, out of, away from . . . with the place or thing from which separation takes place. (BDAG)

The word very clearly means "out of." "Drink ye all of it," in Greek, has to mean "All of you drink **from** it," or "All of you drink **out of** it."

But "of" doesn't mean that in our English. I already showed this above. I got out of order. So sue my editor.

Growing up, I misunderstood the words of institution at the Lord's Supper every time they were spoken to me, because I speak contemporary English, not Elizabethan English. I bet that a pastor or two did try to explain to me, but I'm not certain.

I'm telling you right now: I'm not relishing the job I've given myself. Looking through the OED entry on "of" is going to be huge.

Yup. A full sixty senses in sixteen categories. Rest assured, this was the work of a dedicated person who spent months, even years, on "of." And this work, I feel certain, was built on later by other nerds.

I tried, I really tried (while on a late evening flight after an exhausting trip!) to find The One Sense of "Of" to Rule Them All. I think I did find the right one at last, but I was comforted to hear the OED editors observe near the end of their massive entry,

> Many former uses of *of* are difficult to class. Some of these arose from employing it as a literal rendering of French *de* (or of Latin *ab, ex, de*), in phrases where English idiom would have required some other preposition.

You might have noticed that I don't tend to name the Hebrew and Greek words we look up in this book. But I can't avoid it this time: It just so happens that the Greek word we looked up earlier was *ex*, which is very similar to the Latin *ex* the OED editors mentioned.

I *don't* think the KJV translators used "of" in "Drink ye all **of** it" instead of what English idiom required. That's because I think this sense of "of" fits:

> with *borrow, buy, gain, get, have, receive, steal, take, win,* etc. Now replaced by *from,* or archaic and regional.

"All of you drink from it" is what Jesus meant. And I feel certain that is what the KJV translators meant. I believe "of" is a false friend in "Drink ye all of it" that ends up helping create a syntactical false friend in the word "all." ("Of" is a common false friend in the KJV. Hint: Look for places where "from" now seems to work better than "of.")

The Lord's Supper

To this day, almost every time I think of the phrase "Drink ye all of it"—a phrase I heard countless times growing up, of course—I have to force myself to remember what it really means. I have to untangle the syntax and remember that the "of" is acting funny again.

If I'd read Tyndale's translation from a century before the KJV, I would have understood that one phrase better:

> And he toke the cuppe/and thanked/and gave it them/sayinge: drynke of it every one. (Matt. 26:27 Tyndale)

Let me repeat: The KJV translators did nothing wrong here. Let me also repeat: I was not a dummy to misunderstand this phrase, and neither were you (if indeed you misunderstood!).

Pop quiz! What do you make of these two KJV phrases that—like "drink ye all of it"—contain the word "all"? Does your training in false friends help you? Look for answers in the footnotes.

"In many things we offend all." (James 3:2)[1]
"The love of money is the root of all evil." (1 Tim. 6:10)[2]

36. Oppose

> The servant of the Lord must not strive; but be gentle unto all men, apt to teach, patient,
> In meekness instructing **those that oppose themselves**; if God peradventure will give them repentance to the acknowledging of the truth;
> And that they may recover themselves out of the snare of the devil, who are taken captive by him at his will. (2 Tim. 2:24–26)

What do you think "oppose themselves" means in this verse?

THERE ARE SOME WORDS and phrases in the KJV that puzzled me for years. For many of those years, I simply didn't know to look them up. I didn't know *how* to look them up. Once I gained those skills, it took me a while to *think* to look up all of

1. This is a syntactical false friend, because it places "all" in the place in the sentence where modern English speakers would expect a direct object. The phrase sounds like it's saying that we (James and his readers) tend to offend everybody else in many areas of our lives. But that's not what the Greek says, and that's not what the KJV translators meant. The fact that "offend" is also a false friend isn't helping. The NKJV says to a contemporary audience what the KJV translators said to their contemporary audience: "We all stumble in many things." The SKJV has "In many things we all offend."

2. "All" is almost certainly a false friend here—though I struggled to find explicit validation in the OED. It means "all kinds of evil." The verse is not saying that all evil in existence stems from the love of money. The NKJV says, "The love of money is a root of all kinds of evil."

those words and phrases. One that took me a particularly long time was the one in Paul's second letter to Timothy quoted above.

The servant of the Lord is supposed to be gentle, patient, and meek when instructing "those that oppose themselves." What would it mean to oppose yourself? Is Paul talking about dual personalities, ancient Jekyll and Hyde types?

(Before going through my standard process, let's get one small thing out of the way: "That" here means "who." In older Englishes, "that" served as a relative pronoun in some cases, not just a demonstrative one. So, we're talking about "those *who* oppose themselves.")

Fishing for a False Friend

Do you detect the difference I do between the apparent meanings of the KJV and the NKJV?

> And a servant of the Lord must not quarrel but be gentle to all, able to teach, patient, in humility correcting **those who are in opposition**. (2 Tim. 2:25 NKJV)

The KJV speaks of "those who oppose themselves"; the NKJV speaks of "those who are in opposition." Do you see the difference?

It sure used to sound to me like Paul was saying, "Meekly instruct people who oppose their own selves"—that is, "people who stand in opposition to their own interests." *These people who need to be given repentance, who need to be recovered from the snare of the devil, think they are opposing falsehood,* I thought. *But actually, they are just opposing themselves. They are spitting on an image they hate, but they're spitting at the mirror. They are swinging a bat and hitting their own heads.*

It seemed to me like the NKJV is saying something simpler, less rich: "those who are in opposition"—that is, people who oppose you, your opponents. Not people who "oppose themselves." Was my understanding correct? Let's go fishing.

Responsible original-language lexicons tell me that this word means "opponents." This gets a bit complex, but the word is a participle; it's basically a verb used as a noun—what we call a "substantive" in the biz.

To get a bit more complex, this verb is in what's called a "voice"—not active nor passive, the voices we have in English; it's in "middle voice." What that generally means is that, well—let me quote a scholar who has studied this kind of thing carefully:

> Defining the function of the middle voice is not an easy task because it encompasses a large and amorphous group of nuances. But in general, in the middle voice the subject performs or experiences the action expressed by the verb in such a way that emphasizes the subject's participation.[3]

This leaves us with a bit of difficulty that I'll try to clear up as we go on. But for now I'll pose this question: In what way are the "opposers" involved in this action? Is this action essentially reflexive? They are "opposing themselves"? Or is the involvement of the subject something else? (Hint: I think it is, though I'm not going to tell you what I think just yet!)

Here's what we're left with at this point: The Greek word here means "opponents," but there's some uncertainty and complexity attached to it, because it's in the somewhat unexpected and sometimes fuzzy middle voice.

Now, next step: What does "those who oppose themselves" mean in contemporary English? Here we run into another difficulty, because what I really want to look up is the phrase, not the individual words. What does "oppose themselves" mean in our English?

---

3. Daniel B. Wallace, *Greek Grammar Beyond the Basics: An Exegetical Syntax of the New Testament* (Zondervan, 1996), 414.

NOAD doesn't list a "reflexive" use of "oppose." It says that "oppose" means "disapprove of and attempt to prevent, especially by argument" or "actively resist or refuse to comply with (a person or a system)." This would mean that Paul is speaking of "people who actively resist themselves." Right?

Let us turn to the OED, my friends.

A holy hush comes over the crowd of lexicographers as the great OED volumes are brought into view and opened by the twenty beautiful priestesses who have charge of the precious volumes—one priestess per volume. The first priestess is named A–Bazouki, but it's the tenth priestess, Moul–Ovum, whose opportunity it is to bask in the limelight of our attention.

And lookee here: There's a sense of "oppose" that does directly address our question. It's marked as "transitive," which "oppose themselves" is—in other words, there's something that receives the action of the word "oppose." But it's also marked as "reflexive," meaning that the persons doing the opposing are also the object—they are the thing being set in opposition.

Here's the sense:

> transitive (reflexive). To act or set oneself in opposition, antagonism, or resistance to or against.

Is any light dawning? "Those who oppose themselves" are "those who set themselves in opposition"—opposition to Timothy, opposition to sound doctrine, not opposition to *themselves*.

I cannot say that this is an obsolete construction. The OED doesn't mark it as such. It even finds a sample use from 2001: "Grandmother was a very wise woman and never opposed herself to the ideas that we children had."

That's recognizably the same construction. I think it's the addition of the prepositional phrase, however, that helps the phrase make sense to us. Imagine if the KJV had, for example, "those who oppose themselves *to the truth*." Then I don't think the "people opposing their own interests" idea would occur to anyone.

A Preacher Opposes His Sermon

But that idea has occurred to others, not just to me. I went looking for preachers online who had covered this passage, and who had preached it from the KJV, to see how they fared.

I will not name names, because I'm not here to embarrass anyone. But I found that, yes, absolutely, there is at least one KJV preacher who built his whole sermon around what I can only call a now-obvious-to-me misunderstanding of this passage, a misunderstanding I shared until very recently, when a YouTube viewer brought this passage to my attention.[4] This preacher preached a sermon on "Those That Oppose Themselves."

He said,

> You know, sin not only is opposition to God; this verse says that it's in opposition to yourself. . . . The middle voice of this participle . . . has a reflexive idea, which means they're opposing themselves. They are receiving the ill effects of their own opposition. The fact that it's a plural participle means many people do this. As a matter of fact, I believe that all of us who sin, every time we sin, we are actually in opposition to ourself.

This poor brother has misunderstood the middle voice—he took one of its possible meanings over the one that was actually in operation *because of the false friend in the King James*. Misunderstanding the Greek middle is a very forgivable sin, of course. But this is also why we check commentaries and other versions. He let his reading of the English overrule the careful study he did do in the Greek (genuine kudos to him for even checking

4. Thank you, Aaron Neighbour!

the Greek). But I believe he was tripped up by a false friend. His whole sermon ended up being structured around the ways sin hurts us—the ways it is, unbeknownst to the sinner, self-harming. Sin is opposition to oneself, to one's own interests, he kept saying. This is all true, and he had much that was wise and good to say. It just wasn't what Paul was saying to Timothy.

And that is our job in preaching and Bible teaching. If we say true stuff but don't clearly source it in the intent of the biblical authors, we sever the connection between us and our authority. We all do this sometimes, because we're fallen and finite. But one of the major goals of Bible training is to help Bible teachers not do this.

The warmhearted and diligent commentator Matthew Henry (1662–1714) saw this passage the same way I do now; he interpreted the older English correctly in his commentary. Note that he shows his understanding by adding a prepositional phrase ("to the truth"):

> Those who oppose themselves to the truth are to be instructed; for instruction is the scripture-method of dealing with the erroneous.[5]

It's sad to me to see this passage misunderstood due to an archaism, because all pastors and surely all laypeople who go online need to be reminded of this passage all the time. I know I do. Hear it in the NKJV again:

> And a servant of the Lord must not quarrel but be gentle to all, able to teach, patient, in humility correcting those who are in opposition, if God perhaps will grant them repentance, so that they may know the truth. (2 Tim. 2:24–25 NKJV)

5. Matthew Henry, *Matthew Henry's Commentary on the Whole Bible: Complete and Unabridged in One Volume* (Hendrickson, 1994), 2,363.

Now, let me ask: Do all pastors do this in their churches? We can't possibly know. But often enough, the way they treat online opponents doesn't give me hope that they're following this verse in their churches. A great essay I read recently argued that too often adults go to social media to basically acquire the moral right to be angry and then to take revenge. People let you get away with nasty behavior if you successfully demonstrate that you're just responding, not starting the fight.[6]

The New and Old Testaments alike show a different way: Gentle and meek replies are usually what the Bible calls for. There are exceptions, but to cut to the chase, you're probably not in one of them. Most of the time, instruct your opponents with gentleness, maintaining hope—and, I'd add, prayer—that God would grant them the repentance that results in their acknowledgment of the truth.

---

6. Elizabeth Bruenig, "The Limits of Forgiveness," *The Point*, accessed February 25, 2026, https://thepointmag.com/examined-life/the-limits-of-forgiveness/.

Folk Etymologies

FOLK ETYMOLOGIES ARE WHAT HAPPENS when language change makes one word accidentally "rhyme" with another. For example, the word "belfry"—bell tower—comes originally from the Germanic word *bergfrid,* meaning "defensive place of shelter" (the -frid on the end is still visible in the German names "Gottfried" and "Sigfried"). The word *bergfrid* was used to refer to a small shelter used in sieges to protect the occupants from arrows and other airborne weapons. But somehow *bergfrid* became *belfery* and *belfray* when it arrived in English (through Latin and then Old French). It still referred to shelters of protection. But English speakers began to assume that the "bel-" on the front of the word referred to "bells" (that's the folk etymology), and the word gradually came to refer exclusively to shelters for bells—bell towers. It is no use telling English speakers that they are wrong, that *belfry* properly ought to mean "siege tower." If everyone for time out of mind has used *belfry* to mean "bell tower," then it means "bell tower."

Folk etymologies can be funny, but they are a real force in language. This is true because, as Moisés Silva has said, "We must accept the obvious fact that the speakers of a language simply know next to nothing about its development."[1] And that is not a criticism; it would be literally impossible for even a minority of English speakers to learn even a minority of etymologies for our words. Words mean what groups of people use them to mean, not what they once meant in other times and places.

37. Replenish

> The ships of Tarshish did sing of thee in thy market: and thou wast **replenished**, and made very glorious in the midst of the seas. (Ezek. 27:25)

What do you think "replenish" means in this verse?

"REPLENISH" IS ONE of the false friends most often sent to me by YouTube viewers. It's significant because of precisely one of the seven places in which it appears in the KJV:

> And God blessed them, and God said unto them, Be fruitful, and multiply, and **replenish** the earth, and subdue it: and have dominion over the fish of the sea, and over the fowl of the air, and over every living thing that moveth upon the earth. (Gen. 1:28)

Put very simply, this seems to be saying that the earth used to be full of various things and God's going to refill it. Indeed, several

1. Moisés Silva, *Biblical Words and Their Meaning*, rev. ed. (Zondervan Academic, 2010), 38.

influential figures have used this apparent meaning to support a "gap theory" that finds time—perhaps immense time—in a "gap" between Genesis 1:1 and 1:2. Clarence Larkin, famous progenitor of large dispensationalist charts, writes:

> In the words "replenish the earth" we have unmistakable evidence that the earth had been peopled before it was thrown into a chaotic condition, and that its inhabitants in some way had been destroyed. It does not follow, however, that those inhabitants were human beings like ourselves. No human remains have been found antedating the creation of man.[2]

A well-respected teacher of the recent past, J. Vernon McGee, said something similar:

> And now, [God] says to [Adam], "Replenish." And, that's an interesting word. That would seem to indicate that this earth had been habited before by other creatures. And God says, "Replenish the earth" because whatever the other creatures were, they'd been destroyed. They'd disappeared.[3]

Yet another popular Bible teacher on YouTube—one with eight hundred thousand subscribers as of this writing—has also argued that "replenish" probably means "refill."[4] He acknowledges what we're about to find out (spoiler alert), that "old dictionaries" say that "replenish" meant "fill" in 1611. But he argues that the next use of "replenish" in the KJV, Genesis 9:1, suggests that the word means "refill" in its first mention:

---

2. Clarence Larkin, *Dispensational Truth: Or God's Plan and Purpose in the Ages*, rev. ed. (Clarence Larkin Estate, 1920), 34.

3. J. Vernon McGee, "Genesis 1:26–2:3," *Thru the Bible*, April 22, 2021, www.oneplace.com/ministries/thru-the-bible-with-j-vernon-mcgee/listen/genesis-12623–883398.html. I owe this citation to YouTube viewer Jeff Paul.

4. "The Gap Theory," YouTube video, 1:03:03, uploaded by Robert Breaker, February 5, 2016, https://youtu.be/E4bZ5bVt660. He seemed to favor his read of "replenish" meaning "refill," though he wasn't dogmatic.

> And God blessed Noah and his sons, and said unto them, Be fruitful, and multiply, and **replenish** the earth. (Gen. 9:1)

Noah was, of course, "refilling" an earth that had been wiped clean. So, does "replenish" in Genesis 1:28 mean "refill" or just "fill"?

Fishing for a False Friend

Well, one might notice not only that it's odd for God to be refilling the earth in the middle of creating it in the first place (a contextual conflict) but also that very few other significant English translations use the word "replenish." One is the light KJV revision called the SKJV. Even the pre-KJV Geneva Bible uses the word "fil." The NKJV also uses the word "fill," not the word "replenish."

As perceptive readers might be expecting, the Hebrew word translated "replenish" in the KJV does not mean "*re*fill." It just means "fill" (HALOT).

For the third step, I hardly need to mention that "replenish" in today's English means to "fill (something) up again," to "restore (a stock or supply) to a former level or condition" (NOAD). Waitstaff replenish water in empty glasses; bakers buy flour to replenish their depleted bins; people who like lard replenish the larder.

When we turn to the OED, we find that it offers a sense for this word, of course, that fits the Hebrew and the context:

> to stock or supply (a place) abundantly with people or animals. . . . Now rare. In later use chiefly with allusion to Genesis 1:28, "And God said unto them, Be fruitful, and multiply, and replenish the earth" (King James Bible).

There is no indication that the "re-" on "replenish" meant "again" to the KJV translators. Instead, "re-" on this word had its other sense as an intensifier, something like "thoroughly" or "completely."

In contemporary English we have words like "resplendent," which means thoroughly shining—not "shining again." Likewise, to "receive" something is not to "ceive" it again; to "recommend" something is not to "commend" it again; to "reduce" something is not to "duce" it again. In words like "recreation" or "religion," the "re-" prefix simply no longer means anything. To "request" or "require" something doesn't mean that you "quested" or "quired" it once before. One nerdy website comments that "in many of the older borrowings from French and Latin the precise sense of re- is forgotten, lost in secondary senses, or weakened beyond recognition."[5]

So, to "replenish" in 1611 was to thoroughly fill (in Latin, the *plen-* root means "fill"), not to "refill." Here's a very old sentence the OED editors found in which "replenished" clearly can't mean *re*filled:

> With pitefull scriches she repleneshyd the hole mancion.

In modern spelling: "With pitiful screeches she replenished the whole mansion." Clearly, the mansion (or rather the room; see word 29) was not previously empty of screams and needed to be refilled. No, this just meant that she *filled* the room with screams.

So, what happened to "replenish"? Here's my educated guess: I think that people somehow started to mistake the "re-" for its more common meaning of "again" or "back" or "over again." In other words, a sort of silent folk etymology developed in which English speakers as a group forgot that "re-" doesn't always mean

5. See "Origin and History of *Re-*," Etymonline, accessed January 26, 2026, www.etymonline.com/word/re-. It is from this site that I draw most of the examples given in this paragraph.

"again." They started reinvesting the "re-" in "replenish" with its much older meaning.

Nobody noticed that English was fine with "receive" and "request" and "require" and "recreation."

And all of a resudden, we have a false friend.

The Usefulness of the Original Languages

The YouTuber mentioned earlier noticed perceptively that "refill" makes a good deal of sense in Genesis 9:1 when Noah is told to "replenish the earth." The earth has been emptied; it needs to be refilled. Therefore "replenish" means "refill" in Genesis 1:28. Right?

But this YouTuber has omitted another possibility: that "replenish" means "fill"—and not "*re*fill"—in *both* Genesis 1:28 and Genesis 9:1. That's what the Hebrew says, and that's what the OED reveals.

Knowledge of Hebrew and Greek is not required for good theology, good Bible reading, or a life of faith, hope, and love—and it sure doesn't seem to have solved all of the theological disputes in the Christian church. Apparently, knowledge of the original biblical languages doesn't automatically deliver good Bible interpretation.

Here's where I find Hebrew and Greek to be most concretely and demonstrably useful: not in telling us what the Bible means but in telling us what it doesn't mean. The original languages show that some interpretations—often interpretations based solely on English (or French, or Russian, or Urdu) translations—are impossible. The Hebrew shows here that "replenish" in the KJV in Genesis 1:28 doesn't and can't mean "refill."

Those who find a gap between Genesis 1:1 and 1:2 may be right, of course (though I don't think they are). But those who find that gap because of the word "replenish" in Genesis 1:28 and 9:1 in the KJV are simply and clearly wrong.

38. Help Meet

> And the LORD God said, It is not good that the man should be alone; I will make him an help meet for him. (Gen. 2:18)

What do you think "help meet" means in this verse?

LEXICOGRAPHERS ARE USUALLY harmless drudges, silent and impassive figures who prefer to remain in dark corners amassing obscure citations. But every once in a while, emotion breaks through their cold, taciturn exteriors. On rare occasions, those hidden people who give us The Dictionary must let the whole world know what they truly feel inside. But I'm afraid lexicographers have only one feeling in their hearts: acrid disgust for all the plebes out there who are killing English dead.

Observe the OED entry for the word "helpmeet":

> a compound absurdly formed by taking the two words help meet in Genesis ii. 18, 20 ('an help meet for him', i.e., a help (help n. 2) suitable for him) as one word.

Feeling broke through the descriptive logic at one point there, like magma through a crack in the earth, in that word "absurdly." I'm sure the poor lexicographer who wrote this definition was emotionally exhausted after such an eruption and had to stay in bed for a fortnight.[6]

6. And that's too bad, because "fortnight" is a lexicographer's only fun. They all get together once every two weeks and build forts to see who can isolate themselves most effectively from social contact with other humans.

Fishing for a False Friend

What we've got here is a folk etymology that has created a false friend, and I've let the OED editors be the ones to alert us to it this time.

Way back in the days of the first real English Bible, 1382, Wycliffe used this phrase in Genesis 2:18: "an helper like him." But really, he wasn't setting a course for future translators so much as following one begun by the Latin Vulgate (from which he translated). The Hebrew here is a bit opaque; it says, if I may be painfully literal for a moment,

> Then the Lord God said, "It is not good that the man should be alone; I will make him **a help as before him**." (Gen. 2:18 PLV)[7]

The word "help" does appear elsewhere in the Bible, of course. It means assistance, service, or benefit. It's a common word. It even shows up within names like "Azariah" and its shortened form, "Ezra," meaning "the Lord has helped."[8]

But that phrase "as before him" occurs in only one other place and is therefore obscure. That place happens to be in the very same passage, just two verses later. This is pretty much all we have to go on for what "as before him" means:

> The man gave names to all livestock and to the birds of the heavens and to every beast of the field. But for Adam there was not found **a helper as before him**. (v. 20 PLV)

Whatever it means that Eve was a helper "as before" Adam, it has to mean that she was able to help him in ways that animals couldn't. Interpreters through the centuries have read this

7. Every once in a while, I must provide a "painfully literal" translation of a given Hebrew or Greek phrase in order to make a point. I call this the PLV.

8. It's also in the New Testament name "Lazarus," a Greek transliteration of the Hebrew for "helped by God."

to mean that Eve was a helper "fit for" him or "corresponding to him." Coverdale's early translation, 1535, gave "an helper, to beare him company." The KJV gives "an help meet for him," but it puts in the margin, "Hebr. 'as before him'" to acknowledge that the phrase is obscure. Some newer translations have gone with "helper comparable to him" (NKJV) or "helper suitable for him" (SKJV). I think all those choices are fine. They're all shooting at the same target from different angles. But, undoubtedly, the KJV's "help meet for him" has—because of language change—ended up causing some confusion.

I don't think we need to look up "help" or "helper." "Meet" is causing the trouble here. Contemporary dictionaries like the *New Oxford American Dictionary* say that "meet" once meant "suitable; fit; proper"—and that fits the Hebrew and the context quite well. But NOAD goes on to say that this word is now archaic.

I don't actually think that anyone will read this as saying that Eve is M-E-A-T for Adam, like he was going to boil her and eat her. I also don't think anyone but the most lackadaisical reader will think it means he's "meeting" her for the first time. But I do think that lots of KJV readers are making at least a little mistake when they read this phrase, "an help meet."

The OED shows that people misunderstood this word "meet" very early on, and that their misunderstanding created a new English word that has made it even more likely that contemporary readers will misunderstand Genesis 2:18. That word is "helpmeet." Look how the OED explains this:

> Already in the 17th century the Scripture phrase is found with the two words improperly hyphenated; which led the way to the use help-meet, [or] helpmeet without "for him."

Did you catch that? This lexicographer is pointing out that "a help meet" doesn't make any sense without the full phrase: "a help meet for him." It would be like calling her "a help suitable." A help suitable . . . for *what* or *whom*?

The OED goes on:

> [Helpmeet's] recognition as a [separate] "word" is chiefly of the 19th century: it is unknown to [Samuel] Johnson, [the legendary and first real English lexicographer, and to other lexicographers such as] Todd, Richardson, and . . . Webster.

Then the OED gives a fantastic parallel: "sweetheart." You can imagine how that word began. First came the phrase "She is my sweet heart." But soon the two words were put together, and "sweetheart" became a word and underwent what's called a "backshift" to prove it. The emphasis went from *heart* back to *sweet*. This happens frequently in language: Boy *Scouts* becomes *Boy* Scouts. Web *site* becomes *web*site. That's what happened with help meet. "Help *meet* for him" became "*help*meet for him."

Then this word took a further step. "Helpmeet" doesn't make sense to people etymologically. As language changed, people stopped knowing what "meet" meant. So, at some point they started assigning it what we call a "folk etymology." They imagined a history for the word by pronouncing and then spelling the word as "helpmate." That makes sense. *She's a mate. She's a help. She's a helpmate.* NOAD tells me that this word came into use in the early 1700s.

A misunderstanding of this phrase became a word. That word became another word. And that word's existence now trips people up when they read the KJV in Genesis 2.

From "Help Meet" to "Help Mate"

You can hear people trip up when they read the "help meet" verse. I'm not going to pick on anyone by giving actual quotes from real sermons, but I surely and truly could. The very first sermon on this passage I found on SermonAudio.com was preached by a famous traveling preacher whom I know personally, a godly and skillful man whom I respect and like. Nonetheless, he suggested to me by the way he pronounced this phrase that he didn't understand it. It's subtle. If you know what the phrase means, you'll read it like this, without the pronunciation backshift: "The Lord God said, It is not good that the man should be alone; I will make him an help *meet* for him."

But I clearly heard this preacher say, as I regularly hear other KJV readers say, "I will make him an *help*meet for him," as if the two words were one, with the stress on the first syllable of that word-that-isn't-a-word. Go listen for yourself to online sermons on this passage. I'm prepared to guarantee that you will easily find preachers who, when they read this verse from the KJV, will demonstrate that in their minds "help meet" is effectively one word. I bet you'll even hear a few pronounce it "helpmate."

The dominant sense of a word is the one that is uppermost in our minds, and if it works in context, we don't go seeking another one. "Helpmate" works—of course it does. It was born in the KJV in this very passage.

Paul and Genesis

Does this really matter? Should we care if people aren't pronouncing things right in the KJV? Not if we're just being persnickety elitists spilling our acrid linguistic disgust everywhere like a lexicographer on their worst day. But we're not doing that. I'm not. That little word "meet" means something. And it doesn't mean "mate." It means "fitting" or "suited." As one interpreter said in Reformation times, when celibacy was held up as an ideal, the phrase means that "woman is given as a companion and an associate to the man, to assist him to live well."[9]

Our culture is obsessed with male and female roles. Loud parts of Western culture insist that there shouldn't be any differences. Tasks in marriage and in society should be apportioned according to a gender-blind meritocracy—or maybe by dice rolling? If the question is about gender *equality*, this passage most certainly doesn't deny that equality. As I said, and as many have pointed out, God is called our "helper" in Scripture and that doesn't make him inferior to those he helps. Calling the wife the "helper" of her husband does not imply inequality. Both are made in the image of God. Neither does the passage deny that the husband should also help the wife. Ephesians and 1 Peter speak of things the husband can do to love and serve his wife.

But I have to end this chapter with some countercultural biblical teaching: The original pattern of marriage, the pattern to which Jesus himself appeals in Matthew 19, makes the wife a help fit for her husband in a way that isn't reversible. I don't know all that this means; it is beautifully suggestive rather than oppressively detailed. But I do know we can't flinch, as Western culture does, when other parts of the Bible take this passage and explain it to mean that the woman was "created . . . for the man" (1 Cor. 11:9). Paul says that "the woman is the glory of the man" (v. 7), and not vice versa. And he reasons this way: "Neither was the man created for the woman; but the woman for the man" (v. 9). Paul draws contemporary conclusions from the ancient biblical words about Adam and Eve; he treats these words not as informative but as normative.

9. John Calvin, *Commentary on the First Book of Moses*, vol. 1 (Logos Bible Software, 2010), 129.

Genesis is not saying, and Paul is not saying, that all women were made for all men, or all women must submit to all men. This is a common smear against biblical teaching. But this passage does tell me that my wife was made for me; she is a helper befitting me. It is a travesty if I treat her as an imposition and not a blessing, if I fail to love her self-sacrificially—because when I love her, Paul says, I am loving myself (Eph. 5:28). Every good I do for her only helps me. She is my glory. She bears my very name. My wedding ring says on the inside, in Greek from the New Testament, "Nourish and cherish your wife."

In such a foundational passage as Genesis 2:18–20, every word in the description of the marriage relationship is precious. I don't want any of them being misunderstood because of the vagaries of language change over the last four centuries.

Conclusion

Brethren, What Shall We Do?

I HAD A BRIEF PHASE in early high school in which I fished a lot. I lived in a large DC suburb that was built around a man-made lake. My home was on one of the less expensive outer rings, but I could ride my bike past the wealthy houses on the water and fish and swim to my heart's content.

I don't recall the specific rules, but I believe that if certain fish didn't weigh enough, you were supposed to throw them back into the water. I did this many times. To be honest, I think I did it every time. . . . I'm not sure I ever caught a fish that weighed enough to be worth keeping. They all went back into the drink.

So, how do we weigh the benefits of using the King James Version against the difficulties presented by dozens of KJV words we don't know we don't know? In other words, what are you supposed to make of this book?

I see several options that equally sincere, doctrinally sound Christians can take, and several major ways in which we can weigh the current value of the good things we have in the King James Version against the difficulty of people having to learn words they don't realize they're misunderstanding.

But I'm not going to tell you what those options are, because this is where Christians really start to disagree—and even get angry and upset. And I am determined that this book should provide a point of unity and not of further division. I am dead set as a doornail: I want people who by conviction read only the KJV to be able to read this book with joy and not with grief. Discovering the meaning of Bible passages you've previously misunderstood is a joy; let's focus on that.

I'll tell you only two things.

Firstly, I certainly haven't thrown the KJV back into Lake Montclair. As of this writing, I'm reading through the KJV yet again, and I just finished one of my very favorite portions of it, the Psalms.

Lastly, what you have learned and heard and seen in this book, go and teach others also. Preachers, especially: Teach your people these false friends, and (this, I think, is essential) teach them how to fish. Word lists in a little booklet or on a website don't help when people don't realize they're misunderstanding. They need to be taught how to fish, or they won't do it.

I just want people to understand their Bibles.

Acknowledgments

I'M AFRAID THAT I would miss some examples or get some wrong if I named precisely which false friends were given to me by which true friends. I'd like simply to thank the following people who submitted false friends to me that were included in this book or in my "150 False Friends in the KJV" YouTube series: Dustin Burlet, Freddy Castaneda, Brian Collins, Eric Couture, Josiah Dennis, Caleb Friske, Marcus Gale, Scott Sanjay Hayes, Joseph Hons, M. A. Moreno, Rob Pettifer, Isaiah Reid, Caleb Richardson, Caleb Schaaf, Omar Schrock, Sam Sinclair, Layton Talbert, David Todd, and Kendra Vanstone.

Also, Marcus Moreno, Dustin Burlet, Brian Collins, Eric Couture, Caleb Richardson, David Lowry, Sam Sinclair, Josiah Dennis, and Omar Schrock all read this manuscript and provided valuable feedback. Any errors left in this book are not the fault of these good brethren, but they're clearly not my fault either.

Appendix 1828

Dictionaries

I USE A KEY SET OF DICTIONARIES and other lexicographical (dictionary-related) tools in this book. Here they are, ranked for their importance in each category, followed by a note about why I don't use certain other resources. For time's sake, I give some very frank assessments here. If I were speaking to the editors of these works, I'd coat my words with more sugar. But everything I say here is the fruit of years of careful, extensive, obsessive work.

Contemporary English Dictionaries

✔ **NOAD**: The *New Oxford American Dictionary* has become my most trusted resource for describing contemporary American English. I have compared it repeatedly to the other two contemporary dictionaries on this list, both of which have a valuable place on my (digital) shelf. What I have found is that NOAD does the best job of describing English as it truly, empirically *is*, not as it once was—or was in 1980 or 1930. NOAD also comes installed automatically on every Mac, which makes it handy for some readers. The *Collins English Dictionary* (see below) has the same aim as NOAD, but (a) it is a little less accessible to me than NOAD, and (b) the name "Oxford" carries some weight when I'm teaching others.

✔ **MW**: *Merriam-Webster Unabridged* does not set out to describe English merely as it is; it self-consciously includes descriptions of English as it once was. This is valuable if you know what you're looking at, but I believe it can be confusing for readers who don't keep language change in mind. Also, the entries for the free online version of this dictionary do not always include the full list of senses in the unabridged version. I have sometimes paid for a subscription to the full dictionary online, and this is a good thing to do if you simply cannot afford the OED. Sometimes (such as on the words "hell," "communicate," and "constantly") I have found that MW includes the particular obsolete sense I need in order to understand the KJV. But it's hit-or-miss. I find that a combination of NOAD for contemporary English and the OED for KJV English meets almost all my needs for looking up English words.

✔ **AHD**: The great value of the *American Heritage Dictionary* (which is now defunct, though the website is still operative) was its "usage panel," a set of experts—including an excellent linguist whom I'm honored to call a personal acquaintance, John McWhorter—who weighed in on difficult bits of English usage. This will occasionally be useful for study of the English of the KJV, but the AHD has naturally fallen behind the current state of English usage as its fifth (and last?) edition was put out in 2018. The AHD also tends to preserve some older senses of words that I feel are no longer in use, just like (though not as often as) MW. This also means that it is less useful as an OED substitute. In my experience, the AHD cannot be relied on to give now-obsolete senses of KJV words.

✔ **Collins**: The *Collins English Dictionary* is especially focused on staying current, but that doesn't mean it's full of slang. It relies, instead, on a 4.5-billion-word "corpus," or body of written English, that enables its lexicographers to scientifically describe the way English is written today by real people. Every dictionary uses some kind of corpus, even if an informal one, but this feature of Collins makes it well suited for step 3 in this book. I use NOAD instead for mostly practical reasons.

✘ **Dictionary.com**: I do not use this site, because I find it lacks some tools I need and because I can't stand the garish ads. But it does appear to be put together by responsible people, and it is possibly better than what's provided for free at Merriam-Webster (though probably not better than the paid MW service).

Contemporary English Corpuses

✔ **The NOW Corpus**: News on the Web (NOW) is a linguistic corpus—a collection of over fifteen billion words of English articles—that enables the general public to do what linguists and lexicographers do (see www.english-corpora.org/now/). With a corpus, you can examine the way English writers—writers who don't know they're being observed by linguistic analysts—use the English language in written form. What really defines contemporary English is not any dictionary; dictionaries *observe* contemporary English. And what they observe is found in corpuses like NOW. See chapter 4, "miserable," for an example of how this corpus might be used to study KJV English.

✘ **COHA**: The Corpus of Historical American English (COHA) is very useful for people who are studying the period of English that it covers (see www.english-corpora.org//coha/). Which is not us. This corpus stands between the English of the Elizabethans and the English of you and me. It is of comparatively little value for study of the KJV.

Historical English Dictionaries

✔ **OED**: The *Oxford English Dictionary* (OED) is the only dictionary of historical English we need for the purposes of this book. It is a landmark achievement. It describes English at all phases of its existence, and it provides millions of valuable citations—examples of the way a given word was used, along with the date and author and other important information. There simply is no alternative to the full, twenty-volume OED if you wish to do serious work on KJV words. The two-volume edition, produced in microprint and packaged with its own magnifying glass, can be found for a reasonable price; I personally have electronic access through my local library system.

✘ **LEME**: I do not use the Lexicons of Early Modern English (LEME) site in this book; I believe the OED is far more valuable than this collection of early dictionaries. But as the LEME site says, "Any contemporary's testimony about the meaning of his own words has an undeniable authority."[1] The site's own introduction, however, acknowledges that the "lexical insights" of those who put together these early dictionaries "may at times seem misguided to us." I agree. Nonetheless, the LEME is the (very) poor man's OED.

✘ **MED**: I do not use the *Middle English Dictionary* (MED) that is available freely online, provided by the University of

1. "Introduction," Lexicons of Early Modern English, accessed January 26, 2026, https://leme.library.utoronto.ca/help/intro.

Michigan.[2] For one thing, my wife is from Ohio. For another, the MED covers English only from 1100 to 1500, making it mostly irrelevant to the study of KJV English.

✘ **Webster's 1828**: If all you have is one dictionary to read the KJV, Webster's 1828 is probably better than a contemporary dictionary, because it was created closer in time to the release of the KJV.[3] But Webster's work records the state of English about halfway between 1611 and now, which will cause some confusion. Webster himself felt that English had changed enough by his day that the KJV needed an update. In the Webster Bible of 1835, America's most legendary lexicographer, Noah Webster, actually names the concept of false friends (he calls them "false ideas") and gives examples.

Greek-English Dictionaries

✔ **BDAG**: *A Greek-English Lexicon of the New Testament and Other Early Christian Literature*, by Walter Bauer, Frederick W. Danker, William Arndt, and F. W. Gingrich (BDAG), is the key, standard Greek-English lexicon. Everyone who has any Greek training should own it. I have used it nonstop for over two decades. Those who cannot read Greek should skip this resource unless they get it electronically and put some time into learning how to use it. A major strength of BDAG is that it provides definitions and not just glosses (translation equivalents). It also divides words into senses, each of which gets a prose definition.

2. See Middle English Dictionary, University of Michigan, accessed January 26, 2026, https://quod.lib.umich.edu/m/middle-english-dictionary/dictionary.

3. An even better choice may be Samuel Johnson's 1755 dictionary, which is even closer to 1611 and is now available at JohnsonsDictionaryOnline.com. But Webster's 1828 is widely available (and used) in print, so I mention it here.

✔ **LN**: Louw-Nida (LN) is an excellent Greek-English dictionary produced by Johannes P. Louw and Eugene Albert Nida; its complete title is *Greek-English Lexicon of the New Testament: Based on Semantic Domains* (United Bible Societies, 1996). Note that the website Marble.Bible makes (a version of) LN available for free. Though I use BDAG most commonly in this book, Louw-Nida is an excellent more or less free alternative. It is also noticeably more accessible than BDAG.

✔ **NIDNTTE**: Moisés Silva, editor of the latest edition of the *New International Dictionary of New Testament Theology and Exegesis* (NIDNTTE) (Zondervan Academic, 2014), is my favorite Christian writer on the use of the biblical languages. I confess, however, that I have not used his dictionary because of cost, time, and my particular needs. I trust Silva so much, however, that I wish to recommend this resource.

✘ **TDNT**: The *Theological Dictionary of the New Testament* (TDNT), edited by Gerhard Kittel and Gerhard Friedrich and translated by Geoffrey W. Bromiley (repr. Eerdmans, 1990), is something of a status symbol on preachers' shelves. But I wonder how often it gets used. Moisés Silva (and James Barr before him) have given excellent critiques of the whole-kitchen-sink approach of TDNT. It invites readers to find too much meaning in New Testament words. I cannot recommend it except to specialists who know how to weed through it.

✘ **GE**: GE is the official abbreviation for *The Brill Dictionary of Ancient Greek*, by Franco Montanari, Madeleine Goh, and Chad Schroeder (Brill, 2015). This work (sometimes also called Brill-DAG) is based, in turn, on the work of Liddell-Scott-Jones from the nineteenth century. I find that its definitions are too short to be of reliable use for the purposes of this book. If it's all you have, however, it is a responsible resource.

✗ **Thayer's** and **Strong's**: I do not use Joseph A. Thayer's nineteenth-century *A Greek-English Lexicon of the New Testament*, nor do I use any of the iterations of James H. Strong's *Greek and Hebrew Dictionary of the Bible*. These are outdated and, especially in the case of Strong's, regularly misleading.[4] Not a few times have I seen people mistake Strong's list of KJV glosses as a set of definitions. If in God's providence you must use a free resource, Thayer's is definitely better than nothing (you can find it online at the Blue Letter Bible), and it includes citations—but the lexicons at Marble.Bible are definitely preferable to Thayer's.

✗ **Vine's**: I may sound like a killjoy, but I cannot recommend *Vine's Complete Expository Dictionary of Old and New Testament Words*, by W. E. Vine, originally published in 1940. It is guilty too often of reading theology into words, of piling too much theology onto words that don't bear it. I could go on in great detail; instead, I'll give you a fat footnote.[5]

4. See my article "How to Use Strong's Concordance and What to Use Instead," *Word by Word* (blog), March 30, 2023, https://logos.com/grow/min-strongs-concordance-and-what-to-use-instead. This article has also been shot as a video on my channel. See "How to Use Strong's Concordance and What to Use Instead," YouTube video, 21:03, uploaded by Ward on Words, August 3, 2023, https://youtu.be/XmLPFOZzSRQ.

5. Moisés Silva's *Biblical Words and Their Meaning* has had a profound impact on my Bible reading and on the course of my life. Along with James Barr's *The Semantics of Biblical Language* and D. A. Carson's *Exegetical Fallacies*, Silva taught me to be wary of "theological lexicography," or reading all terms in the Bible as technical and chock-full of theological meaning. This initially sounds like exactly what you ought to do: These are God's words, after all. But Silva (along with Barr and Carson and others) shows that what actually happens when interpreters view the Hebrew and (especially the KJV) Greek this way is that they inadvertently smuggle theology into their Bible interpretation. This, too, may seem like not such a bad thing. And frequently, in practice, it isn't. The theology that evangelical interpreters smuggle into given passages is evangelical theology, so they don't form wrong theological conclusions. But they still end up smothering the actual message of given texts and

✘ **Mounce's**: I regret having to give a negative assessment of *Mounce's Complete Expository Dictionary of Old and New Testament Words* (Zondervan Academic, 2006), because I know Bill Mounce a little bit personally, and I think highly of him. But he didn't write this dictionary; his students did. I reviewed it many years ago, and I was glad to see in his preface some of the wisdom I tried to provide in my fat footnote about Vine's. But when I turned to the entries in Mounce, I was disappointed to find that some of the students had fallen too far from the tree; they had written too much like Vine's—the very resource they were supposed to be replacing.

Hebrew-English Dictionaries

✔ **HALOT**: *The Hebrew and Aramaic Lexicon of the Old Testament* (Brill, 1994–2000), by Ludwig Koehler, Walter Baumgartner, and Johann Jakob Stamm, is the preeminent Hebrew-English dictionary. It is complicated, difficult, and incredibly valuable. It is definitely less accessible to the layperson than BDAG. Do not purchase this expensive resource unless you have studied biblical Hebrew. If you have studied it, purchase this expensive resource right away. It is what I typically appeal to in this book.[6]

✔ **CHALOT**: *A Concise Hebrew and Aramaic Lexicon of the Old Testament* (Brill, 2000), edited by William L. Holladay, is, naturally, more accessible than HALOT. But not much. There

imposing on them something God said elsewhere. This severs the connection between the preacher or Bible teacher and their only real authority. If this whets your appetite, take some Greek and read Silva. His book *God, Language and Scripture* (Zondervan Academic, 1991) is also fantastic.

6. For this fact I am somewhat apologetic. When it comes to fishing for false friends, the most difficult deep-sea fishing task involves looking up Hebrew words, and I do not model the use of accessible tools in this book. But what I do with the difficult tool can almost always be done with a more accessible one, especially Marble.Bible. The model will still work. Don't throw out the fish with the seawater.

is simply no avoiding the complexity and difficulty of using a dictionary that describes an ancient language using an unfamiliar script.

✔ **DCH** and **CDCH**: David J. A. Clines's *Dictionary of Classical Hebrew* (Sheffield Academic Press; Sheffield Phoenix Press, 1993–2011) and its little brother *The Concise Dictionary of Classical Hebrew* (Sheffield Phoenix Press, 2009) are, in my judgment, a bit more accessible than HALOT/CHALOT. But they are still difficult.

✔ **BDB**: *The Brown-Driver-Briggs Hebrew and English Lexicon* (Clarendon Press, 1977), by Francis Brown, S. R. Driver, and Charles A. Briggs, is arguably more accessible than any of the options above, and it's available for free online in multiple places. It is old, but it is responsible.

✔ **Marble.Bible**: The best free Hebrew-English lexicon is the *Semantic Dictionary of Biblical Hebrew* at Marble.Bible, put together by a personal acquaintance, Reinier de Blois. A Dutch Christian scholar of Hebrew, de Blois is a remarkable man who has extensive Bible translation experience and linguistics training.

✔ **NIDOTTE**: Like my usage of its New Testament counterpart, my usage of the *New International Dictionary of Old Testament Theology and Exegesis*, edited by Willem A. VanGemeren (Zondervan, 1996), has been limited. I cannot speak with detailed knowledge of its contents. But the few times I've picked it up it seemed responsible, and several trusted friends love it.

✔ **TWOT**: I have used the *Theological Wordbook of the Old Testament*, edited by R. Laird Harris, Gleason L. Archer, and Bruce K. Waltke (Moody, 1980), on many occasions, and it nearly always gives me what I came for: an evangelical explanation of a word rather than a dry, academic recital of lexicographic information. I use TWOT as a shortcut when I don't have time to dig into commentary literature on a word. All the same, readers need to know that some commentary—some interpretation—is getting mixed in.

✘ **Strong's**: Strong's for Hebrew, most commonly from some edition of *The Exhaustive Concordance of the Bible,* originally published in 1890, is just as unreliable as Strong's for Greek. I am not casting aspersions on a man who did great good for the church with his justly famous KJV concordance. I am saying that I have seen Strong's dictionary misunderstood and misused so often that I cannot recommend his work.

Appendix 1982

The Three English Bible Translations Used in This Book

MANY CHRISTIANS TODAY are nervous about using more than one Bible translation. The KJV translators were not. Their work was "Translated out of the Original Tongues, and with the Former Translations Diligently Compared and Revised," or so says their title page, and was itself a revision of the 1568 Bishops' Bible. They checked multiple English and foreign language translations in the course of the work.

In this book I use only English translations that are based on the Masoretic Hebrew Text for the Old Testament and the Textus Receptus (TR) for the New Testament. There are numerous historical and contemporary translations of these texts into English. The main three are the following (the first is rather obvious).

✔ **King James Version (KJV)**: The KJV is obviously an important tool for studying the KJV. There are multiple editions of the KJV, and there are minor differences among them. The main revision of the KJV that "stuck" was that of Oxford's Benjamin Blayney in 1769. It does not matter which edition of the KJV you use. Because the differences are so minimal, *What Saith the Lord?* will still be useful to you! Personally, my favorite editions of the KJV focus not so much on the text ("Pure Cambridge" vs. other options) as on the layout. Though I don't favor the drop caps, the Schuyler Treveris KJV (Schuyler, 2019) and the KJV Store's Reader's Edition Bible (KJV Store, 2025) are single-column, paragraphed editions of the KJV with verse numbers in the margins. I really love this format. I think it is the one most conducive to careful, contextually sensitive Bible reading. The *New Cambridge Paragraph Bible* (Cambridge University Press, 2005) is also an excellent way to read the KJV. It's beautiful and tasteful, and it returns the KJV to the intentions of the 1611 translators.

✔ **New King James Version (NKJV)**: The NKJV is a careful update of the KJV. Many people who love the KJV do not realize that the NKJV is based on the Masoretic Hebrew Text and Textus Receptus just like the KJV. Its preface makes the latter clear:

> Because the New King James Version is the fifth revision of a historic document translated from specific Greek texts, the editors decided to retain the traditional text in the body of the New Testament.[1]

Unfortunately, its preface also makes the former unclear. The NKJV preface says that its textual basis for the Old Testament is the Biblia Hebraica Stuttgartensia. This is *not* a critical text of the Hebrew Bible. It is what's called a "diplomatic text." It's the Leningrad Codex, which is the Masoretic Text.[2]

1. *Holy Bible: The New King James Version* (Thomas Nelson, 1982), x.

2. What's more, James D. Price, who worked on the New King James Version, has said in an unfortunately (to my knowledge) unpublished paper that in the eight

Also unfortunate: Some marketing language was apparently used at the 1982 release of the NKJV that has proven to be simply untrue—the NKJV is not a mere English-only update to the KJV. There are some places where the NKJV translators opted for a slightly different interpretation than did the KJV translators (Matt. 7:13–14 is one such place: Can you spot the difference?). But every time this is done, it is done for responsible reasons—for the very reasons the KJV translators themselves placed alternate translations in the margins of their 1611 edition. The KJV preface explains that there are sometimes translation difficulties that require this.[3] In those places where the NKJV does not appear to match the KJV, sometimes my concept of "false friends" will show that they do not, in fact, disagree (see "honesty" in ch. 10). But sometimes the KJV and NKJV translators looked at the very same Hebrew and Greek words but came to slightly different conclusions about how best to translate them.

✔ **Simplified King James Version (SKJV)**: The SKJV is a very light revision of the KJV that aims to update English archaisms. It comes in tasteful editions that explain in some detail what has been updated—or "translated"—and why. I do not know who did this work, but it appears to me to have been done responsibly. People who wish to use a KJV update alongside the KJV—such as in Sunday school classes, in small groups, or in church congregations—may find that the SKJV will cause slightly less

---

minor places where the Hebrew text underlying the KJV differs from that of the *Biblia Hebraica Stuttgartensia*, he adjusted the text back to match the underlying text of the KJV.

3. "Some peradventure would have no variety of senses to be set in the margin, lest the authority of the Scriptures for deciding of controversies by that show of uncertainty should somewhat be shaken. But we hold their judgement not to be so sound in this point." You can easily read this section of the KJV preface online, and you should. Read at least up until, "They that are wise had rather have their judgements at liberty in differences of readings than to be captivated to one, when it may be the other." (Norton, *New Cambridge Paragraph Bible*, xxxii–xxxiii.) The KJV preface is full of very difficult prose—and very valuable counsel.

confusion than the NKJV, because the SKJV is simply a lighter revision of the classic KJV. I don't know of a light KJV revision that comes in nicer editions than the SKJV.

✘ **Modern translations not based on the TR**: This book does not quote modern English translations that base their New Testaments on something other than the Textus Receptus. Even when the underlying text of such versions matches the TR perfectly, these versions are not quoted. I wish for this book to be perfectly usable by Christian people whose consciences lead them to the TR and only the TR.

Appendix 50

150 False Friends in the King James Version

MY ONE CONCRETE GOAL when I started a YouTube channel in 2020—the same year everyone else started a YouTube channel—was to expand the relatively short list of false friends that I included in *Authorized: The Use and Misuse of the King James Bible*. I wanted to prove and refine the concept with more examples. I also wanted to place real emphasis on teaching others how to fish. And I wanted to learn new things myself—new old things; namely, the meaning of KJV passages that, because of language change, I had previously misunderstood.

So, I launched a playlist called "Fifty False Friends in the KJV." All along I felt that it would be great if I could reach seventy-five, not just fifty. But fifty false friends seemed like a big enough goal. And the title just works, you know?

When I reached fifty-one on my list of fifty, I couldn't bring myself to change the playlist name. But at some point, I decided to stop at one hundred. Then, at the very last moment, I did a massive, two-hour video with fifty more—and finally, officially stopped. No one died and made me King of KJV False Friends. But I don't see anyone else angling for the title. So, for what it's worth, here are all one hundred and fifty of my Fifty False Friends in their "official" order.[1] The ones included in this book are bolded.

1. Halt
2. Apt
3. Variance
4. Emulations
5. Seditions
6. Heresies
7. Cattle
8. Meat
9. Commend
10. **Miserable**
11. Convenient
12. Wait On
13. Remove
14. Careful
15. Spoil
16. Equall
17. Incontinent
18. Enlargement
19. **Judgment**
20. **Honest**
21. Excess
22. **Overcharge**
23. **Communicate**
24. Want
25. **Prevent**
26. Let
27. Conversation
28. Corn
29. Fetched a Compass
30. Fair
31. Sorrow
32. Quick
33. Experience
34. **Moderation**
35. **Suffer**
36. **Help Meet**
37. **Watchings**
38. **By and By**
39. **So That**
40. **Bastard**
41. **Bowels**
42. **Ass**
43. **Holy Ghost**
44. Moisture
45. Fray
46. **Study**
47. Quit
48. **Coasts**
49. **Counsel**
50. Host
51. **Sodden**
52. By Myself
53. **Science**
54. **Mansions**
55. Flowers
56. **Offend**
57. Rumor
58. Condemn
59. Entreat

1. I'd like to thank Nathan Stockwell for carefully watching all of my videos and compiling most of this list. He even noticed that I did videos on "study" twice (oops!), and that I failed to assign a number to certain other false friends. We've fixed those errors. Quite a number of these false friends were sent to me by YouTube viewers; I apologize for not being able to thank them all by name.

60. Which
61. **Occupy**
62. **Of**
63. Affect
64. That
65. Wealth
66. **Peculiar**
67. Road
68. Followers
69. Taxed
70. **Curiously**
71. **Bruise**
72. Brethren
73. **Passenger**
74. **Constantly**
75. You
76. **Lewd**
77. **Outlandish**
78. **Oppose**
79. In
80. Of Purpose
81. Rage
82. Imagine
83. People
84. **Sincere**
85. Creature
86. Will Worship
87. **Replenish**
88. Discover
89. Debate
90. Devotions
91. Dispute
92. Difference
93. Shew
94. Closet
95. Issues
96. Apple of the Eye
97. Nephew
98. Cousin
99. Virtue
100. **Hell**
101. Charity
102. Staggered
103. Desired
104. Require
105. Confound
106. Convinced
107. Conversation
108. Great Waster
109. Dishonesty
110. Message
111. Commune
112. Turtle
113. Delicacies
114. Grudge
115. Other
116. Admiration
117. Observe
118. Lust
119. **World**
120. Reins
121. Dispensation
122. Hail
123. Grief, Grieve
124. Minister
125. Scholar
126. Master
127. Mean
128. Freely
129. Doubts
130. Room
131. Naked
132. Allow
133. Disallow
134. Table
135. Amaze
136. Comfortably
137. Spirit
138. Confusion
139. Sensual
140. Mourn
141. **Evil**
142. Comprehend
143. Doctrine
144. Duke
145. His
146. Generation
147. Rid
148. Target
149. Naught
150. Naughtiness

"The judgment of the judicious" (to borrow a phrase from the KJV translators) may decide to eliminate a few examples from my list. "Moisture," for example, is rather obscure and, frankly, debatable. "Apple of the Eye" may, I admit, have a worm in it. But then, there are more false friends in the KJV; I'm certain of it. I have a long list of potential candidates in my files.

Now you must go fishing in the highways and byways of the King James Version. Compel the false friends to come in. Send them to me through comments on my YouTube channel, Ward on Words. I *love* it when people catch fish I didn't even know were there.

Now, hopefully, thou understandest what thou readest in the King James Version a little better.

Mark Ward, PhD, is a video Bible teacher on YouTube @WardOnWords. He also teaches on RightNow Media and in assorted schools. He has written hundreds of Bible-nerdy articles for various publications and is the author or editor of multiple books and textbooks including *Basics for a Biblical Worldview* (BJU Press, 2021) and *Authorized: The Use and Misuse of the King James Bible* (Lexham Press, 2018). His next books are *The Parallel King James New Testament* (forthcoming from Bethany) and *Words Gone Wrong: Bible Study Errors and How to Fix Them* (forthcoming from Zondervan Reflective).

CONNECT WITH MARK

WardOnWords.com

YouTube @WardOnWords